Theodore Meyer Greene, Hartley Burr Alexander Professor in the Humanities at Scripps College, is one of the outstanding liberal scholars, teachers, and writers of our day. Born in 1897 in Constantinople, Turkey, the son of missionaries, he received the B.A. degree from Amherst College in 1918 and the Ph.D. degree from the University of Edinburgh in 1924. For many years he was a member of the faculty of the Department of Philosophy at Princeton, and later Yale. He is the author of several books, notably *Liberal Education Reconsidered* (1953), and articles on aesthetics, philosophy of religion, and liberalism.

Liberalism

ITS THEORY AND PRACTICE

THE RUSHTON LECTURES

The Rushton Lectures originated with the establishment of a memorial trust by the sons and daughters of the late James Franklin and Willis Roberts Rushton in memory of their revered father and mother, who contributed so much to the social, economic and spiritual growth of the city of Birmingham, Alabama. The funds in this trust provide for a series of public lectures which, in the past several years, have been given in co-operation with Birmingham-Southern College.

It has been the aim of the Trustees to present eminent authorities in the various disciplines in order to stimulate the community and to make its people aware of the latest developments in the scientific and humanistic fields.

The lectures of Dr. Theodore M. Greene constituted the fourth presentation in the Rushton Lecture Series. The previous lecturers were Howard Mumford Jones, Karl T. Compton, and Arnold J. Toynbee.

LIBERALISM

Its Theory and Practice

BY THEODORE MEYER GREENE

AUSTIN : UNIVERSITY OF TEXAS PRESS

© 1957 by Theodore Meyer Greene

Library of Congress Catalog Card No. 57-7558

Printed and bound in the United States of America

TO

Alexander Meiklejohn

LIFELONG IMPASSIONED LIBERAL

Preface

WHAT IS a liberal? What is the essence of liberalism? Is it merely an attitude of tolerance and a faith in critical inquiry? Or do this attitude and this faith presuppose certain beliefs regarding man's dignity and value? If so, what are these beliefs, and how may they be justified? Can liberalism ever become a powerful creative force in this country and throughout the world unless liberals can band together in a common faith? Yet how, if at all, is such a common faith possible in our half-secular, half-religious American society and in a world of many conflicting ultimate beliefs? How, finally, may liberalism be more effectively exemplified and implemented institutionally in this country—in government; in home, school, and church; and in business and industry?

These are some of the questions which this book attempts to answer. Their urgency was perhaps more obvious a year or two ago, when our civil liberties were being flagrantly violated in many quarters and when few spoke out boldly in their defense. That dangerous wave of fanaticism has, fortunately, largely subsided. But who can tell when the next will arise? More important, what weakness in our body politic and our cultural ethos occasions such waves of overt un-American illiberalism? And what can we do now, before it is too late, to revitalize and strengthen our traditional love of freedom and our century-old hatred of all forms of tyranny? These are questions that must deeply concern all of us who cherish our heritage of freedom. They are at least as crucial today as they were yesterday and are likely to be tomorrow.

There is, I trust, nothing original in the following pages. It is my hope, rather, that the reader will find that my answers to the foregoing questions at least partially express his own deepest liberal convictions. All I have tried to do is formulate and defend, as simply and directly as possible, what thoughtful and loyal Americans have always believed and still believe about liberty and the conditions and expressions of liberty. These beliefs are indeed old, but they are not old-fashioned. Today they stand in great need of reaffirmation and clarification.

This book is a considerable expansion and revision of three Rushton Lectures delivered in 1949 in Birmingham, Alabama. The central theme is the same, but the argument has been developed and strengthened. I hope that this reworking may, in some measure, compensate for the unavoidable delay in publication.

THEODORE MEYER GREENE

Scripps College
Claremont, California
January, 1957

Contents

PART I

*Liberalism and
the Liberal Attitude*

Introduction

Most of us will aknowledge the vital importance of our liberal heritage when we stop to think about it, and especially when our own freedom is challenged or when we see the rights of others blatantly violated. But we seldom take the time or make the effort to re-examine the meaning of liberalism and to review its basic presuppositions. We therefore tend to minimize or ignore the many ways in which subtle changes in our basic institutions and in our national ethos threaten to undermine our freedoms and jeopardize our hard-earned rights. We are inclined to be apathetic and indifferent when we should be acutely alive to present danger and future menace, particularly in a period of cultural crisis such as ours.

Our first task in this book must be to see why liberalism is so important an issue in our time. Why are our freedoms so precious and how are they being threatened today at home and abroad?

We must then ask whether the terms "liberalism" and "liberal" are the best we can find for the clarification of this vital issue. Have these terms been hopelessly spoiled by misuse and should they be abandoned? Are other terms available and preferable?

We must also consider with care whether the specific freedoms that we have come to regard as our inalienable rights are of equal importance, or whether one of them, freedom of speech, may perhaps be more crucial than the rest. If it is, what gives it its special priority? How is this freedom related to man's age-old search for truth? And why is a true understanding of ourselves and our environment so essential to our individual and corporate welfare?

Finally, we must face early in our study whatever major obstacles con-

front us as we attempt to maintain and strengthen a society that is both free and cohesive. Some people believe that freedom and social solidarity are incompatible. Are they right? Many liberals are still convinced that authentic liberalism is merely an attitude of critical tolerance and that such an attitude necessarily precludes a common liberal creed and program of action. Must we agree? Others grant the desirability of such a creed and program but believe that our American society is too divided on basic issues to have a common faith and a common over-all policy. Is this true? Are we too hopelessly divided to become a spiritually unified nation?

These are some of the preliminary questions to which we must address ourselves seriously before we consider in detail the affirmative theory and practice of liberalism.[1]

---

[1] Cf. Theodore Meyer Greene, *Our Cultural Heritage* (The Elsevier Press, Houston, 1956).

Chapter 1

The Crucial Problem of Our Time

THE "Great American Experiment" was a quest for liberty. Our Founding Fathers crossed the Atlantic to escape religious persecution and secular restraint. They were determined to be free to worship God as they chose and to enjoy the fruits of their own labors. They sealed this determination with their blood in the Revolution. Thereafter, they were free to rule themselves politically. Their first act was to draft a Constitution designed, so far as possible, to guarantee and implement their new hard-won political and civil liberties.

The American Experiment was continued by succeeding generations —in the slow consolidation of the Eastern seaboard, in the hazardous westward migration and settlement, in agricultural expansion and industrial growth, in the gradual maturing of American culture. Amid these mighty changes, and despite ever-new threats to freedom and equality of opportunity, our ancestors steadfastly maintained their passion for liberty—political and religious, economic and civil. The nation they were creating was for them and increasingly for the whole world "the land of the free." Step by step they extended and strengthened its freedoms—by the Bill of Rights, by legislation and judicial procedure designed to correct social injustice, by liberal education and the liberalizing of the churches, by the abolition of slavery and the enfranchisement of women, and by the welcoming of harassed aliens to these shores. When, finally, in the present century, all freedom-loving nations, including our own, were challenged to the supreme test, we joined hands in two bloody wars around the globe to defend not only our own liberty but that of all men everywhere.

What has happened to our traditional love of liberty during the last decade? Why has a "liberal," that is, a lover of liberty, become suspect today? Why has "liberalism," which for us should be a synonym for sound American conservatism, become a term of condemnation and abuse? Why is "liberal" education, designed to free men from the tyranny of ignorance and prejudice, being replaced by "general" education? Why is religious "liberalism" so widely repudiated today in our churches, political "liberalism" so hated, social and economic "liberalism" so savagely attacked? Have we Americans lost our faith in liberty, our traditional passion for freedom? Are we, at this late date, repudiating our heritage and abandoning the Great American Experiment?

No doubt many will immediately protest that we are doing no such thing. All that has happened, they will insist, is that the *terms* "liberal" and "liberalism" have quite properly fallen into disrepute because they have come to designate individuals and signify doctrines that are today judged to be harmful to the national welfare. The modern "liberal," they say, is dangerous because his professed "idealism" is irresponsible. He threatens the economy by his "unrealistic" crusade for social justice. He challenges national sovereignty by his "un-American" insistence on international co-operation. He is unorthodox theologically and utopian educationally. He is a "subversive" and a "fellow-traveler" because he endorses some of the criticisms that our great enemy abroad is leveling at us. It is only the modern "liberal" and his "liberalism" that are therefore, justifiably, under attack—so goes the argument.

Is this the correct answer? Do we, as a people, still have a passion for liberty? How well do most of us understand the true meaning and conditions of freedom? How willing are we to pay the price, and run the risks, of maintaining the heritage of liberty?

We can certainly be proud of the stamina and courage of our young men on the field of battle and of our efficiency and morale on the home front in time of war. Nor need we question our deep unconscious loyalty, as a nation, to all the basic freedoms. The love of liberty is in our very blood stream; indeed, it is so much a part of us that we take it for granted. We feel in our bones that what has happened to other freedom-loving peoples cannot happen to us.

This uncritical assumption that nothing can rob us of our cherished freedoms is both healthy and dangerous. It does bespeak our deep-seated affinity for freedom and our profound repugnance for all forms of tyranny. But it also reflects, at least to some extent, our failure to realize that the freedoms we prize are not part of the natural endowment with which we are born but are painfully acquired blessings which we can easily lose.

We still refer to the civil rights that are safeguarded by the Constitution as "inalienable," and we tend to believe that they will therefore automatically remain ours forever. They are indeed inalienable in the sense that it is man's true nature and proper destiny to be free. But they are not inalienable in the sense that all men necessarily possess them and enjoy them. We know that most of the peoples of the world have never known freedom as we know it, that no people has ever won freedom without sustained effort and bitter sacrifice, and that, in our own time, nations have lost the freedoms that once were theirs. We should realize that we too, as a nation, can lose our freedoms, not only by subjugation by a foreign tyrannical power but also by slow attrition from within—by passive submission to petty local tyrannies, indifference to violations of civil rights, progressive loss of respect for the traditional safeguards of liberty. It took the blood of our ancestors to make us free. We cannot hope to remain free without corresponding effort and sacrifice.

Today our freedoms are in fact in grave double jeopardy. We are confronted externally by a ruthless enemy engaged in its own "great experiment" at home and apparently determined to dominate the entire globe. We need not here attempt to assess its major policies, which deviate so profoundly from our own. What alone concerns us is the growing might of Soviet communism and, in particular, its radical repudiation of the freedoms we value—freedom of speech on all controversial issues and the right of honest dissent, freedom of worship and the rights of religious minorities, and all the other freedoms the Constitution and its amendments seek to protect. We know what has happened to these freedoms in the countries Soviet Russia has drawn into its orbit and made its satellites. We also know how strenuously and cleverly Communist doctrine has infiltrated other nations, including our own. We are, as a nation, finally aware of this growing threat and are taking steps to protect ourselves against it.

But there is also a grave internal threat to our freedoms against which we are not yet sufficiently on guard. The most dramatic symbol of this threat is the hunt for Communists in our midst by methods that flagrantly violate the very freedoms we profess to cherish. These methods include the assumption of guilt until innocence is proved, public trial without the safeguards of orderly legal procedure, attack by accusation without adequate opportunity for self-defense, and repudiation of the Fifth Amendment by use of the maligning label "Fifth Amendment Communist." What is so alarming is not so much the recourse of a few elected representatives to these tactics. In times of unusual danger there will always be unscrupulous demagogues ready to turn public anxiety to their own advantage. What is alarming is the wide public support these men have elicited, the failure of leaders in every walk of life to protest and resist these practices, and, above all, the atmosphere of fear and suspicion generated by such tactics throughout the nation. The danger of Communist infiltration is indeed real and urgent; we must, of course, make every proper effort to identify those who would betray us and neutralize their efforts. But the danger of losing our rights and freedoms in the very effort to defend them is far greater.

Even more serious is our growing disposition to hold in disrespect all minority opinions on controversial issues, to confuse "heresy" and "treason" (to use Sidney Hook's useful distinction), and to brand all honest dissent as "subversive" if not actually "treasonable." Witness recent denunciations of leaders of past administrations as "traitors" and the ominous failure of most of our present political leaders instantly to condemn such irresponsibility. Witness, too, the widespread assumption, open or implied, that anyone who criticizes current political and economic policies and practices is *ipso facto* a disloyal American. The current hostility toward political and economic "liberalism" reflects this very tendency. "Liberals" are judged to be wrong in what they sincerely advocate for the common welfare; they are also accused of disloyalty and subversion for speaking out their honest convictions. How long can the freedoms of speech and conscience prevail if decent and responsible citizens adopt this attitude to minority opinion and honest disagreement?

Let us push our analysis a step further. What is happening to our traditional faith in man himself and his basic rights? Are we witnessing a change not only in our prevailing ethos—our climate of opinion—but in our corporate moral and spiritual fiber as well? Are we today in danger of losing confidence in ourselves and faith in the Great American Experiment? This crucial question was well put by Secretary of State John Foster Dulles in his book *War or Peace*. I quote Dulles at some length in the hope that his diagnosis will carry weight with those who are presently so suspicious of all "liberals": [1]

Something has gone wrong with our nation, or we should not be in our present plight and mood. It is not like us to be on the defensive and to be fearful. That is new in our history. . . .

Our nation was founded as an experiment in human liberty. Its institutions reflected the belief of our founders that men had their origin and destiny in God; that they were endowed by Him with inalienable rights and had duties prescribed by moral law, and that human institutions ought primarily to help men develop their God-given possibilities. We believed that if we built on that spiritual foundation we should be showing men everywhere the way to a better and more abundant life. . . . [But] as our material power waxed, our spiritual power seemed to wane. We appeared to be less concerned with conducting a great experiment for the benefit of mankind and to be more concerned with piling up for ourselves material advantages. Our vision seemed to contract, and our sense of mission to lessen. Others began to think of us more as a possible source of money and material things and less as a source of inspiration and of guidance. . . . What we lack is a righteous and dynamic faith. . . . The difficulty is that we, ourselves, are unclear as to our faith and the relationship of that faith to our practices. . . . At home, our institutions do not attract the spiritual loyalties needed for their defense. There is a confusion in men's minds and a corrosion of their souls. . . . Our faith lacks the power and clear definition that would make it contagious in the world.

The contrast Dulles draws between our influence and that of the Soviet Communists is painful but inescapable:

While our influence and security have been declining, those of Soviet Communism have been rising. This is not primarily due to the fact that Russia as a nation has great power, although the Red Army is a background threat. It is rather due to the fact that Soviet Communism has a creed, a creed of world-wide import. It is a creed in which the hard core of Party members believe fanatically, and which they are spreading with missionary zeal throughout the world. . . . They can and do implement policies with the portrayal of a "great Soviet Communist experiment" with which, during this century, they are catching the imagination of the people

[1] John Foster Dulles, *War or Peace* (The Macmillan Company, New York, copyright, 1950), pp. 253–58. Used with permission of The Macmillan Company.

9

of the world, just as we did in the nineteenth century with our "great American experiment." . . . We cannot successfully combat Soviet Communism in the world and frustrate its methods of fraud, terrorism, and violence unless we have a faith with spiritual appeal that translates itself into practices which, in our modern, complex society, get rid of the sordid, degrading conditions of life in which the spirit cannot grow.

This is a devastating indictment of our whole way of life, our basic spiritual outlook and temper. Is it a fair diagnosis of ourselves and of the Communists in the world today?

Mr. Dulles is surely right in stressing our historical indebtedness to the Hebraic-Christian heritage and in declaring that the essence of this heritage is a living faith in a living God and a lively concern for man. It was this faith and this concern that led men and women of the early Christian community to martyrdom and that has always animated the Christian church when it was true to its high calling and exemplified what it preached. It is still the faith and the way of life of dedicated Christians today. But for how many of us, even in the churches, is this faith really dynamic enough to motivate and direct our daily actions? To what extent is this so-called "Christian people" committed to a vital belief in God and animated by a compelling respect and love for fellowmen?

Our cultural heritage had its source not only in Palestine but also in Greece and Rome. Greek philosophy set the stage for modern science, and Roman law, in conjunction with Christianity, gave rise to the modern democratic movement. Hence the "modern" western allegiance to truth and justice—to truth as the goal of scientific inquiry and the key to man's control of nature; to justice as the goal of democratic legislation and judicial action and the key to social welfare. Men have also suffered martyrdom for truth and justice, and mighty efforts have been made to discover and implement new truths and to promote the cause of justice. America's dedication as a growing nation to both truth and justice has been notable. We too have esteemed our scientists for their dispassionate search for truth. We too have been aware that justice is more than power and that all men are entitled to justice. But how strong is our dual allegiance to truth and justice today?

Our concern for both does seem to be perplexed and wavering. In sophisticated circles there is considerable skepticism about the reality of objective justice and a strong tendency to identify "justice" with the laws and legal procedures actually operative in a society at any given time. Many politicians seem to be more anxious to cater to the special interests of their constituents than to promote the cause of justice throughout the land. Many of us as citizens and private individuals exhibit little respect for law as such, or for justice when it entails our loss. We are inclined to evade an irksome law if we can get away with it. Nor can we as a nation lay claim to a steadfast allegiance to truth and intellectual honesty. We show no great desire to face, as realistically as possible, unpleasant facts about ourselves and our society. We hate to acknowledge the colossal price of adequate military preparedness and the need for eternal vigilance if we would preserve our civil rights and freedoms. We prefer the flattery of advertisers, the easy reassurances of politicians, the comforting words of priests and ministers. We have come to believe that we are entitled to luxuries, that the economically less fortunate among us usually get what they deserve, and that, all in all, we are the finest people on earth.

In short, our unparalleled prosperity does seem to have made us intellectually and spiritually soft. We dearly love the comfortable way of life, and we try to shut our eyes to the injustice and misery in our midst. We like democracy but give little thought to its basic preconditions, structure, and implications. We make little effort to cultivate and strengthen the underlying faith which created our democracy and without which it cannot survive.

Dulles believes that the growing might of communism is due primarily to the fact that it has a creed of world-wide import in which the hard core of party members believe fanatically and which they are spreading with missionary zeal throughout the world. We know how heavily the Politburo relies on seductive promises and how ruthlessly it resorts to regimentation, imprisonment, torture, and liquidation to hold the masses in line. But Soviet communism could not possibly have achieved what it has achieved both at home and abroad had not its appeal been addressed to certain basic human needs. What are these needs and how has communism tried to satisfy them?

The original Communist creed did express, in its own perverted way, a certain idealistic passion for justice and human welfare. It did become a rallying call supporting the many (the proletariat) and opposing the

11

few (the exploiters of the many), supporting social equality and opposing prejudice. Despite its repudiation of objective justice and its cynical reliance on arbitrary force, communism still seems to echo something of the idealistic concern for the common man that was evident in the writings of Engels, Marx, and Lenin. This remnant of an earlier idealism, however partial and hypocritical it may be today, is still widely proclaimed and still appeals to man's deep craving for justice and his hatred of ruthless exploitation. This at least partly explains the apparent success of much Communist propaganda against what it calls "capitalistic" exploitation of the masses.

In its own ruthless way, communism also tries to satisfy man's deep-seated need to belong to a cohesive community bound together and motivated by a common faith. Man is not made for solitude or loneliness. If he is left too much to his own devices, too independent of social ties and allegiances, he becomes lost, miserable, and ineffective. He is essentially a social creature, craving close bonds with his fellows. He is also naturally inclined to believe rather than to doubt, to hold strong, affirmative beliefs, and to believe wholeheartedly rather than hesitatingly. He is happiest when he can direct his actions toward positive goals whose value he does not question, particularly when others cherish those goals as unquestioningly as he does. In its own misdirected and violent way, communism offers its adherents just such a tightly knit community dedicated to a common goal and committed to a common program of action. This in itself must make a powerful appeal to all who prefer membership in any closely organized community, however tyrannical, to solitary drifting; who crave positive beliefs they can share with others rather than a state of disbelief and cynical skepticism; who demand a positive social program, however ruthless and dangerous, that will direct their own daily conduct, in however unpleasant a way, rather than the "freedom" of social chaos and personal irresolution. Here again, paradoxical as it may seem to us, the strength of communism lies in its positive answer to a positive human need.

Communism has a third spiritual arrow in its quiver. Despite man's natural preference for security and comfort rather than danger and sacrifice, there is also an aspect of human nature that welcomes a demand for self-sacrifice. We await a challenge, clear and unqualified, to identify ourselves with an active group in support of a vital cause. A cause must seem worthy of our loyalty to challenge us, but our impulse to be loyal is often stronger than our impulse to examine carefully the merits of the cause in question. We crave a challenge so compelling that we can respond to it without question, a cause so vital that we ourselves become intensely alive by identifying ourselves with it. We can then actually glory in the sacrifice required, since the very pain of this sacrifice seems to guarantee the value of the cause that demands it and to justify the loyalty that it evokes in us. This too helps to explain the powerful appeal of communism as a cause. Many members of the party must wonder whether the goal of communism really justifies the brutal methods employed, but the challenge is so unambiguous, the orders are so clear (at any given time), and the personal sacrifices required are so great that the value of the ultimate goal must seem indubitable.

These are some of the powerful spiritual resources of the communism we are seeking to resist and compete with throughout the world. The leaders of the party, the rank and file of party members, and even some who are not members of the party seem to possess a philosophy, a program, and a passion that, in combination, present us with an impressive challenge. Do we today face communism and the rest of the world with a comparable philosophy, program, and passion? How deep and how informed is our devotion to our cause, our Great Experiment?

History seems to have played an ironic trick on us. Would not an impartial observer, surveying the two opposing camps in the world struggle that is going on today, expect to find greater loyalty and zeal, a firmer belief and a more passionate dedication, among us, with our historic faith in a God of righteousness and love, our traditional respect for all men as men, and our age-old search for objective truth and justice? Would he not expect the materialistic philosophy of communism, with its repudiation of all civil rights and freedoms, its reliance on false propaganda, its universal spying, rigid regimentation, and wholesale liquidation of enemies, to engender fear and revulsion among its own party members, in the peoples it has subjugated, and in all the neutral nations in the world today? Yet it is the Communists who seem to have the missionary zeal, we the indifference; it is they who have a shared philosophy and a common creed, which we seem to lack; it is too often they, not we, who seem today to be capturing the imagination of men and women who are in desperate need and are looking for a solution

13

to their own most urgent problems. Could anything be more paradoxical than that the Communists should apparently be able to evoke more sacrificial loyalty and zeal than can we, whose traditional faith in God and respect for man would seem ideally suited to man's loftiest hopes and ultimate loyalties?

Can we Americans do anything to improve this dismal situation? We pride ourselves on being a practical people, and practical people are usually not willing to sit back and contemplate paradoxes. We are also a fundamentally honest, energetic, and courageous people whenever circumstances—for example, a fighting war—compel us to bestir ourselves. Our distinctive problem seems to be to get ourselves to face the facts regarding ourselves and our world, to recognize our assets *and* our liabilities, both physical and spiritual, and then, while peace (such as it is) still prevails, to do whatever may be necessary at whatever cost to recapture or create a vital faith we can really live by. But this will require all the hard thinking, imagination, and will power at our disposal.

Such is the major challenge of our times. We are living in a period of unprecedented world-wide tension. We have received a wonderful heritage of religious faith and loyalty to justice, truth, and liberty, but our corporate understanding of this heritage is inadequate and our loyalty to it is bewildered and weak. We are confronted by an enemy with a dynamic philosophy, program, and passion, which, for the moment, we cannot match with a corresponding philosophy, program, and passion of our own. We are not yet able to meet in our way, as communism has so far been able to meet in its way, man's perennial need for a faith to live by, a community to belong to, and a cause worthy of great sacrifice. Can we achieve a steadfast common faith, a liberal equivalent of the Communist Manifesto? Can we recapture our ancestors' faith in liberty? That, I believe, is our crucial problem. It is the challenge to liberalism today.

Chapter 2

The Terms "Liberalism" and "Liberal"

How shall we label or name the philosophy of life, the working faith, we are seeking to define and promote?

To raise this question at the outset may seem unnecessary or premature. Why bother with a label at all? And how, in any case, can we intelligently decide how to label a position we have only begun to explore?

We must remember two facts: that our present inquiry is part of a widespread search going on right now in this country and that key labels operate powerfully in the definition of issues and the resolution of problems. The issues at stake are of growing concern to thoughtful men and women throughout our land and throughout the world. We must conduct this inquiry amid all the pressures and prejudices of the forum and the market place where goals are being sought, policies determined, and methods of procedure debated. In this context, the key terms employed may be of great importance in determining what issues are brought into focus and what conclusions and attitudes emerge. The words we use to designate what we believe in, or do not believe in, tend to acquire a life of their own and a power over us. They take on emotional overtones, and these overtones can generate in us attitudes appropriate to the objective meaning of the terms themselves.

It behooves us, then, to pick with care the labels under which we seek to define and promote our cause. Mere labels will not, of course, really unite us, but we shall be better able to achieve a united front and work together with the requisite loyalty if we succeed in finding appropriate descriptive terms for our common bonds and goals. And since we are trying to discover and vitalize a single embracing position to which we can all be loyal, it is most important that we get the best possible single label for it.

The labels now in common use are all relevant and helpful but have certain limitations. "Democracy," for example, has emotional overtones that are so affirmative today throughout the world that Russia has been impelled to adopt it for its own use, even though this involved a complete reversal of its western meaning. It signifies for us that type of political organization and procedure which has proved so useful in safeguarding our basic rights and liberties and in promoting the values we most cherish. However, political democracy is not valuable for its own sake; it is valuable only in so far as it functions effectively as a means to these ends. We believe that these ends are equally valid and valuable for all peoples and all nations, but we know that there are still many societies on our globe whose traditions and state of culture make them, at least for the time being, unqualified for what we regard as responsible political democracy. To label our common cause "democratic" would imply that political democracy, presumably in its present American form, is what we Americans most prize. The use of the term in this context would tend to blind our own eyes to the great merits of other forms of political democracy, such as the British, to the present unavailability of any form of political democracy to some peoples, and to the fact that our own political democracy is bound to evolve, gradually taking on new forms in the hands of future generations. It would also invite a dangerous confusion, both at home and abroad, of ends and means; it would attach too much importance to political structure and process and too little importance to the ultimate ends all political devices should serve.

The phrase "social democracy" is somewhat more inclusive in its meaning, but the adjective "social" seems to stress society at the expense of the individual—a stress that is completely alien to our traditional aims. Like "democracy," the phrase also has the disadvantage of unduly exalting the political aspect of our common life. The longer phrase, "our democratic way of life," is still more inclusive in meaning and points to some sort of common faith. But, besides being long and clumsy, it tells us nothing about this implied common faith save that it is "democratic."

More serious objections can be raised to such labels as "capitalism," "private enterprise," and "bourgeois culture." "Capitalism" designates only one aspect of the economic component of our way of life. Moreover, this is the facet that has been the prime focus of criticism in recent years. We have done much to mitigate the past abuses of capitalism and most of us are prepared to defend it, in principle at least, with major or minor qualifications, but few of us would wish to have our whole way of life identified with, or symbolized by, capitalism. We are not eager to play into the hands of the Communists, who have so successfully caricatured us as nothing but a selfish capitalistic plutocracy. Similarly, we have valued and notably exemplified "private enterprise" since the earliest colonial days, and we shall, I hope, continue to value all private initiative that is not predatory but is socially oriented. Even at its most vital and responsible, however, private initiative is only one aspect of our total attitude and pattern of behavior.

As regards "bourgeois culture" (were it to be seriously considered as a useful label), no label that includes two such sophisticated terms could possibly gain popular currency. Even if we ignore this liability, the term "bourgeois," though it has some descriptive merit, would be very misleading for our purposes. The term does distinguish our culture from the aristocratic cultures of the Greek city-state, the Roman Empire, and medieval feudalism. It also has the merit of indicating that in our culture it is the great middle class, rather than the upper or lower class, that has come into its own. Surely, however, we do not want to do the very thing that Communist propaganda tries to get us to do—defend the privileges of a middle class *against* the rights of the manual workers whom the Communists refer to as the "proletariat" or *against* the rights of the more successful. It is the Communists who have repudiated the essential dignity of man as such, who have set class against class, and who, in alleged defense of the proletariat, have submitted so many millions of men, women, and children to imprisonment, torture, and death merely because they were members of the bourgeoisie. We cannot afford to define our objectives in such class terms.

All these labels have the further disadvantage of denoting secular aspects of our culture in complete disregard of its important religious component. Phrases such as "our Christian culture" are, of course, as unfair and misleading in the opposite direction. We must admit America's marked cultural heterogeneity—the fact that we are partly religious and partly secular. We are trying to find and briefly designate what, if anything, is common to *both* these rival or complementary approaches to life. One way to phrase our problem is to ask ourselves: "What is most significantly distinctive about American secularism *and* American religion at their best? In what common cause can members of both groups unite with complete integrity and genuine enthusiasm? Under what banner can they march forward arm in arm, honoring their differences and complementing their respective deficiencies?"

I can suggest no better single term for our common faith than "liberalism." Like those already mentioned, it is far from perfect. It too is shopworn from overuse and careless use, but unfortunately all the basic words in our vocabulary tend to get shopworn in a society committed to freedom of speech and therefore inundated with public utterances that are both informed and ignorant, precise and careless. In an age in which we are bombarded by a perpetual stream of emotionally charged labels, every label has become a tired horse. The term "liberalism" has probably been no more misused and is no more tarnished today than the terms "God," "nature," "freedom," and "democracy." In any case, unless we want to invent a brand-new label, we must select the most suitable term we can find and try to reburnish it by clarifying its meaning and putting it to work in support of a worthy cause.

"Liberalism" and "liberal" have indeed acquired various misleading associations and meanings that must first somehow be sloughed off if these terms are to serve our purposes. For example, "liberalism" became identified in nineteenth-century England with a political position and finally a political party that espoused specific social and economic reforms in opposition to conservative forces that leaned heavily on tradition and were committed to the defense of certain vested rights. This association of the term with a specific type of policy still prevails in this country; there is still a strong tendency to define a "liberal" as one who supports certain political and economic policies in opposition to others. This fact explains much of the current opposition to liberalism—an opposition often charged with bitter hatred.

This well-established meaning of "liberalism" is in a sense salutary. A real liberal is by nature a social reformer, the champion of the exploited underdog and the foe of all predatory vested interests. There are such vested interests in every society; there are always the haves who are determined to preserve their privileges and power and who are prepared to fight for them to the end. Any reformer who crusades for greater social justice and for the rights of the have-nots is bound to incur the enmity of the vested interests. Yet capitalistic owners have no copyright on predatory selfishness; well-organized labor, embracing many millions of workers, can be just as predatory and just as dangerous to the common weal. The courageous liberal will therefore incur the wrath of labor no less than that of capital in his fight against *all* exploitation and *all* social injustice. That the term "liberalism" is today associated with the espousal of unpopular causes is, therefore, an asset rather than a liability; liberalism is by its very nature a fighting cause that will inevitably arouse the hatred and resistance of all who stand to benefit from an unjust status quo.

But this is only half the story. We must not forget man's tendency, as strong as his natural selfish egoism, to conceive of his analysis of a situation as the only valid analysis, his reform policy as the only policy that is right and socially beneficial. If liberalism becomes wholly identified with any specific political, economic, or social policy, it is doomed to the status of mere partisanship and is, as a consequence, bound to generate in its supporters the same kind of self-righteousness that so often characterizes the defense of vested interests. The cause we are here seeking to define is that of social justice, whatever specific policies may promote it best; the cause of open inquiry and free speech, however diverse the results of such inquiry and various the policies publicly defended. Only if "liberalism" can come to be identified first and foremost with ultimate allegiance to freedom, justice, and truth can it serve as a useful label for what we as a nation should cherish most deeply.

It is important that this point be made quite clear. Every "liberal," as here defined, should be characterizable in two ways—as one who excels in open-mindedness and a sense of fair play and whose ultimate objectives are freedom, justice, and truth, and also as a man who believes that certain specific beliefs and policies will best safeguard freedom and increase social justice. He is bound to have specific convictions and policies that differ from those of many of his fellow-citizens. But he, like his opponents, may be wrong both in his definition of a specific goal and in his choice of means to achieve this goal. Such mistakes, if they are honest mistakes, do not in and of themselves make him any less a liberal, nor do the comparable mistakes of his opponents, if they too are honest and sincere, automatically damn them as illiberal. Here, at the level of specific belief and specific policy aimed at specific goals and involving specific implementing devices, is where we are certain to encounter honest differences of opinion that every true liberal will wish to respect.

These clashes of honest opinion differ in principle from the superficially similar internecine clash of selfish vested interests, which are essentially predatory and can be defended only hypocritically by an appeal to general social welfare. They also differ in principle from the inevitable clash between the claims of vested interest and the efforts of social reform. The marks of the true liberal are, first, his determination and ability to rise above the scramble for special privilege, above the struggle for pork-barrel loot or any other kind of loot; second, his resolve to dedicate his life and fortunes to unceasing warfare against all plundering; and third, his profound respect for the most diverse opinions regarding specific goals and methods, provided these goals are sought and these methods are employed with a genuine concern for social welfare. The natural enemies of the liberal are, so far as they can be identified, the enemies of mankind; his natural allies are all men and women who, in their different ways, are doing what they can for the common good.

"Liberalism," so defined, is neither Republican nor Democratic; it may achieve notable exemplification in members of both political parties. It is neither secular nor religious; men and women of both persuasions may or may not be liberal. It is not identifiable with any specific doctrine or set of political, economic, social, or theological doctrines, though every thoughtful liberal is bound to take sides on these controversial issues. In politics a liberal will vote as his conscience dictates—alone, as a member of a minority, or with the majority; but he will cherish the democratic process more highly than victory, freedom of speech above the rightness of his personal views. On social issues he will value the cause of social justice above all else, and he will have the humility to admit that his most considered opinions on any controversial issue may be wrong. He will also have his convictions about religion and, if he is a member of some religious body, he will take sides on various doctrinal and ecclesiastical disputes. But here, even more than on secular issues, he will remember his own finitude and not presume dogmatically to identify his own beliefs with *the* truth. In short, his dominant attitude will be that of profound respect for all men and for their honest beliefs and their true welfare.

The liberalism here defended differs essentially from both extreme antisocial individualism and extreme anti-individual totalitarianism. English nineteenth-century liberalism did espouse the cause of the individual and of free enterprise, but it did so at a time when this cause was in need of militant support. In this country liberalism also came to be identified with the philosophy of rugged individualism—a philosophy that was congenial to the tough pioneering spirit of the early settlers and the westward movement. This spirit still persists and still retains its value once it is purified of its predatory antisocial associations. Ruthless individualism ("Every man for himself," said the elephant, dancing among the chickens) never was defensible, but a kind of self-sufficient private initiative was justifiable and valuable in an era of expansion as it no longer is today in our very different society. As Dulles the "conservative" has himself reminded us, nineteenth-century laissez-faire liberalism is outmoded today.[1] Our present task is to redefine the essential role of private initiative within the context of social co-operation, that is, in terms of a free community of responsible persons.

The widespread tendency today to identify the liberal with the "leftist," the "radical," the "pink," or the "fellow-traveler," is stupid and uninformed. The true liberal may find himself defending a conservative tradition as often as he is impelled to resist some traditional attitude or procedure. Who, for example, are the more truly "conservative" today in the light of our American tradition—the liberals who defend our traditional freedoms or those "100 per cent Americans" who would override these freedoms in the alleged interest of national security? Liberals are bound to be attacked for their "radicalism" whenever they have the courage to fight vested interests. If the cause of social reform is defined as "leftist," liberals will of course find themselves constantly in the "leftist" camp. If the championing of traditional rights and values is defined as "rightist," the liberal will join forces with the "right." But under no conceivable circumstances will the true liberal merit the label "pink" or "fellow-traveler," for there is no one more utterly opposed to the spirit and temper of totalitarian regimentation than he. Authentic lib-

[1] John Foster Dulles, *War or Peace* (The Macmillan Company, New York, 1950), pp. 257-60.

eralism is, in essence, at the extreme opposite pole from communism, and a genuine liberal is the most convinced opponent one can imagine of communism and fascism in any form. Here again it is of the utmost importance to distinguish a basic attitude from the endorsement of a specific policy.

A ruthless and ingenious enemy like Soviet communism, intent to fight us on every front and to undermine our strength in every possible way, will in the course of time level at us some criticisms that are just and valid, along with countless charges that are utterly false and unfounded. Like every society, we too are vulnerable; we too are guilty of social injustice and race prejudice; we too have our faults. The mere fact that some of these weaknesses of ours are noted and criticized by an alien camp does not transform them into virtues or relieve us of responsibility for them. When, therefore, sincere social reformers recognize these deficiencies and strive to correct them, this effort, even though it involves agreement with Communist (or other) criticism of us, should in no way carry with it the further implication that these reformers are themselves Communists, or even distantly sympathetic to communism. The justice of a cause never depends upon who happens to support it or attack it. No specific, isolated policy is automatically wrong because it has received Communist support; none is automatically right because the Communists have attacked it. Nothing, in short, could be more contrary to the spirit of liberalism than to give up one's own best judgment and decide issues solely on the basis of what the Communists or any other group have said about them. Such a policy would imply subservience to those whom we are most concerned to resist. What could be more illiberal and un-American?

It is true that a few self-styled "liberals" have really capitulated to Communist propaganda and have more or less identified themselves with the Communist movement. So did twenty-one soldiers in Korea—twenty-one young Americans who, so far as we can tell, were anything but enlightened liberals.[2] No one in his right mind would hold all young Americans or all members of the armed forces suspect because of the deplorable decision of these tragically mistaken youngsters. It would be

[2] See Virginia Schmitz Pasley, *21 Stayed: The Story of the American GI's Who Chose Communist China—Who They Were and Why They Stayed* (Farrar, Straus and Cudahy, Inc., New York, 1955).

as stupid to condemn all liberals because of the essential illiberalism of an infinitesimal minority or to stigmatize all liberalism as "pink" because of the confusion or even the treachery of a few misguided individuals. All men are fallible and prone to grievous error—even those who seek to espouse the cause of liberalism. What is at stake for us is the cause itself, that basic philosophy of life which is so profoundly hostile to its great contemporary competitor. Let us not obfuscate this vital issue and jeopardize this vital cause by irresponsible smears and name-calling. Nothing, I repeat, could be more completely opposed to all forms of tyrannical absolutism, whether secular or religious, than what I have sought to describe as the essence of true liberalism.

The term "liberalism" has much to recommend it affirmatively. It is brief and familiar, and it has useful adjectival and adverbial derivatives. More important, its generic meaning is precisely right for our purposes. For, divorced from unhappy associations and overtones, it signifies an open, receptive, and generous attitude—an attitude essential for all free social co-operation and human progress. It signifies a critical rather than a subservient attitude to tradition and convention—yet an attitude hospitable to whatever in a tradition is worthy of preservation. It also suggests, at least by historical association, the supreme value of liberty as a prime condition of individual creativity and free social solidarity, and the ultimate threat slavery presents to all human aspiration and advance. It points to the life of the spirit and its ultimate values without committing us to any dogmatic formulation of these values or to any specific means for their realization.

If liberalism is to move us as dynamically as communism moves the Communist, it must indeed acquire for us a richer and more precise meaning than it now has. In the following pages I shall attempt to indicate ways in which this meaning can be circumscribed and deepened. I shall use the term "liberalism" and its derivatives to signify that attitude and those basic beliefs which most sharply differentiate us from all authoritarians, Communist or Fascist, secular or ecclesiastical, and which make us a people traditionally dedicated to the defense of genuine liberty and of all that liberty implies.

Chapter 3

Freedom of Speech and Man's Search for Truth

THE LIBERAL ATTITUDE is the natural expression of a faith in freedom. If we believe in freedom we shall wish to act without restraint; we shall regard this freedom as our right, and we shall defend the corresponding right of others as sedulously as we do our own. However much we may disagree with our fellows, our attitude toward them will reflect our deep respect for their freedom as well as for our own. The liberal attitude is the subjective expression of our belief in objective freedom. We cannot have freedom unless we believe in freedom, and such belief must express itself in a liberal attitude toward others.

The liberal attitude will, in turn, reflect a prior concern for freedom of speech. We can clarify our own thoughts only by expressing them and testing them against the expressed thought of others; we can work together for a common cause only if we learn to understand each other by speaking our minds openly and candidly. Only thus can a free society achieve any degree of responsible and informed corporate self-consciousness.

But we can take freedom of speech seriously only if we value truth and therefore honor honest speech for whatever truth it may contain. For all speech, like all reflection, is ultimately man's attempt to get at the truth. The participants in any serious conversation normally assume that what is being said is being honestly expressed and contains at least enough truth to merit attention. They feel that they owe it to the speaker to let him have his say, and they remain hopeful that what he says may be worth listening to. Why is an ultimate concern for truth so essential for man, and how is this concern related to free speech and a liberal attitude?

For our purposes, we may define truth as the quality of propositions that "do justice to" or are "adequate to" the aspect of reality—to the actual situations or matters of fact—to which they refer. That is, truth is the distinguishing characteristic of what a conscious mind really knows or might know about whatever is real. Reality itself is not "true"; it simply is what it is. Were there no knowing mind, finite or infinite, the problem of truth would never arise. It is only when consciousness is directed to something that is real in its own right and has a character of its own that the possibility of truth and error arises. When a conscious mind more or less seriously misapprehends what it seeks to know, it falls into that degree of error. When, on the other hand, its apprehension of its "object" is more or less adequate and accurate, it has to that extent grasped the truth.

Why does man take his search for truth so seriously? Partly, no doubt, because of his innate curiosity. We are so made that we are fascinated by our environment and derive intrinsic satisfaction from knowing as much about it as possible. But the chief reason for man's preoccupation with truth is more practical. True awareness of things is his most effective way of adjusting himself to them and of controlling them for his own welfare.

Adjustment based on conscious cognition is not, of course, the only way in which living creatures can cope with their environment. The lower animals rely on instinct and automatic reflexes to adjust themselves to their environment. Such instinctive response may be more or less conscious, but it is never really reflective. Animals "know" or "learn" without reflection how to propagate, nourish themselves, and protect themselves against their enemies. Man too inherits certain basic aptitudes of this type, but in him they are largely unspecialized. He has, instead, a far greater ability to learn from experience, that is, from observation, reflection, and experimental action. It is man's reason that above all enables him to learn the ways of nature, to adapt himself to it, and thus to induce it to satisfy his needs. He encounters nature with his senses, but it is with his reason or power of reflection that he interprets what he sees and hears, touches, smells, and tastes and then decides how to act.

25

Man's progressive exploration of nature and his increasing use of its resources is, furthermore, an essentially social enterprise. He could learn very little singlehanded; it is only in lively co-operation with his fellows that he can hope to explore nature's intricate regularities and put them to his own use. Our knowledge of nature is the cumulative product of centuries of corporate effort—of multiple observation, pooled reflection, and the transmission from generation to generation of an ever growing body of factual information regarding the physical world. The culmination of this long process is modern science, and it is science, of course, that has made modern technology possible. The value of scientific truth is today incontrovertible.

But nature is not the whole of man's environment. He is also deeply involved in a human society; if he is to survive and prosper he must understand his fellow-men and learn how to adapt himself to them and their ways. He must, in short, come to terms with his social as well as his physical environment; he must be able to deal with individuals and to play his part in a variety of group enterprises. Even in the most primitive societies we find complex social institutions and mores whose function it is to enable men to live and work together with some degree of harmony. In advanced societies such as ours, this knowledge is formalized and perfected in what we today call the "social sciences" and, at the practical level, in those specialized skills which enable us to conduct our many, infinitely complex social enterprises. Here, then, is a second area of "reality" with a character of its own which it behooves man to know as truthfully as possible if he would live and prosper.

A third area of inquiry is opened to man by his unique ability, not shared by other living creatures, to reflect upon his own essential nature and the ultimate character of the universe in which he finds himself. Since earliest times he has tried to peer through the veil of appearances to what lies behind all appearances and explains their nature and behavior. Primitive man conceived the world of nature to be animated by spirits whom he could propitiate in various magical ways. His myths and rites were the precursors of what we today know as science, philosophy, and the "higher" religions. Science has solved many of man's problems and relieved him of many of his fears, but it is still unable to fathom the ultimate what and why of things. Religion at its enlightened best relies heavily on man's distinctive "religious" experiences and the in-

spired insights of great spiritual leaders and offers finite man a variety
of faiths to live by. Philosophy studies all ultimate enigmas with systematic rigor and tries to explain them as reasonably as possible. Here,
then, is a third area or dimension of reality with which man, despite his
finitude, tries to come to grips.

Each of these aspects of man's total environment—the world of nature, human society, and the ultimate depths of reality itself—not only
pique man's curiosity and invite his perennial inquiry but also present themselves to him from the very first as full of human import,
that is, as profoundly affecting his well-being. He is forever judging
them and assessing his reactions to them in terms of their value or disvalue, their significance for him as a conscious selective agent. He learns
very early to discriminate between nutritious and poisonous foods, between efficient and inefficient means of attaining warmth and shelter,
and, among his fellows, between friends and enemies. As his society
becomes more complex, he tries to draw finer distinctions between harmful and beneficial mores and beliefs and develops complicated hierarchies
of virtues and vices. Even his speculations regarding ultimate reality are
evaluative; he is convinced that the more truly he can apprehend the
ultimate nature of things, the better will he be able to relate himself to
it. In short, his apprehensions and his evaluations are coterminous:
he assumes that everything he encounters in nature, behind and beyond
nature, and in human society is pregnant with potential good or harm,
value or disvalue. He is therefore deeply concerned to know as truly as
possible what in nature, in his fellow-men, and "behind" nature is good
or evil, of potential help or harm. He is eager to find out what types of
response to nature, to his fellows, and to the supernatural are most likely
to help him or injure him in his attempt to survive and prosper.

The answer to the question: "Why do men value truth?" is therefore
clear. Men seek knowledge partly for its own sake, in curiosity and wonder, and partly for practical reasons, in order to live and live well. Egre-
gious ignorance of nature spells instant death; notable error dooms men
to a state of bare survival. Only as we come to know nature more and
more truthfully are we able to adapt ourselves to it with scientific and
technological competence. Only as we come to understand ourselves and
our fellow-men can we adapt ourselves to our society and learn to live
with our fellow-men in peace and harmony. Only as we fathom the dark

mysteries that underlie nature and constitute the inner essence of reality itself can we learn how to discipline our ultimate beliefs into conformity with things as they really are and to conduct our lives with realistic long-range wisdom. Without truth regarding both "fact" and "value" we are doomed to frustration and failure.

This brings us back to the importance of freedom of speech. If truth is so essential to mankind, and if the discovery of new truths and the preservation and use of older truths are so dependent upon social co-operation, it is essential that men speak their minds freely and exchange ideas without restraint and with intellectual and moral integrity. Respect for freedom of speech and respect for truth and truthfulness thus imply one another. Freedom of speech is not an end in itself but an essential means for the attainment and communication of truths men must have to survive and flourish. To suppress freedom of speech would put the entire process of cultural advance into reverse: it would eventually force men back into a primitive state of barbarism, superstition, and fear. Allegiance to free speech is thus no arbitrary whim or mere convention. It is rooted in and demanded by human nature itself and man's perennial need to know himself, his fellow-men, the world of nature, and ultimate reality so far as they can in fact be known.

If man's need for truth is so imperative, what basic propositions does his search for it presuppose? How must men regard one another and their diverse opinions to make possible the efficient corporate search for truth and the effective use of it? The following four presuppositions are basic to man's search for truth and therefore to the liberal attitude.

1. All human beings are fallible; all man's apprehensions of the truth are therefore necessarily partial and inadequate. Man's finitude reflects itself in his most advanced corporate understanding of reality and in his highest-funded wisdom. Even when we pool all our cognitive resources and combine our most assured insights, we still fall far short of perfect comprehension or absolute certainty. The cognitive limitations of any single individual, however brilliant and industrious he may be, are even more pronounced. What could the greatest intellectual genius imaginable learn about himself and his total environment in a long and active life lived in complete solitude without benefit of any cultural inheritance—without any language, any accumulated knowledge, or any contact with other human beings? In ripe old age he would be more ignorant than a young child of normal endowment in a normal human society.

Even under optimum conditions of free social intercourse perfect knowledge is impossible. Each culture and historical period has its own provincialisms and prejudices. Moreover, each individual in any culture looks at life from his own special perspective and interprets what he sees and hears in terms of his own temperament, needs, and interests. Each of us is also bound to be influenced by the limited perspectives of the various social groups and institutions with which he is identified— his family, his local community, his class, his political party, and his nation. All these and other affiliations not only affect the scope and accuracy of our knowledge but also profoundly influence all our evaluations and our ideal standards, as well as our appraisal of concrete situations and specific actions and policies.

2. *Man can benefit by pooling his fragmentary insights and by correcting his provincialisms through contact with others.* The only corrective for a limited perspective is free intercourse with others whose perspective, though often no less limited, is at least different. Only thus can contrasting temperaments and social backgrounds be made to correct and complement each other. Your limited experiences can supplement mine; my evaluations can be rendered somewhat less warped by being compared with yours; together we can achieve a wider perspective and a greater degree of objectivity than either of us could possibly achieve without the other's help. This is the only cure available to man for the many provincialisms that bedevil him, distorting his vision and putting him in potential or actual opposition to his fellows. Only as men enrich their own experiences through vicarious participation in the experiences of others, only as they match opinion against opinion in a common effort to transcend individual prejudice, only as they test their respective interpretations of their total environment by pitting them against each other in a critical and constructive spirit—only thus can their understanding of reality broaden and deepen and their evaluations become more responsible and objectively defensible. No finite being and no group of finite beings can ever know *the* truth. But we can most closely approximate this ideal by using, as it were, a kind of social triangulation that will enable us to move confidently toward the goal of ever greater truth.

3. *Diversity of human perspectives and beliefs is an asset rather than*

29

a liability, provided such diversity is put to constructive use. If perfect knowledge were available to any finite being, all divergent opinions would be false and difference of opinion would have to be condemned as an unqualified evil. Those who believe that they possess absolute truth or truths deplore diversity of opinion and do their best to force others to agree with them. Omniscience cannot tolerate diversity of opinion or outlook, of interpretation or evaluation. But if we are finite we are of necessity fallible, and fallibility should welcome diversity on the principle that two finite heads are better than one. We can easily test the truth of this principle. From whom do we learn the most—from those whose experiences, background, opinions, and prejudices most nearly resemble our own, or from those who look at the world through fresh eyes, with other interests and from a different perspective? History points to the same conclusion: it has always been the great crossroads of the world, where commerce has flourished, where cultures have commingled, and where the most diverse opinions have clashed, that have been the chief historical centers of intellectual and spiritual fermentation and advance.

These benefits have accrued, however, only when men of different persuasion were willing to listen to one another and learn from one another. Mere diversity of belief achieves nothing; the clash of dogmatically held opinions merely intensifies the dogmatic intolerance of the disputants. What is essential to the co-operative search for truth is genuine humility rooted in a profound sense of finitude and the genuine open-mindedness of those who are eager to learn from others and, with their help, in some measure to transcend their own finite limitations. The *sine qua non* of fruitful intercourse is the valuing of diversity for the truth that it may yield.

4. *It is to man's advantage to discover and agree on truths that are relatively abiding.* However valuable diversity of opinion may be, the implicit if not the explicit purpose of all talk and argument is the enlargement of areas of significant agreement. The reason for this is obvious. Despite all their diversities, men do have a common human nature, and the reality they confront does have its constants. Each of us, no doubt, has his unique problems, and many of our needs, if not unique, are more or less specialized. But all these unique problems and special needs are, after all, variants of man's recurrent problems and ubiquitous

needs. All of us must somehow cope with man's universal predicament of life and death; whether we like it or not, we must all face the common challenge of sickness and health, growth and decay, misery and welfare. The closer we come to the real truth in any area of human concern, therefore, the more universally valid will be our apprehension and the more closely will men of intelligence be able to agree. This is the major premise of mathematics, the pure and applied sciences, all the social sciences, and even theology and philosophy. The last-named, no less than the former, are orderly attempts to approximate as closely as possible *the* truth—in this case, regarding Deity and his relation to man and reality as a whole and man's place in it. Indeed, the more closely a controversial issue touches our welfare, the more urgent is our human need for the best possible solution of the issue and the widest possible acceptance of its resolution. We can afford to ignore or laugh off differences of opinion on minor issues, but on matters of major human concern we must regard serious differences of opinion with real apprehension because they indicate how far we still are from the truth.

Emphasis on the value of agreement should not, of course, be construed as approval of agreement for its own sake. Agreement in error is more dangerous than the clash of one erroneous opinion with other opinions that are equally erroneous. Such agreement is likely to confirm us in our error, whereas a clash of opinion may well help us to discover the error and impel us to dig deeper for the truth. Nor does our praise of agreement contradict what has just been said regarding the value of complementary finite perspectives, of contrasting experiences, of diverse interpretations of the same "facts" and "values." Diversity of perspective and opinion is inevitable because men are finite and fallible; in and of itself it betokens discord and disharmony. It is of value in our search for truth only when men listen to one another, combine their limited perspectives, and thus together achieve a more embracing vision. Disagreement has no intrinsic value; rather, it is a measure of our ignorance, the result of our failure to apprehend truth clearly enough to agree. Rational human beings tend to agree, not disagree, in proportion as they succeed in knowing things as they really are and in articulating that knowledge. Our goal is a knowledge of reality so adequate, or so close to the truth, that all reasonable men can agree on it.

There is thus no need, and indeed no valid excuse, for absolutizing either our agreements or our disagreements. The radical skeptic falls into the indefensible and suicidal error of supposing that since men differ so widely on so many subjects no reliable knowledge is possible at all—that no truths are knowable, even partially, and that all opinions are wholly arbitrary, nothing but the expression of a unique individual perspective conditioned by social prejudice. Such skepticism is indefensible because the record of man's advancing knowledge refutes it at every turn. It is suicidal because a thoroughgoing skeptic can defend his own skepticism only on the contrary assumption—that his skeptical denial of all truth is itself true, that his reading of man's cognitive predicament is at least more nearly true than any alternative account of it.

The absolutist falls into the opposite error by ignoring man's essential finitude and fallibility and by absolutizing certain truths that, by their very nature, must be partial and inadequate. The absolutist is justified in believing in absolute truth and in searching for it; he is also justified in believing that some men are closer to *the* truth than others, that is, that their apprehensions of reality are more adequate than the apprehensions of others. But he commits the inexcusable fallacy of "misplaced absoluteness" when he ascribes to any of his opinions the finality and perfection that can pertain only to that absolute truth of which he is in search. He forgets that absolute truth, whether we conceive of it as a Platonic essence or as the omniscience of God or as a humanly created ideal, is for us a necessary but largely empty point of reference. It is merely the ultimate goal of all our cognitive striving, a goal whose content we finite beings can never fully comprehend and of which we can at best get only fleeting and partial glimpses. As Paul put it, we do see, but only in a glass, darkly. We do have some apprehension of *the* truth, but we can never attain an absolute or perfect comprehension of it. The dogmatic assurance of the absolutists is indefensible not merely because both secular and religious absolutists disagree so radically but primarily because their absolutism ignores man's finitude. Both extreme positions, in short, are unnecessary and intolerable—the absolutist's absolutizing of the incorrigibly relative no less than the relativist's relativizing of the absolute. Sanity lies squarely in between. Man can and does know something, but not everything, and what he knows he can know with increasing pragmatic assurance but never with dogmatic certainty.

Such, then, is the underlying rationale of free speech. As liberals we must cherish freedom of speech because without this freedom men cannot competently search for the truth that alone can make them free. Freedom of speech is not an end in itself, but it is the only means whereby we can realize ourselves as beings endowed with reason. The liberal will therefore defend this freedom above all other freedoms as the *sine qua non* of human welfare and advance. His liberal attitude will always reflect this deep conviction and concern.

Chapter 4

Is a Free yet Cohesive Society Possible?

*I*F WE REALLY WANT to come to grips with liberalism in our time we had better start with a realistic recognition of several major problems, each of which is in its own way unique to us as a freedom-loving people. Each is occasioned by our own distinctive conception of human nature and human liberty. Communism, with its very different conception of man and reality, is not embarrassed by these problems as we are.

CAN A FREE SOCIETY ACHIEVE SOCIAL SOLIDARITY?

A society that cherishes freedom labors under a grave disadvantage in competition with communism. Can it establish and maintain the closely knit community, the social solidarity, that men seem to crave without doing violence to its cherished liberties by coercing its members into a common faith?

People cannot work together as a group unless they are somehow able to agree on certain common objectives and procedures. No family, business, industry, school, or church can function without them; and what is true of these less inclusive groups is no less true of the most inclusive group we know, namely, a nation or state. The smaller the group and the more specialized the objectives of its members the easier this task is without resort to coercion. But a modern nation like our own is gigantic in size, and the interests of its members are infinitely various. How, under these circumstances, is a free cohesive community possible? Indeed, is not such a community a contradiction in terms?

Communism, in sharp contrast to democracy, has three resources that greatly facilitate the creation and maintenance of such large-scale solidarity. It has the machinery for forcible regimentation, the technique of propaganda, and, above all, a good conscience in using both force and propaganda without restraint.

The Soviet state has in constant use a powerful secret police force to maintain peace and conformity within her own frontiers. We know how ruthless and efficient these policing methods are. We know how effectively Soviet spies watch every official and every organization and how they insinuate themselves into the intimacy of the home. There seems to be no corner into which the long arm of forceful Communist control does not reach.

These controls are powerfully supported by a program of organized propaganda unprecedented in world history in scope and intensity. Never before have a few powerful men been able to control all their state's sources of information, all public speech and newsprint, the whole course of education, and, to a marked degree, all expression of opinion, even in the home. We can obtain some slight sense of the cumulative effectiveness of such propaganda by noting the effect of high-pressure advertising upon ourselves. Despite its puerility, its self-righteousness, and its wearisome repetitiousness it does influence our attitude toward products, try as we may to ignore and resist it. Such methods are highly successful even in a land in which there is still freedom of speech and the right to challenge and criticize. What might we not believe if all public utterance were rigidly controlled, if we could read and hear and learn only what a ruthless Politburo permitted us to read and hear and learn, and if the beliefs it favored were dinned into us by endless repetition and without contradiction?

Communism can use the two devices of brute force and unlimited persuasion so effectively because its ideology has given absolute priority to "security" over freedom. The security it seeks is safety not only from foreign aggression but also from want—one of the four basic freedoms proclaimed in the Atlantic Charter during World War II. Communists are convinced that both types of security depend essentially upon absolute uniformity of opinion on all basic political, economic, social, and philosophical issues. They do seem to permit criticism and dissent on questions that are not judged to be vital to the common good, but these questions are severely limited in number and scope. Even their artists, scientists, and technicians have been censured for failure to follow the party line. The higher freedoms which we most cherish and to which we believe all men have an essential right are the very freedoms they regard as most dangerous and to which, in their view, men have no right whatever.

It is not surprising that communism has been as successful as it has in achieving that type of social solidarity which is the hallmark of the efficient monolithic state. Our task as a free nation is the very reverse of Russia's—to create and maintain enough social solidarity for external defense, internal harmony, and economic well-being without extensive reliance on a police force, without forceful propaganda of any kind, and with full respect for the three other freedoms that communism so cavalierly abrogates—freedom from fear, freedom of thought, and freedom of worship. We rely on a small police force, which is at least theoretically restrained by constitutional safeguards and legal procedures. We are committed to free speech, free press, and free or "liberal" education—in short, to persuasion pitted against counter-persuasion, to belief opposed to contrary belief. How can we preserve allegiance to these freedoms and still achieve social cohesion based on a common faith?

Our problem is acute in different ways in war and in peace. During a war a free society must partly imitate a monolithic society by temporarily abrogating certain freedoms. We are willing to give our leaders special powers "for the duration" and to subject ourselves to considerable regimentation and censorship. At such times the problem of corporate solidarity is largely solved for us by a common external threat and our common goal of victory. The danger is, of course, that we will become habituated to these war-time controls and that the partial abrogation of our freedoms will turn out to be less temporary than was intended.

The opposite danger threatens a free society in times of peace. For then, often in the very name of freedom, predatory individuals and groups seek to exploit the public and may succeed in doing so for lack of adequate governmental restraint. Rugged individualism in its most antisocial forms may flourish unchecked by popular indignation or official action. Social injustice affecting large minorities may be ignored by a complacent majority; governments may refuse to raise urgently needed funds through taxation; and the public, lulled into a false sense of security, may decline to practice self-restraint and fail to make the effort requisite for national strength and health.

The defense of freedom is particularly difficult for us because we must ultimately rely not on a small group of self-appointed rulers but upon a whole society of self-disciplined citizens who have taken upon themselves the ultimate responsibility of governmental power and social control. Nothing is more difficult than to raise the general public conscience to the level requisite for resolute action in restraint of vice and in furtherance of the general welfare. Many oligarchies have been ruled for a time by small, able, and beneficent groups. Our problem is the colossal one of self-rule. The vast majority of our many millions of citizens must be informed enough, wise enough, concerned enough for the welfare of others, and self-disciplined enough to rule themselves and one another.

One thing is clear: no society can achieve uncoerced social solidarity unless it makes freedom itself its cornerstone. History has shown how relatively easy it is to achieve social cohesion *at the price of* freedom, and how hard it is to achieve it and maintain it *in terms of* freedom. Yet this is our task; for us, union at the expense of freedom must be utter defeat, not victory. Whatever else we do, we must weave our basic freedoms and our allegiance to freedom itself into the very fabric of our society. Here no compromise is possible.

Liberalism, defined as unswerving loyalty to the principle of liberty, lies at the very heart of our common venture. A free society must be liberal; an illiberal free society is a contradiction in terms. Such liberalism will express itself most clearly in a liberal attitude of mutual respect and tolerance—not the tolerance of cynical indifference, not partial tolerance on minor issues, but that basic tolerance which respects and welcomes radical disagreement on questions of major human import. It is easy to be tolerant of conflicting opinions if one believes that nothing really matters and that, in the last analysis, one opinion is as good as another. It is also easy to tolerate inconsequential and trivial beliefs and practices. Real tolerance manifests itself only when crucial issues are at stake. This is the tolerance of the genuine liberal and the tolerance requisite for a really free society.

IS THE LIBERAL ATTITUDE SUFFICIENT?

A second major difficulty concerns the full meaning and scope of the term "liberalism." All liberals will agree that it necessarily involves the liberal attitude and that this attitude, in turn, entails not only genuine tolerance but lively criticism of others and self-criticism. The question is: "Does the liberal attitude, so defined, constitute the whole of liberalism?" Is such a liberal attitude self-explanatory and self-sufficient? Can it be divorced from a more basic underlying faith? Should it be asked to generate a common program of social action?

There are many people today who would call themselves "liberals" who sincerely believe that liberalism is indeed merely an attitude of tolerance and critical inquiry. They are convinced that such an attitude is self-sufficient, that its value is self-evident and self-authenticating. They believe that any attempt to justify the liberal attitude by relating it to a more basic faith in man or in the universe or in both is contrary to the very spirit of liberalism and an inevitable lapse into the dogmatism deplored and resisted by authentic liberals. They also believe that liberalism by definition precludes the very idea of a common program of action. In short, liberalism is here reduced without remainder to the liberal attitude of universal tolerance and unceasing criticism.

This conception of liberalism has been well expressed by the late Morris R. Cohen in his book *The Faith of a Liberal:* [1]

> Liberalism is too often misconceived as a new set of dogmas taught by a newer and better set of priests called "liberals." Liberalism is an attitude *rather than* a set of dogmas—an attitude that insists upon questioning all plausible and self-evident propositions, seeking not to reject them but to find out what evidence there is to support them rather than their possible alternatives.
> . . . The liberal temper [is], above all, a faith in enlightenment, a faith in a process *rather than* in a set of doctrines, a faith instilled with pride in the achievements of the human mind, and yet colored with a deep humility before the vision of a world so much larger than our human hopes and thoughts. . . . The real liberal believes that life is important only as the condition or opportunity for the good life, and prefers not to live at all if he must live as a slave or in degradation.

This is an admirable description of the liberal attitude of tolerance and critical inquiry. It reflects man's faith in his own cognitive and critical powers and, no less, his recognition of his own inescapable fini-

---

[1] Morris R. Cohen, *The Faith of a Liberal* (Henry Holt and Company, Inc., New York, 1946), pp. 437, 468–69. Italics supplied.

tude in the face of cosmic mystery. It is therefore an attitude of open-mindedness rather than dogmatic certainty, of self-reliance rather than servility, of humility rather than arrogance. The true liberal is one who is imbued with the Socratic temper of unremitting search; he believes that "the unexamined life is not worth living." The liberalism that permeated our western heritage and that we want to recapture, revitalize, and reaffirm must, at the very least, be defined in terms of this Socratic attitude.

The crucial question, however, is whether this liberal attitude is self-sufficient or whether, on the contrary, it itself depends upon certain basic beliefs regarding man and the universe. Why, for example, does Cohen, in company with other liberals, believe so firmly in "enlightenment"? Why does he put such faith in the process of critical inquiry? Is not the answer to these questions to be found in his conception of man as a rational being whose "good life" depends essentially upon the free and untrammeled use of his mind? The liberal attitude, as Cohen himself describes it, is by no means independent of and indifferent to his underlying interpretation of human nature and of man's proper destiny. If we repudiate this interpretation we undercut the attitude that reflects it and essentially depends upon it. It is *because* man is capable of examining his life and *because* he can realize his true nature only by critical inquiry that the unexamined life is not worth living. Cohen's deep faith in the liberal attitude is itself rooted in his anterior belief in man as a conscious and reflective being.

Or again, why does Cohen believe that the truly liberal attitude is "colored with a deep humility"? Is it not because, to quote his own words, man has a "vision of a world so much larger than our human hopes and thoughts"? It is because the world, as we encounter it with intelligence and imagination, confronts us with mysterious vistas and depths we cannot encompass that we are impelled to humility. Deny man's sense of human finitude in the presence of cosmic infinity, and humility promptly loses its appropriateness. Humility per se makes no sense; it makes sense only in a larger context, that of finite man facing a universe too complex and mysterious for his complete understanding.

Or, once again, why is freedom so precious to man and why is slavery so abhorrent a degradation? The slavery of complete regimentation does not seem abhorrent to the Communist because he conceives of man as craving and needing security at any price. Freedom for the Communist is not what it is for the liberal—the pearl of great price—because of his radically different conception of human nature and human destiny. It is for him not only a useless luxury but a positive threat to what, in his reading of human nature, constitutes man's basic need—the need for economic and social security. The liberal does not minimize this need but subordinates it, in his reading of human nature and in his hierarchy of values, to man's need for the higher freedoms, to think with intellectual integrity and to believe and worship with moral and spiritual integrity. Here too the attitude of liberalism seems to be rooted essentially in an underlying conception of what man is in his essence.

I can see no way of avoiding the conclusion that the liberal attitude is not self-explanatory or self-sufficient but that it is, on the contrary, derived from prior beliefs regarding human nature and the cosmos and that it is defensible only by reference to and in terms of these prior beliefs.

Cohen's account of liberalism raises another question of equal importance: whether or not a liberal attitude precludes all firmly held beliefs. Cohen, in company with many liberals, is apparently convinced that all firm beliefs must be held blindly and uncritically as "doctrines" or "dogmas" and that they are therefore necessarily inconsistent with the liberal attitude. Is this correct? Is it impossible for a man to hold a belief so firmly that he can decide and act on the basis of it and yet simultaneously subject it to the critical scrutiny dictated by the liberal attitude? Are real conviction and real open-mindedness radically incompatible? Is reflective commitment impossible?

It is interesting to note that Socrates, whose eulogy of the examined life is always being invoked by liberals, managed to combine a lifelong critical analysis of the current beliefs of his day and of his own progressively formed opinions with such ringing spiritual affirmations as: "Be assured that no harm can befall a good man, either in this life or the next" and "I do believe in the gods, indeed, more sincerely than do my accusers." [2] He did achieve reflective commitment to a notable degree— a wholehearted commitment that was at the same time thoroughly self-critical and humble. Such reflective commitment has also been achieved by others in our tradition, by philosophers like Plato and Kant, by theo-

[2] See *Crito* and *Phaedo*.

logians like Augustine and Pascal, by statesmen like Jefferson and Lincoln, and by countless scientists, explorers, and venturesome men of affairs. Firm belief and critical inquiry need not be mutually exclusive.

They are compatible, of course, only if the beliefs in question are held with an open-mindedness reflecting a real conviction that man and all his works are inescapably finite and that all man's knowledge is therefore essentially partial and fallible. In one way or another all authoritarians deny this basic major premise by accepting the infallibility of a secular or religious institution, of a document such as the Bible or the Constitution, of human reason at its purified best, or of man's conscience or basic intuitions. Whatever their locus of infallibility, they accept it without reserve or question and assign absolute authority to its pronouncements. They regard these pronouncements as literally certain, that is, as being of such a nature that their opposites are utterly inconceivable. Those who believe that absolute and indubitable truths of this type are available to man and that they themselves actually possess them will, of course, be unable to subject such truths to challenge or criticism. They will also be quite incapable of tolerance in these areas, for how can one who is absolutely sure of the truth tolerate what by the same token is radical error? Such dogmatic—that is, systematically unchallenged—assurance must issue in a spirit of intolerance and give rise to an attitude completely antithetical to what we have described as the liberal attitude.

But "firm belief" need not be authoritarian in this sense. It can take the form of "moral assurance" or "certitude," that is, an assurance strong enough to enable a man to live by it, and if necessary die for it, without a claim to any degree of infallibility. This is the temper of the spiritual affirmations by which Socrates lived so triumphantly and died so serenely. Socrates did not claim to have ever "proved" them ultimately, nor did he ever insist on the inconceivability of their opposites. Indeed, he carefully explored the possibility that they might be completely wrong. But, having tested them to the best of his ability, he was content to accept them as the tenets of his ultimate "philosophy of life."

Is not this the spirit of wholehearted religious faith at its reflective best? It remains a "faith" to the very end because it can never be proved with finality, but it can, as we well know, lead to the greatest sacrifice, including martyrdom. Is not this also the distinctive quality of the scientist's faith in his scientific method and of the philosopher's faith in dialectic? Confidence is, of course, pragmatically enlarged by every new scientific discovery and fresh philosophical insight. But the scientist can never prove in any final manner that there is a world of nature, or that it is orderly through and through, or that his human mind is qualified to explore and apprehend this order, or even that the effort to apprehend it is in itself worth while. These are all ultimate acts of faith on his part—not blind faith, for he has an impressive body of scientific knowledge and intrinsic satisfaction to justify this faith—but faith, nonetheless, rather than absolute certainty. The same is true of the philosopher's ultimate faith in an orderly reality and in his ability and obligation to explore it as best he can with his finite mind. The fact that philosophy can neither start from nor issue in absolute certainties is no impediment to philosophical inquiry; philosophers too have suffered and died for their "moral certitudes."

What is true of religion, philosophy, and science is equally true of every other human enterprise. The common man who makes no pretensions to expertness in any of these areas can test this for himself. None of us can be absolutely certain that a husband or wife or lifelong friend is loyal, or that the faith he lives by is valid, or that his basic values are as sound as he takes them to be. Only a naïve dogmatist (and there are many such) will deny the fallibility of his deepest moral certitudes; only a fool will refuse to rely on these certitudes and base his life on them.

It seems clear, then, that firm belief defined as "moral certitude" is possible in every walk of life and at every level of erudition. It is not only possible, it is necessary as the essential precondition of such activities as religious worship and philosophical speculation, scientific inquiry and the normal living of one's life.

It is equally clear that our faith can be validly strengthened only by more insight and understanding and that these are the product of an ever continuing critical inquiry. I say "validly strengthened" because faith can indeed be emotionally intense in the virtual absence of knowledge and reflection. Pathological hopes and fears are the extreme instance of such intense, irrational belief. In contrast, belief is rational only in so far as it is well grounded and well tested. This means that we dare not leave any of our beliefs, particularly our most basic and cherished

42

beliefs, unexamined and uncriticized, for if we do so we are bound to lapse into the dogmatism of thoughtless acceptance. It also means that we can hope to render our beliefs more rational only if we, in co-operation with our fellows, persist in the search for new evidence and greater intellectual clarity, however painfully this search may force us to modify the beliefs to which we have clung, it may be for a lifetime. The surest mark of a mature liberal is his willingness to submit a lifelong belief to this crucial test and, if necessary, to abandon it or radically modify it in his later years.

I submit, then, that those who insist that all firmly held beliefs are necessarily blind dogmas are fundamentally in error. We can hold such beliefs firmly yet critically, resolutely yet humbly. Man can and does, at his creedal and critical best, declare: "Here I stand—I can do no other!" without, in the process, surreptitiously playing God and claiming for himself even a fragment of divine omniscience.

CAN ANY FREE SOCIETY HAVE A COMMON FAITH AND A COMMON PROGRAM?

Two further questions must now be considered with care. The first relates to the possibility of a free society's achieving a common faith capable of undergirding a strong common allegiance to the liberal attitude. The other concerns the possibility of devising and putting into operation a practical program of united liberal action. A liberalism hanging in a void, without a philosophical base and without practical implementation, would seem to be condemned to sentimental vagueness and ineffectiveness, particularly in a world like ours of militant ideologies and violent economic and political tensions.

The characteristic answer of many liberals is that, for better or worse, this is the fate liberalism cannot avoid. All that a liberal can do, they insist, is advocate the liberal attitude in and for itself and then leave it to the individual liberal to root his own liberalism in whatever ultimate faith suits him best and translate his liberal attitude into whatever concrete policies and actions recommend themselves to him as an individual. The liberal society thus envisaged would be, to all intents and purposes, an anarchistic society in which the only bond holding men together was their common loyalty to the principle of inquiry and tolerance.

43

Liberals of this persuasion would abandon all hope for any other common faith. They would also object on principle to any effort to achieve such a common faith, on the grounds that free men are bound to disagree in their ultimate beliefs; that such disagreement is natural and salutary, the very condition of man's spiritual health and social progress; and that radical disagreement can be avoided or overcome in only one way—the fatal way of totalitarian regimentation.

They would also reject both the possibility and the desirability of joining forces at the practical level by setting up a concrete program of action to implement a common liberal creed. Not long ago several of my friends and I explored the feasibility of getting together some prominent liberals in different walks of life—political, industrial, educational, theological, and so on—to discuss our common problem and to see whether we might be able to formulate a creed of liberalism and create a united front in support of our basic freedoms. The answer of a prominent lawyer, declining our exploratory invitation, was typical and illuminating.

I think it would be a waste of time for eight or ten convinced intelligent liberals from different walks of life to get together for several long week ends to discuss this crucial problem, to map a course of practical action, prepare a liberal manifesto, form an effective pressure group, work on many fronts, and try to give a lead to liberals in our country and throughout the world.

. . . Frankly, I think it impossible through one week end or many of them to form your united front of liberalism. *That seems to me almost a contradiction in terms.* For example, I regard Justice Frankfurter, Justice Douglas, and John Lord O'Brian as liberals. I can imagine them standing together on many issues. But (even assuming they were otherwise free to do so) I cannot imagine their subscription to such a united front. . . . Their several viewpoints are basically too divergent. [Italics supplied.]

This letter is ambiguous in two important respects. It is not clear precisely how the writer conceived of a "united front" or what he meant by the last statement about divergent viewpoints. It may be that he had in mind controversial political or economic policies on which intelligent men are bound to differ, and that a "united front" meant for him some sort of democratic counterpart to the Communist party line, which dictates not only ultimate objectives but also the practical means by which these objectives are to be pursued. If so, his protest was well founded. Liberalism must indeed repudiate any such regimentation of belief and action.

However, his statement seems to go much further than this. He seems to be denying the very possibility of a long-range liberal program at any practical level. He grants that certain liberals may be able to stand together on certain issues at any particular time, but he seems to be convinced that such agreement and united action must be accidental in the sense of being unpremeditated and unplanned. Apparently they must also be temporary, with the expectation that the next issue that arises will, or at least may, provoke disagreement among those who may have found themselves in agreement on a previous issue. An "independent" congressman would seem to typify the liberalism here defended—a congressman who acknowledges no party affiliation, accepts no long-range party policy, and votes on each bill simply as his own conscience dictates.

This basic repudiation of the very idea of a common liberal faith underlying the liberal attitude and of the very notion of a common program designed to implement such a faith and attitude is widely prevalent among the liberals of our day. Small wonder that liberalism has of late been relatively ineffective in its opposition to well-organized secular and religious forces at home and abroad—forces with not only passion for their cause but, in addition, a basic philosophy and a practical program.

In our further analysis of liberalism we may be driven to define it in these restrictive terms. If so, I believe we shall have to conclude that liberalism cannot provide us, either as individuals or as a nation, with a sustaining and guiding philosophy of life. No man can live his life solely on the basis of open-minded inquiry and charitable tolerance. Really to live, deeply and fully, we must have certain affirmative beliefs regarding ourselves, our fellow-men, and the universe, and we must find some way of expressing these beliefs in action, some way of working toward our goals. The liberals I have been describing would doubtless agree that this is true for any given individual. But is it not equally clear that no society can survive, particularly in the same world with communism, without some common beliefs, objectives, loyalty, and program of action? However precious may be the spirit and temper of liberalism as an attitude, that attitude cannot suffice as the only basis for communal life and corporate endeavor. A society without common fundamental beliefs is not a community but a mere aggregate of individuals existing in a cultural and spiritual vacuum. And just as nature abhors a physical vacuum, so human nature abhors a spiritual vacuum. In a period of doubt and skepticism such as our own, men will adopt any corporate beliefs they can find. If liberalism cannot provide us with such beliefs today, our people will certainly look for them elsewhere in order to make their own lives meaningful and to make possible whatever bold corporate action may be deemed necessary. No one can predict precisely where they will look or what they will find, but it is a safe guess that they will finally adopt some type of illiberal authoritarianism, secular or ecclesiastical, that will be profoundly hostile to the spirit of free liberal inquiry and genuine tolerance.

Our task is clear. We must search for those beliefs which explain and justify the liberal attitude itself, for beliefs so basic that they constitute the very presuppositions of free inquiry, democratic procedure, legality and human decency—in short, for the beliefs that already in some measure constitute the working creed of a free people. We must also consider with care the possibility of working out some common program in and through which liberals can join forces in promoting their common cause.

IS A COMMON FAITH POSSIBLE IN OUR HETEROGENEOUS SOCIETY?

Were we a culturally homogeneous people this question would not be so acute. We are, however, a deeply divided people. We are most nearly in agreement about the enduring validity and value of our democracy and of science, though even here we differ widely among ourselves in our understanding of both processes and of their implications. Many of us attach great value to the continuing humanistic tradition, the search for wisdom, and the creation and enjoyment of significant art, though most of us pay them little more than lip service. It is our religious heritage over which we as a nation differ most radically. This is the locus of our deepest cultural cleavage.

There are those among us whose religious faith, Christian or Hebraic, is for them of supreme importance. There are others no less intelligent and sincere who reject all variants of traditional religious belief with equal conviction and fervor. There is also a large group of "indifferent-ists" who ignore religion both in theory and in practice, who fall short of convinced atheism on the one hand or convinced theistic faith on the other, and who are agnostics more by default than by reflective decision. It is these indifferentists who, in company with the relatively small band of convinced skeptics and atheists, constitute the "secularists" in our midst. It is their beliefs or half-beliefs or lack of positive religious be-liefs that make us today so largely a secular society. For we are by no means a religious nation, fundamentally committed to a common reli-gious faith and way of life; we are, at best, a nation half-religious and half-secular.

The bold dichotomy between the "religious" and the "secular" is, of course, only a rough preliminary classification of the enormous variety of vital beliefs that motivate us. The terms "religious" and "secular" are both omnibus terms embracing widely deviant beliefs and attitudes.

The term "religious" includes not only Roman Catholics, Protestants, and Jews but also Roman Catholics who differ notably among them-selves on many crucial issues, Protestants of many different sects, and Jews whose religious beliefs and practices differ no less widely. The term "religious" can also be applied to those who belong to what Paul Tillich has called the "latent church," that is, to those sincere and humble search-ers after God who rightly or wrongly find it impossible honestly to affili-ate themselves with any traditional religious body but who believe in and worship God, the Object of their quest, in their own private and individual ways. Finally, there are endless private variations in doctrine and practice and in intensity of belief and dedicated social concern within each of the religious groups just mentioned. What we actually find is precisely the wide diversity of doctrine and ritual, individual and corporate behavior to which our cherished "freedom of worship" was bound to lead.

The term "secular" is no less ambiguous and catholic in what it is made to embrace. It includes, on the one hand, the considerable group of impassioned "humanists" who insist on man's distinctive dignity and intrinsic value. These humanists fall into two camps: those who believe that the basic values of truth and goodness, justice and beauty are in some sense "objective," somehow imbedded in the universe, not man-made but awaiting man's progressive discovery and actualization in human history; and those who conceive of "nature" or "reality" as neutral, that is, as essentially devoid of all value, and who therefore believe that the values men envisage and seek to actualize are essentially man-made, not anterior to man or awaiting his discovery.

The "secular" also includes in its domain those "naturalists" who ascribe primacy to "nature," who conceive of nature solely in terms of the findings of the natural sciences, and who therefore define human nature in strictly naturalistic terms. They disagree with the humanists chiefly in their refusal to admit any difference in kind between man and the higher animals; he differs from them only in degree—that is, in complexity of structure and behavior, not in intrinsic value. But naturalists, too, differ greatly among themselves, some going much further than others in reducing man to the status of a mere complex psychophysical organism and nature to mere spatiotemporal process. Some, like Spinoza, are impressed by man's distinctive characteristics and find in nature those infinite depths which impelled Spinoza to equate God and nature in his famous phrase *deus sive natura*. Despite their doctrinal heterodoxy according to all orthodox theistic criteria, the genuine piety of these spiritually minded naturalists might well justify us in adding them to our mixed group of religious believers.

Finally, the term "secular" must be made to include all those among the religious indifferentists who have found a secular god to whom they give their highest loyalty and whom they serve with quasi-religious fervor. These include the men and women who give their ultimate allegiance to science or art, to the cause of political democracy or social reform; all impassioned "nationalists" who virtually worship the United States as a sovereign nation; those who believe that a world government will usher in utopia; or, finally, those who make humanity itself their god. There are also those whose secular god is far less idealized—who value above all else their own sensuous gratifications, economic "success," social prestige, or power for its own sake. These too have their ultimate loyalties for which they are willing to sacrifice all else. Any of these loyalties can be basic enough to clash with one another and with the diverse ultimate loyalties of the theist, the humanist, and the naturalist in varying degrees and with varying intensity. In short, what we find here is again what we should expect to find in a free society dedicated since its founding to freedom of speech and of ultimate conviction.

Even this description of the wide spectrum of ultimate beliefs in our society fails to take account of the fact that few of us fall neatly into any of these categories. We are all infinitely complex beings with conflicting interests and beliefs, hopes and fears of which we ourselves are only partly aware. Who, save perhaps the rare reflective philosopher or theologian, really knows what he believes with any clarity or why he cherishes the beliefs he seems to hold, or how steadfastly he does hold and consistently act on the beliefs that he openly expresses from time to time? Who can distinguish clearly within himself his own overt and latent, conscious and unconscious, firm and tenuous, important and trivial convictions? And who can relate his multiple attitudes and his complex and often inconsistent behavior to the beliefs he is able to discover within himself and articulate in words? If, then, each of us finds it difficult to know and express his own beliefs, how impossible the task of describing that infinitely complex amalgam of beliefs that constitutes the working faith of the American people.

This problem is clearly one of such gigantic dimensions that we cannot possibly hope for anything like a precise analysis or comprehensive description. We must content ourselves with a few general comments.

The first is that *our creedal heterogeneity is by no means unique to our country or our own times.* There was radical divergence of belief in the early Colonies and in the decades preceding and following the Civil War. We have never been a homogeneous nation on matters of ultimate human concern. Nor do we differ in this respect from other free nations, for freedom breeds diversity of belief, and human interests are as diverse in Europe as they are on this continent. Any society seems to tend in the direction of creedal uniformity when its people are kept ignorant and ideologically regimented; it inclines toward creedal diversity when real freedom of speech and worship prevails. Ignorance and tyranny are the two great historic forces making for a monolithic conformity of belief; education and freedom are the chief sources of creedal diversity.

A second generalization is needed to offset the one-sidedness of the first. *Freedom and education need not produce diversity of opinion or preclude substantial agreement on matters of major human concern.*

49

The history of free religious communities is a record of both agreement and disagreement, among both the theologically elite and the common worshipers. The history of art records continuities in creative techniques and standards of taste as well as creative innovations. The democratic movement could never have arisen and flourished as it has if large numbers of people had not been able to band themselves together for the common task of popular self-government. Despite the radical differences between major philosophical positions, there is considerable agreement among philosophers on the basic nature and value of philosophy, the scope of its perennial problems, and the standards by which solutions for these problems should be judged. In recent times, science is the outstanding example of the extent to which highly educated men, who in their scientific work enjoy the greatest possible intellectual freedom, are able to agree regarding not only the methods of scientific inquiry but also the scientific results of this inquiry. It may therefore not be too presumptuous to assert that men tend to agree rather than disagree to the extent to which their thinking stems out of a common or shared experience, their education enables them to think clearly and cogently, and their search for truth is allowed to proceed without being deflected, warped, or stifled by artificial external restraint.

We can venture a third large generalization regarding the contemporary scene which, if it is at all valid, we shall have to take seriously into account in our ensuing inquiry. *We Americans tend to agree far more on our conception of human nature and man's secular welfare than we do on our conception of the universe and its ultimate import for man.* There is widespread agreement among all decent and thoughtful Americans that human beings, regardless of color, creed, sex, or social status, are in some significant sense beings of intrinsic worth and therefore should not be ruthlessly exploited or cruelly tortured and put to death. We differ sharply, however, when we attempt to explain man's intrinsic value in more ultimate terms. Is this value God-given, or natural, or merely the product of our human tradition? Again, we all recognize the fact that men do value some things more than others, that they entertain ideals and seek to actualize these ideals, and that these evaluations and strivings should therefore be appropriately honored by a humane society concerned with the welfare of its individual members. We are even in considerable agreement concerning these actually cherished values. We approve of health and cleanliness, peace and order, comfort and beauty, decency and justice, truth and love. We disapprove of their opposites; we seek to restrain vice and correct pathological perversity. It is chiefly when the questions arise why these values have merit and whether they are merely social or somehow "objective" and real in their own right that dispute becomes serious.

In short, the issues on which we disagree most profoundly have to do with the ultimate nature of the reality that confronts and encompasses us. Is reality in itself hostile, neutral, or friendly to human welfare and aspiration? Is it indifferent to value or somehow impregnated with value? Is there a God, or is nature itself divine, or does nature possess mysterious depths of holiness that should be differentiated from its finite spatiotemporal manifestations?

It is these questions which have always puzzled mankind most profoundly and which have been the preoccupation of religious thinkers and philosophers in every age and culture. It is these same questions which so profoundly puzzle us today and to which we give such divergent answers with such varying degrees of assurance. It is because these questions concern each of us so vitally that we take our several answers to them so seriously. The irony of man's predicament is that he can know with least assurance what concerns him most deeply. Here, in the light of our human finitude and the inevitable inadequacy of our knowledge of the Ultimate, humility should be the rule rather than the exception; yet it is precisely here that life itself seems to demand of us maximum assurance—an assurance that makes genuine tolerance so very difficult.

The problem of how to achieve a vital common faith is somewhat different at different social levels. At the sophisticated level our problem is one of reconciling conflicting beliefs that are well articulated and plausibly defended. It is the better informed religious believers, on the one hand, and the better informed secularists, on the other, who have come to grips most violently over these issues. Here we find the most dogmatism and intolerance. By and large, the great secular-religious cleavage in our culture is most pronounced at this "higher" level, among this small minority of religious and antireligious enthusiasts. For the great mass of our population, the problem transforms itself into one of spiritual lethargy, the tolerance of indifference, or the intolerance of sheer bigotry. At this level, which is much nearer our nation's cultural

51

center of gravity, the problem of religious belief or disbelief is less urgent in men's minds and hearts. Here the Olympian disputes are echoed in bickerings over conventional mores; here the well-grounded intolerances of the sophisticated reverberate in grosser religious and racial prejudice.

This is not a pretty picture. It is certainly unfair in its neglect of a small minority of really enlightened and tolerant believers and disbelievers and of a much larger minority of genuinely concerned and tolerant folk who have had little or no secular or religious education. These two minority groups are the liberal yeast with which the total lump must be leavened if it is ever to be liberalized. However, we dare not close our eyes to the intolerance of many of our intellectual and spiritual leaders or to the widespread lethargy and bigotry of most of our "common" men and women. Witness the disputes among theologians and academicians; witness the lives and thoughts, hopes and fears, of the "average" American citizen.

Barring a wholesale atomic war, it is hard to see what can happen to us as a nation in the foreseeable future that is likely to change this overall picture radically. Widespread religious evangelism, such as that of Billy Graham, might slightly alter the ratio of "believers" and "disbelievers" in our land, and greatly revitalized churches and synagogues might have a comparable effect. Yet no one seriously expects our entire nation to become religiously oriented in any significant sense, nor is our nation as a whole likely to close its churches and transform itself into a homogeneously secular society. We can also count on the continuation of our vast spiritual indifference and lack of intellectual curiosity, for in all cultures and at all times this has been the characteristic state of most of mankind.

What, then, is our hope? What, if anything, is possible? What can we do to remedy this situation? The only answer we can give is that a slow change for the better is possible if the leavening liberal minority will exert itself hard enough and soon enough to provide our nation with the right kind of forceful and dynamic leadership. Leaders can rely primarily on force and regimentation designed to elicit passive, slavish obedience, or they can rely primarily on rational persuasion, inviting the willing co-operation of the common man. The former type of leadership and response is that of all totalitarian regimes; the latter, the ideal of all free societies. The method of uncoercive and persuasive leadership is inevitably slow, far slower than that of revolutionary authoritarian force, and for the first time in human history, with the discovery of the atom bomb and its devilish progeny, time may be running out on us. It may already be too late for us to save ourselves by the only method appropriate to a free people. But there is still hope, and this hope rests squarely on the shoulders of those whose special gifts and opportunities have put them in some position of leadership in our society. It is the task of the liberal minority to lead the common man wisely, courageously, and efficiently in the direction of more stable peace, more intellectual curiosity, more justice and compassion, more love, more spiritual strength and dedication, more genuine tolerance. This is pre-eminently the task of and contemporary challenge to liberalism.

The "common faith" of which we as a nation stand in such urgent need is not the compelled faith of a monolithic society, nor the faith, however true and potent, of any sectarian religious body or secular movement, nor merely a common acceptance of the liberal attitude. It must be a reasonable faith—not totally provable, but based on evidence and purified by reflection. It must be as "realistic" and unutopian as possible, but it must also do full justice to man's deepest spiritual experiences and his highest aspirations. It must welcome honest diversity of opinion, but it must articulate a common area of agreement broad enough and firm enough to enable us to use it as a basis for our common efforts. It must suffice both to undergird and to direct our lives as free and responsible members of a free co-operative community. It must express itself in a creed that is as clear and as compelling as the Communist Manifesto but differs from it as radically as our ideal of a free society differs from the Communist ideal of a totalitarian society.

Let us beware of utopian hopes. The task we have in view can certainly not be performed with complete success. We are bound to fail in the future as we have in the past, but not necessarily in the same ways or to the same degree. Nor should we believe that this task can be undertaken in only one way, secular or religious. The problem that confronts us is so difficult and so challenging precisely because it is so many-sided, calling for all the wisdom and ingenuity of men and women of the most diverse talents and of very different persuasions. Our goal must be to find a way in which all these talents and beliefs can be put to work in fruitful and co-ordinated harmony.

PART II

A Liberal Creed and Three Areas of Controversy

Introduction

"What is man, that Thou art mindful of him?"

"Man is the measure of all things."

These two famous statements, the one Biblical, the other ascribed to the Greek humanist and sophist Protagoras, set the stage for our inquiry. Both are focused on man; both point beyond man to the reality he encounters; both ascribe intrinsic value and dignity to man. They differ radically, however, in their explanation of the source of this dignity and value. The Biblical account insists that man is nothing apart from God, that he possesses intrinsic value only because he is created and sustained by God and because God loves him as a father loves his children. Protagoras, in contrast, finds in the universe no loving Father, no cosmic source of human dignity and value. Reality, he believes, is indifferent to human aspiration, neutral with respect to all the values man most prizes. Man is therefore strictly "on his own," himself the source of values and the author of his own dignity. It is not man's task to realize his God-given destiny; rather, it is his task to forge his own destiny and make of himself what he can.

This basic divergence of ultimate belief has persisted through the centuries and prevails today in our own land. It constitutes the great spiritual cleavage in our half-secular, half-religious society. By and large, and with all due allowance for doctrinal variations in both camps, the convinced secularists among us subscribe to the Protagorean thesis, the convinced religious believers to the Biblical thesis. Is there any constructive way of mediating between these two camps?

Our problem would be well-nigh hopeless if they disagreed as radically about human nature as they do about ultimate reality. Such, however, is not the case. What we actually find is widespread agreement regarding the sanctity of human life and man's dignity and intrinsic value. Let us start with this area of agreement and try to discover what it is in human nature that gives man the dignity and the value so widely ascribed to him.

Man has three basic potentialities or endowments that we can all accept and prize, however divergent our respective accounts of their ultimate ground. Each raises a distinctive metaphysical problem that has puzzled mankind since serious speculation first started and seems to be as far as ever from definitive solution. In this area of perennial controversy we shall have to agree to disagree in our ultimate faith, while still working together in a free society on the basis of our common reading of human nature.

Our immediate task is therefore clear. It is, first, to state and explain three simple and basic propositions on which it is hoped all liberals can agree and, second, to indicate in each case a related area of ultimate belief and inevitable controversy. The three initial propositions constitute what might be called a liberal creed, particularly when they are taken in conjunction with the three areas of dispute. The careful definition of these areas and the liberal resolve to avoid all dogmatic intolerance within these areas is clearly as important for the cause of corporate liberalism as is common agreement to the three affirmative articles of the creed itself. It is necessary for us to know where and why we cannot hope to agree and, on these issues, to cultivate a mutual tolerance rooted in the humility of acknowledged finitude. It is also necessary for us to reinforce by appropriate formulation and common acceptance whatever affirmative beliefs we do in fact share.

Chapter 5

Man as an Evaluator

*M*AN IS AN EVALUATOR. He is a being who can discriminate between truth and error, honesty and falsehood, beauty and ugliness, justice and injustice, love and cruelty. He can also appreciate the value of truth and honesty, beauty, justice, and love and the disvalue, or evil, of their opposites. In short, he is able to evaluate, to make value judgments; he can discriminate and then consciously approve or disapprove. Of course, he does so only inadequately; his evaluations are often mistaken and never perfect. Nonetheless, he can distinguish between good and evil, and he can abhor evil and cleave to the good.

More than once philosophers have attempted to interpret all values in terms of pleasure and pain, thus reducing man's evaluative capacity to the more primitive ability to feel pleasure and pain and to prefer the former to the latter. In principle this would reduce man's status to that of animals, since they too, at least at the higher levels, seem to feel pleasure and pain and to attempt to act in such a way as to avoid pain and pursue pleasure. In this view man would be nothing more than the most complicated of psychophysical organisms. He would differ from his humbler fellow-creatures only in his capacity for various pleasures and pains beyond their ken. His "morality" would reduce itself to prudence, and prudence would presumably dictate the use of some sort of calculus of pleasures and pains whereby they could be matched and balanced in terms of their duration, intensity, certainty, fecundity, and the like.

This interpretation of man's evaluations would not have persisted through the centuries had it not possessed an element of truth. We do feel pleasures and pains of many different types; we do both consciously and unconsciously try to increase our pleasures and lessen our pains; we do, furthermore, take pleasure in what we judge to be good and experience pain in the presence of evil. The cardinal weakness of such a hedonism, as has been repeatedly pointed out, is that it puts the cart before the horse; it makes the feeling of pleasure and pain the basic source of values and the basic ground of man's evaluative judgments. It assumes the identity of the pleasurable and the good and approves of the pleasurable merely because it is pleasurable. A more searching analysis reverses this conclusion. It sees that men not only discriminate between good and evil pleasures (thus refuting the identity of the pleasurable and the good); it points out that they are able to take pleasure in what they judge to be good because it is good, not merely because it is pleasurable.

The proof of this interpretation is that we are capable of valuing certain "goods" so highly that we feel powerfully obligated to cherish them at whatever cost of pain and suffering up to and including death. It is true that we do, on occasion, pursue pleasure for its own sake, often with a good conscience. We act hedonistically, for example, when we drink for the pleasure of drinking or go to a dentist in order to stop a toothache. The argument against hedonism is that men need not act with this hedonistic motivation and that they can and do exhibit loyalty to certain values even when this loyalty involves great suffering and sacrifice. When hedonists claim that men act in this way only because of the "satisfaction" such loyalty occasions, the answer is, once again, that the satisfaction is the result and not the cause of the loyalty. If we are loyal to truth we will indeed find the pursuit of truth deeply satisfying; but this satisfaction will depend upon our loyalty to truth itself; we are not loyal to it merely because its pursuit gives us pleasure. It seems indubitable that men, unlike animals, can and do apprehend values as values and that they are capable of wholehearted loyalty to them for their own sake.

We must now note a further characteristic of the values that claim man's loyalty. They are directly encounterable only in concrete contexts and, in these contexts, only partially and incompletely; hence man's inevitable tendency to conceive of them also in their abstract perfection. For example, we never encounter abstract justice in all its purity. All that we can directly experience are concrete instances of justice —in a person, a law, a human transaction, and so on. But these concrete instances of justice never seem to us to exhaust its nature; if our evaluations are at all sensitive we shrink from declaring any individual, law, or transaction to be absolutely just. Why is this possible? It is possible only because we are able, however vaguely, to conceive abstractly of a more nearly perfect justice by reference to which all concrete instances of justice are seen to be inadequate exemplifications or approximations.

All values, then, have a curious ambivalence for the sensitive evaluator. He can cherish them in their concrete manifestations—in more or less beautiful art or nature, in more or less just or loving persons, in more or less true human judgments—which always fall short of perfect beauty or justice, love or truth. But he must also deplore the inadequacy of all such manifestations and make every effort to actualize ideal values more adequately. Hence the artist's ceaseless effort to achieve greater beauty in his work, the scientist's endless quest for truths not yet captured and formulated, the reformer's eager efforts to promote greater justice and purer love in his society. We value all concrete instances of value, however partial and defective they may be, but we always feel more or less powerfully impelled to try to make good their deficiencies. Values thus evoke our loyalty at both the concrete and the abstract levels. In doing so they create in us a sense of tension between the ideal and the actual. This sense of tension is our sense of obligation: the more sensitive we are, the more do we feel inwardly impelled or obligated to improve whatever we think and do and create—to strive for more perfect art, more adequate truth in every area of life, a purer justice, mercy, and love—in short, for more perfect "goodness," of whatever type, in all our creative ventures.

This is surely one of man's basic characteristics that contribute to the dignity and value we in the West so typically ascribe to him. We ascribe intrinsic value to him because he can apprehend values and respond to them with loyalty, and also because he can sacrifice everything for the values he most highly cherishes.

The differentiation of man from the higher animals need not imply a cynical unconcern for their own value and welfare. We can love a favorite dog for himself, freely acknowledging his many canine virtues and cherishing him to the point of real sacrifice. But in doing so we value him and respect his canine rights as he himself is unable to value or respect himself or other dogs or other living creatures. His responses are, we must believe, merely instinctive and conditioned. We cannot ascribe to him or to other nonhuman living creatures the ability to appraise concrete situations in terms of what to us is good and evil, to envisage ideal values abstractly, or to feel reflectively obligated to make the actual conform more closely to the ideal. The line between us and the higher animals may not, indeed, be absolute, but the differences between us and them seem in this and in other respects so great as to amount to a difference in kind. It is these differences that justify us in conceiving of man as unique among living creatures—unique in intrinsic value because of his unique capacities.

THE STATUS OF VALUES

The foregoing account of man as evaluator was intended to be as descriptive and objective as possible. Its purpose was to point to a universal characteristic of man which anyone can verify for himself and about whose factuality there should be no serious question. A great deal of controversy has arisen over the interpretation of this human trait and its implications. This controversy has been mainly focused on two issues —the status of values and the nature of evaluation. We can formulate the issues as follows: (1) Are values in any meaningful sense "objective," awaiting man's discovery and inviting his loyalty? (2) If so, how and to what extent can he discover them? If not, what is the significance of his evaluations?

Naïve common sense tends to assume quite uncritically that values do exist in their own right and that their discovery constitutes no special problem. It assumes that of course there is such a thing as truth or justice and that of course right-minded men and women can discover them with a little education and reflection and can agree on what is true and just, beautiful and right. This position can conveniently be labeled "naïve realism."

The trouble with naïve realism is that it fails to take into account the very wide variety of things to which people have given their approval and disapproval. Historical and anthropological research during the past century has abundantly confirmed earlier suspicions that men differ greatly in their judgments about what is true and false, beautiful and ugly, right and wrong within any given culture and that they differ even more radically in different cultures and different historical periods. There is scarcely a belief or a mode of conduct that has not been approved in some culture and disapproved in another, and even in the same culture man's evaluations have often been radically modified or reversed with the passage of time. In fact, the highest common denominator of agreement among all men at all times is so low as to be negligible. As regards sex, for example, about the only universal concensus we can find is the need for some sexual controls and tabus; even incest, which is frowned upon in most societies, has been accorded a limited sanction in some, for example, in ancient Egypt in the case of the royal family.

These considerations have impelled many thoughtful people to adopt a completely relativistic position regarding values and the act of evaluation. They deny the existence of objective values having a character of their own and awaiting human discovery. They insist that what are called "values" are merely human ideals that men in different circumstances and on different occasions have quite naturally envisaged in radically different ways. They recognize that every culture has its own values, its own standards of conduct and its own beliefs, and that every society has its own ways of impressing such values upon its members, either by persuasion or force. Accordingly, they stress the conditioning process whereby individual members of a society, however different their temperaments and abilities may be, are induced to conform to the orthodoxies of the group. They recognize the possibility of approving or disapproving of specific beliefs and acts within a given culture or society by reference to that culture's dominant standards; such standards, they admit, possess a kind of "social objectivity" that any competent observer can discover and describe. They also recognize individual deviations from these social norms, but they believe that such deviations merely reflect the individual's partial uniqueness. They conclude that all human evaluations are nothing but individual preferences more or less molded by social convention and that they therefore necessarily lack epistemological validity or truth. It is, they believe, quite impossible to transcend one's own personal perspective and one's own social conditioning. It is therefore impossible to assess the values of any culture by reference to more objective transcultural standards. All that can be done is to evaluate beliefs and acts within a culture by reference to the standards of that culture, or, alternatively, to evaluate one society in terms of the standards of another society. Neither type of evaluation, however, can possess any objective validity, because there are no objective standards or values and because, even if there were, we would have no way of discovering them.

The implications of this extreme relativism are momentous. If all human evaluations are merely individually and socially conditioned, that is, if they merely reflect individual temperament and social mores in combination, there is no possible way of preferring, on any reasonable objective basis, one culture to another or even the evaluations of one individual to those of another individual within the same culture. As regards Soviet Russia and ourselves, for example, this relativism would necessitate the conclusion that the evaluations of the Communists merely reflect their cultural background as ours merely reflect our cultural background, that we and they are therefore equally prejudiced and provincial, and that there simply is no transcultural standard, no higher court of appeal, available for the adjudication of our quarrel. All that they or we can do is resort to irrational emotive persuasion, that is, to propaganda, and, if that fails, to force. Neither side can claim any objective validity whatsoever for its position. Ours is no more a righteous cause than theirs. What they believe and what we believe are in the last analysis equally irrational and indefensible because, in both cases, beliefs and social values reflect nothing but different cultural conditioning. Could anything more effectively reduce our world-wide struggle with communism to meaninglessness and all our sacrifices to ironic nonsense? Could any interpretation of the world scene more surely cut the nerve of our present corporate effort?

The implications of complete relativism are no less far-reaching within a given culture. The denial of objective truth, justice, and goodness automatically makes nonsense of all serious intellectual inquiry and all responsible moral endeavor. If there is no objective truth to be sought for, or if such truth is completely beyond our human reach, man's perennial efforts to apprehend the truth more adequately are *ipso facto* futile and ridiculous, and his conviction that some beliefs must be more nearly true than others is entirely meaningless. Actually, the extreme relativist cannot even claim with any logical justification that the relativism he himself professes and recommends to others is true. All he can do is express his opinions as nothing more than individually and socially conditioned beliefs that, according to his own argument, can possess no more truth or validity than their opposites. The radical denial of objective truth is thus intellectually suicidal; the more successfully the relativist defends his position the more meaningless it becomes. He is like a man who is triumphantly sawing off the tree branch on which he is sitting.

Similarly, to deny the very possibility of objective justice is to reduce all human relations, all social attitudes, and all types of behavior to the status of merely culturally conditioned social conventions and deviations from them. It entirely precludes the possibility of appraising any belief, attitude, or action save in terms of its conformity with or deviation from the ultimately irrational standards of the society in question. To rob the "good" and the "right" of all objective meaning is automatically to reduce "goodness" to mere conventionality and "right" to "might." And when right and might are thus identified, might is not thereby rendered righteous; rather, right loses its meaning and becomes nothing but might. Extreme relativism is thus seen to be as morally suicidal as it is intellectually suicidal. It is, in fact, nihilistic; it empties all our value terms of their intrinsic meaning, destroys the very possibility of intellectual and moral integrity, and cuts the nerve of all intellectual and moral endeavor. Its nihilistic results in the realms of art and religion are the same: beauty and holiness become as meaningless as truth and justice—man's age-old search for both becomes utterly futile. We are well justified in labeling this position "nihilistic relativism."

It is worthy of note that Communist Russia seems to have gone a long way in the direction of such nihilistic relativism. To the extent to which the Politburo has cynically repudiated the claims of objective truth and objective justice it has brought into being a state in which force and force alone has the final say. The more it has denied the scientist's right and obligation to search for and express the truth as honestly as he can, the more has it destroyed the foundations of objective scientific inquiry. The more it has repudiated the concept of objective justice, the more has it undermined the possibility of legal integrity and fair play. The chief justification for our continued resistance to communism is its nihilism, its wholesale repudiation of objective values, and its resultant evolution into a ruthless and inhuman police state. Our opposition to communism would indeed be ironic were we as a nation to embrace the very nihilism it so tragically exemplifies.

If we are to take seriously the concept of man as an evaluator, we must at the very least resolutely reject a nihilistic relativism which denies that there are any objective values and that all we can say about men and cultures is that they differ in their preferences. If this were the whole story, there would be no possible reason, apart from blind, irrational prejudice, for condemning Communist lies and cruelty or for being ready to sacrifice and, if necessary, die for what we believe to be basic human rights and basic human values. A nihilist can have no rational answer to any of the questions that most vitally concern us as human beings; all he can do is confess that he simply prefers to live in a certain way, whatever this way may be.

To reject nihilism is to assert at least by implication that there are, somehow and in some sense, objective values within human reach. But this assertion immediately gives rise to another danger, which is as grave in its own way as the danger of nihilism. It gives the dogmatist a chance, which he is not slow to grasp, to insist not only that such objective values exist and that they are in principle progressively discoverable by human beings but also—and here is the rub—that at least some men can apprehend them and have apprehended them with absolute certainty and finality. In short, the dialectical swing of the argument can all too easily induce us to jump out of the pan of nihilism into the fire of dogmatic authoritarianism.

This authoritarianism manifests itself whenever any individual or group regards any human being or institution as in any sense infallible, or any human opinion or interpretation as final and indubitable. It is essentially a form of idolatry because it ascribes to a finite human belief, person, document, or institution the infallibility that in fact, if it belongs to anyone, belongs only to the Deity. The precise form and content of authoritarianism will, of course, differ from individual to individual and group to group. It may be claimed for the pope, speaking ex cathedra, or for a dictator, a divinely inspired church or Bible, some rationalistic dogma, or man's private conscience. It may even be claimed for what is taken to be "common sense," and it is often claimed for the uncritical prejudices of some group that presumes to speak with final authority in defense of such causes as "100 per cent Americanism," "white supremacy," or some particular economic or political program. Whatever its specific nature and however ignorant or enlightened, unselfish or exploitative, honest or dishonest it may be, it always involves the neglect or repudiation of man's finitude and fallibility and therefore contains some measure of arrogance and pride and lacks basic humility. It stands in radical opposition to a central tenet of all the higher religions (that man is fallible and sinful), to the very spirit of scientific inquiry (which is essentially tentative and humble rather than dogmatic and arrogant), to man's eternal quest for ever greater wisdom (since no man is ever wholly wise), and to a basic axiom of democracy (that power corrupts and that a free society dare not therefore give absolute power to any individual or group). Both secular and religious authoritarianism has indeed manifested itself again and again in the West, but always in opposition to the peculiar genius of our western culture. It is essentially un-Biblical and unphilosophical, unscientific and undemocratic; it is the very antithesis of western liberalism. It too can, in its way, weaken the liberal spirit and finally destroy a free society as surely as can the acids of skeptical nihilistic relativism.

This "rightist" danger is far greater in our own nation today than is its "leftist" counterpart. Among us, the temptation to nihilistic relativism is strongest in certain restricted sophisticated circles, whereas the temptation to self-righteous authoritarianism is strongest precisely in those well-populated groups—ecclesiastical and political, civic and fraternal—which make up the bulk of our society and which most loudly and indiscriminately denounce the "leftism" of college professors. Therefore, as a nation we must be particularly on our guard against it; we can be sure that it will cloak itself with seductive protestations of loyalty to God and nation, free enterprise, and the democratic way of life.

It is not surprising, when one stops to think of it, that Soviet communism, like German nazism and Italian fascism, has managed to combine nihilism and authoritarianism. This apparent contradiction is understandable when one remembers that both doctrines are essentially appeals to the irrational. Each therefore tends to generate and reinforce the other. As a nation gradually succumbs to nihilistic skepticism and paralyzing doubt, a spiritual vacuum is created. It is then that people most crave strong leadership, the more affirmative and assured the better. Hence the quick response to the authoritarian voice of a dictator and the eager submission to his will. The people's eyes are opened to his tyranny only after it is too late to cast off his heavy yoke. Nihilism thus breeds tyranny. But tyranny likewise engenders nihilism. For even the most arbitrary tyranny must have its plausible rationale, and this rationale can be no other than the dogmatic claim that only the ruler knows the truth and that he knows it with authoritative certainty. Hence his right to impose his absolute will on all who are under him and their duty to obey his dictates blindly. The ultimate irrationalism of both nihilism and authoritarian absolutism thus feed and strengthen one another.

The cause of liberalism would indeed be hopeless if there were no middle road between these two extremes. Fortunately there is such a road—one that might fairly be described as the highway the pioneers of our western culture built and traveled. The middle position, which can for convenience be labeled "critical realism," resembles both relativism and authoritarianism yet differs from each in certain crucial respects.

The critical realist agrees with the relativist that all human knowledge is relative to man's cognitive powers and always reflects the unique perspective of the individual knower as well as the conditioning impact of his society and culture. He is therefore at one with the relativist in repudiating the very possibility of infallibility; no human apprehension can ever be absolutely certain or final. What he repudiates in nihilistic relativism is its nihilism—its loss of faith in objective values and in man's ability to apprehend them, however partially and fallibly. Here he agrees with the spiritually affirmative authoritarians, that is, with those authoritarians who do believe in objective values and in man's ability to encounter them. What he rejects in the faith of the authoritarians is not their faith but their authoritarianism—their claim to a type of certainty he believes to be inconsistent with human finitude. In short, the critical realist has faith in objective truth and beauty, justice and love. He also believes that human nature is somehow congenial to these objective values and that man can, with the requisite sensitivity, reflection, and discipline, apprehend them more and more adequately. But he is firmly convinced that no finite human person, document, or institution can possibly comprehend these absolutes without limitation or distortion. Man's knowledge is indeed relative to individual perspective and social conditioning, but it is not merely relative; it is also to some degree authentic and reliable. Man's evaluations are indeed apprehensions of real values, but they must always fall short of perfect comprehension; they may suffice to give him "moral certitude," but they can never give him complete certainty.

In our society, it is the scientist who most clearly exemplifies the middle position and most successfully travels the middle road. The major presupposition, however unconscious, of his scientific quest is that his search for the truth about nature and human nature is not idle and that there is a way (the scientific method) whereby men of science can apprehend this truth more and more adequately.[1] But, as a true scientist, he systematically refuses to claim finality for any of his discoveries; indeed, he is confident that science as a human enterprise will never be able to achieve absolute certainty. For him, science is a wholly finite venture, based on a faith in objective truth and increasingly successful in its approximations to it, but, by its very nature, incapable of transcending the finitude of its proponents. A genuine scientist is therefore both creedal and critical, both assured and humble. He has faith in objective truth and in man's ability to apprehend it more and more adequately, but he also has the humility that is engendered by his abiding sense of human fallibility.

This is essentially the liberal spirit. This is precisely what liberalism demands in every area of human inquiry and creative effort. The liberal believes in a justice that transcends all human justice, past, present, or future, and devotes his life to its more adequate apprehension and actualization in his society. He does not cynically reduce justice to any or all actual legal practices and procedures, nor does he absolutize any such finite approximations to perfect justice. He is forever mindful of the vital tension not only between actual justice and his

---

[1] We must not be misled by the famous theory of relativity, which is in no sense nihilistic in intent. Rather, it is the most adequate account yet devised of the basic spatio-temporal structure of the physical universe. It is today accepted as "true," that is, as *more* adequate to *the* truth regarding nature than any previous scientific theory.

conception of ideal justice but also between his or any other human conception of justice and what justice is in itself. The nihilist denies the very notion of objective justice; the authoritarian absolutizes some finite idea or embodiment of it; the mature liberal accepts all human laws and all legal procedures for what they are—man's best effort in his own society and age to apprehend true justice and give it social embodiment. The enlightened creative artist and the art-lover conceive of objective beauty and finite instances of beauty in the same way. The enlightened theologian is similarly a man of faith and humility; he too believes that man can indeed encounter and apprehend the holiness of the Divine, yet never with infallible certainty. The true philosopher in his way and the democratic statesman in his are animated by the same spirit of confidence and caution, courage and restraint. Their quest for wisdom, whether speculative or practical, is never halting and never ending; theirs is a perpetual discontent with past achievement and an unquenchable hope for more knowledge and wisdom in the future.

Critical realism is thus seen to be a refinement of the naïve realism of the common man. The trouble with naïve realism is not its realistic faith but its naïveté; man must live by faith, but this faith need not remain untutored and gullible. The faith of a critical realist is a faith tested by experience and reflection; it is not the spontaneous faith of the uncritical but a faith toughened and purified by trial and error, success and failure, venture and doubt. It is the faith of the "expert," the man who is able to stand firmly on the shoulders of his predecessors and to reach higher and see farther than most of his contemporaries. Nihilism precludes the very possibility of expertness; authoritarianism endows the expert with an unmerited and unwished-for halo. The critical realist honors the expert for what he is and acknowledges his right to persuasive leadership. He thus endorses the spontaneous conviction of the common man that some men must be wiser than others in their comprehension of truth, justice, beauty, and holiness. A healthy society will honor its experts, its great scientists, statesmen, artists, moralists, prophets, and saints. But it will not deify them or identify their wisdom with the wisdom of God. A healthy democratic society will, by the same token, repudiate Jacksonian egalitarianism; it will espouse the liberal Jeffersonian principle that every society needs leaders and that such leaders must be found, trained, and intelligently followed if the society is to prosper. But it will never forget that the greatest of leaders differs from the humblest of his followers only in degree, never in kind, and that even he is powerless to lead without their loyal yet critical support.

Such would seem to be the minimum implications of responsible evaluation. For how can man's evaluations be taken seriously if there are no objective values to apprehend or if, though real, they remain completely hidden from all men? Or how can any individual value judgment be taken seriously if all value judgments are equally devoid of validity and if it is therefore impossible, in principle, to believe that any value judgment is "truer" or "more adequate" to its referent than any other? Or, finally, how can moral and intellectual integrity have any meaning if fidelity to the good and the true is meaningless because goodness and truth are nothing? Faith in objective values in some sense would therefore seem to be the absolute *sine qua non* of responsible evaluation and responsible living. The case against dogmatic authoritarianism would seem to be equally strong. For, if authoritarian certainty were in fact within man's reach, how can we explain the notorious contradictions among pronouncements alleged to be infallible? And if there is but one genuine authority, by what infallible criterion or sign can this unique authority be identified? And even if such a criterion were available, how could any finite mortal escape the necessity of applying this criterion for himself and therefore of running the risk of being wrong in his use of it?

We must admit that all these considerations leave many sincere and responsible people unconvinced. There are some philosophers, for example, who would defend the possibility and the importance of responsible evaluation and still deny that values are in any sense objective. There are also men of religious faith who with complete religious sincerity and devotion accept as absolute some religious authority without qualm or question. How should a genuine liberal relate himself to these opposing groups? The answer to this very crucial question should be clear. His only course is to retreat to our *modus vivendi,* to the liberal attitude of genuine tolerance for everything except intolerance. He can live in peace and mutual respect with anyone of any persuasion, provided the prerequisites of mutual respect are honored and not themselves repudiated. Even more crucial for liberalism than a man's explicit convictions are his implicit convictions, which reveal themselves in his basic attitudes and his daily conduct. A liberal must resist and seek to overcome any basic cynicism that expresses itself in contempt and irresponsibility as well as any basic dogmatism that manifests itself in self-righteousness and ruthless domination. He should, of course, be as patient and understanding as possible in his dealings with the cynic and the dogmatist as human beings. But only as he himself exemplifies a liberal attitude and only as he encounters a similar attitude of respect and open-mindedness in others can he and they really converse together, work together, and learn from one another. When this liberal attitude does prevail, for whatever reason and on whatever sound or unsound basis, a real meeting of minds can take place, and when minds really meet, co-operative clarification of the most controversial and crucial issues and the testing of the most diverse opinions are always possible.

Meanwhile, those who are prepared to travel the middle road must also explore a further area of controversy. I refer to that congeries of problems relating to the meaning of "objectivity" and "value." I have insisted that "values" must "somehow" be judged to be objective or judged to be objective "in some sense." But precisely how, and precisely in what sense? What do we mean by "objectivity" in general and, in particular, by the "objectivity of values"? And what, more specifically, do we mean by "values"? Are some more "objective" than others? Should some or all be conceived of (as Plato and Santayana would suggest) as eternal essences? Or are they (as Dewey believes) more akin to human ideals? And should we think of them as somehow dependent upon the Deity? These are but a few of the problems to which the sincere believer in objective values must address himself.

The foregoing analysis can now be summarized as follows: The liberal attitude is the *modus vivendi* of a free society. This attitude assumes that man has certain basic traits. The first of these is his ability to evaluate. That man is in fact an evaluator is therefore the first article of the liberal creed. Thus far no serious question arises and agreement among liberals can be assumed.

The assertion that man is an evaluator does, however, raise the vexed problem of the status of values and of our knowledge of them. Three contrasting solutions of this problem are possible, and two of these solutions—nihilistic relativism and authoritarian absolutism—threaten in opposite ways to undermine responsible evaluation and to violate the very spirit of liberalism, whereas the third, critical realism, seems to undergird responsible evaluation and to be wholly consistent with the liberal temper. Nevertheless, liberals can continue to debate the merits of these three positions if they maintain the liberal attitude and if they subscribe, at least implicitly, to man's ability to make responsible value judgments. In short, these positions define an area of inescapable controversy, but such controversy can and should be conducted in a liberal spirit.

Problems relating to the nature of values and evaluation can also continue indefinitely without violating the basic tenet that man is somehow capable of responsible evaluation and therefore without jeopardizing the basis of a free society. There are many ways in which the objectivity of values can be defined and defended; there are alternative criteria by which value judgments can be assessed. These need not be assumed to be equally satisfactory, and progress in clarification, which will facilitate greater agreement, can always be hoped for. But the mysterious depths of ultimate reality are bound to baffle comprehension to the end of human history. Here, then, we must be prepared to agree to disagree—not because these issues are unimportant but because their perfect resolution seems to transcend our finite ability and because these disagreements need not jeopardize our continuing respect for man as a responsible evaluator.

Chapter 6

Man as a Moral Agent

$\mathcal{M}$AN IS A moral agent. He can distinguish between good and bad, right and wrong; moreover, he can deliberately take sides with moral responsibility. He can envisage alternative lines of action, reflect on them, assess them by reference to some ideal standard, decide in favor of one of them, and then express his decision in appropriate action. Man is thus capable not only of responsible evaluation but also of responsible choice and conduct in the light of such evaluation. It is this capacity that so clearly distinguishes a man from a well-trained dog. The dog is incapable of human good and evil because, so far as we can tell, he cannot envisage good and evil, reflect upon them, and deliberately decide to act for or against the good. He is not a moral agent because he lacks the basic requisites of full-fledged moral responsibility.

We make a similar distinction between morally responsible and irresponsible conduct in our judicious treatment of young children, the senile, and the mentally deranged. Though no absolute line can be drawn, we tend to consider children, the aged, and the mentally ill as responsible for their actions only to the extent that we judge them able to discriminate between right and wrong, to reflect more or less cogently, and to decide and act in the light of such reflection.

In our dealings with our fellow-men we also try on occasion to determine which persons are more able and which are less able to differentiate between right and wrong, to reflect rationally, and to decide and act responsibly, taking into account, so far as possible, both native aptitudes and social environment. For example, we are making increasing allowance for juvenile delinquency as we acquire a better understanding of its social causes. We send delinquents to reformatories instead of to prisons, and we tend to blame the family background or the more inclusive social background rather than the individual delinquent. We also try to distinguish unpremeditated acts of violence induced by sudden emotion from premeditated and cold-blooded acts, and acts motivated by urgent need, such as extreme destitution, from acts for which there is no such mitigating circumstance.

The list of such attempts at moral discrimination could be extended indefinitely. They all betoken a profound, and perhaps a growing, bewilderment over the true meaning and extent of moral responsibility. They also serve to underline the crucial importance for us of the problem of freedom to which we must presently give our attention. However, the fact remains that all mature and responsible men and women in our society (and, so far as we can tell, in all other human societies) do believe that somehow, complicating factors aside, human beings are responsible moral agents. Try as we may, we cannot escape our own deep-seated sense of moral responsibility and the ensuing sense of guilt when we have done what we believe we should not and need not have done. We hold others responsible in a similar manner, and we judge those otherwise normal adults who seem to be incapable of a sense of guilt to be less than human, that is, to be pathological. However puzzled we may be regarding the ultimate nature of human freedom and responsibility, we still believe in our heart of hearts that we are somehow free and responsible moral agents. We respect human beings partly because we conceive of them in this way. There can be no question that the affirmation of man's moral responsibility deserves to be listed as the second tenet of our liberal creed.

THE PROBLEM OF FREEDOM

No problem has troubled men longer or more profoundly than the problem of human freedom and responsibility; none is more likely to remain indefinitely a source of perplexity and controversy. Here, as in our consideration of the status of values, we must first outline two contrasting positions that threaten to undermine man's sense of responsibility; we can then define some of the perennial issues that constitute this area of continuing controversy. The two opposing interpretations of freedom seriously threatening responsible morality are extreme determinism and extreme libertarianism.

The extreme determinist traces all human thought and action back to inherited traits and to habits induced by social influences, that is, to factors over which the individual has no control. He thus ends by relieving man of all moral responsibility: man is no more responsible than any animal. However good or evil man's actions, they are all judged to have been absolutely predetermined by his heredity and his environment, over which he has no control. Freedom is therefore an illusion; necessity is the inviolable law of life. Whatever is, must be.

The supporting argument of the determinist is very plausible. Each human being is endowed at birth with various aptitudes and is born into a social situation for which he patently has no responsibility whatever. There is no reason for supposing that we existed prior to our conception, or that we asked to be born, or that we had any say in the selection of our innate endowments or our parents. Nor had we any control over our prenatal environment. As newborn infants we were precisely what our heredity and our prenatal care made us, and for a considerable period after birth we were subjected to physical and social conditioning influences over which, once again, we had no control Thus far, the deterministic argument is unanswerable.

It is quite impossible to know at what precise moment in the life of a growing child he is first able to distinguish between right and wrong and to reflect, decide, and act in what we call a morally responsible manner. There is an indefinite period when he behaves more like a complicated animal whose responses are being "trained" than a free moral agent. Yet somewhere along the line his distinctively human capacities ripen and a "self" emerges; it is this self which, we suppose, makes the first morally responsible decision. How does the determinist interpret this decision?

The determinist maintains that the self that is here presumed to reflect, decide, and act for the first time must be precisely that self which its heredity and his environment have made it. Its first "responsible" choice is not, therefore, a choice for which the self can be held responsible at all; it is wholly predetermined by two factors—the nature (wholly determined) of the deciding self at that instant and the total environmental setting in which this self is placed. This first choice, itself determined, will have its effect upon the self, which presently makes its second "free" decision. But this decision is, in fact, no more free or responsible than the first, for now the acting self is merely the initial self slightly modified by its first decision and its consequences. The same is true of all subsequent decisions and actions of the self, however informed, reflective, and mature it may become. Nowhere, from birth to death, is there any escape from the tyranny of heredity and environment; it is impossible for a self to emerge whose nature, and therefore its reflective decisions and actions, are not completely determined by factors beyond its control. The determinist denies no observable facts. He merely insists (1) that all the reflections, decisions, and actions of any self are wholly determined by what this self is vis-à-vis its environment, and (2) that this self is what it is because of the sum of earlier conditioning factors—its innate inheritance, its total environment from the moment of conception, and the cumulative influences upon it at any instant of its own previous wholly predetermined decisions and actions.

This account of the self clearly leaves no place for really creative spontaneity, for any kind of indeterminism, or for any freedom whatever from causal factors over which the self has no control. Spontaneity becomes an illusion; for though the reflective self, like the unreflecting self, can be said to initiate an act, it does so entirely because it is at that instant what it is (that is, what it has been made into) and because its stimulating environment is what it is. Our frequent inability to know in advance how we will decide and act cannot be accepted as evidence of any objective indeterminism; it only proves how little we know about ourselves and other selves. The more real understanding we acquire about ourselves and other selves, the more certainly can we predict how we and others will decide and act under specifiable circumstances. The better a mother understands her child, the more accurately can she prophesy his reactions. An omniscient Deity could, we must believe, anticipate all human decisions and actions with absolute certainty. This means that the very concept of freedom is ultimately meaningless. No doubt man does differ from other living creatures in structure and behavior and is therefore subject to somewhat different conditioning influences; but he is no freer than they from the universal rule of law and conditioning influence.

The moral implications of this position are readily apparent. Ultimate responsibility becomes totally meaningless. We are what we are and do what we do because of the universe that has brought us into being with certain endowments and has surrounded us with our conditioning environment. Radical guilt and justifiable pride become equally meaningless. How can we intelligently feel guilty for, or take pride in, what we are bound to do? All retributive punishment and all merited praise are similarly ruled out of court, since no one can be said to have responsibly done right or wrong. To be logical we must restrict ourselves to corrective blame and praise, punishment and reward designed exclusively to modify future behavior, as animals and small children are punished and rewarded not to even the score or because they merit such treatment but only to train them for the future. In short, radical determinism completely negates our moral differentiation between responsible adults and infants, the senile, and the mentally deranged. Of course, differences can still be noted between individuals and between human types, and each individual and each type can still be accorded that kind of treatment which is best calculated to achieve certain desired effects; but all must be judged equally lacking in freedom and moral responsibility.

The libertarian position stresses human freedom as stanchly as determinism opposes it. In its more naïve form it simply asserts man's freedom and responsibility without trying to analyze their meaning or explain them. At a more sophisticated level the libertarian usually invokes an entity other than the self, which he calls the "soul." The self, he can then argue, may be as completely determined as the determinist says it is; it is the soul, in contrast, which constitutes man's true essence, which is free and responsible, and which is destined for immortality. It is this soul which experiences real guilt and which merits punishment; in a religious context it is the soul whose ultimate destiny is righteous salvation or damnation.

However worthy the motives of the libertarian may be, under close scrutiny his position is found to be as unintelligible and implausible as that of the determinist is intelligible and plausible. It will suffice to mention a few of the major difficulties his view entails. (1) There is no empirical evidence whatever for the existence of such a soul. (2) Assuming the soul's existence, moreover, one finds it impossible to give any intelligible account of it if, as is claimed, it is completely distinct from and unaffected by the self of which we are aware in self-consciousness and to which we attribute "our" thoughts and voluntary acts. Such a differentiation between soul and self must be maintained if the soul is to be free from all determining influences, both hereditary and environmental, upon the self. But what, then, is a soul that cannot sense, imagine, reflect, decide, or act? (3) If, despite these difficulties, we do endow the soul with any or all of these familiar human capacities, we find ourselves committed to a soul whose radical independence of nature, man, and God must make it an unpredictable and terrifying entity rather than the locus of moral responsibility. The soul has been invented or postulated to explain human freedom, where freedom is defined as freedom from all determining influence, natural, human, or divine. It is therefore condemned to a limbo where nothing and nobody can ever reach it or help it. It cannot be trained or educated, loved or hated, helped or hurt by man or beast or even by God himself. Indeed, to be completely free, it must be conceived of as self-created, as subject to laws (if any) of which we can have no inkling, as "somehow" animating man, and, from time to time, as impelling him to act in a manner that is, in principle, completely unpredictable. (4) All attempts to praise or blame, reward or punish such a soul would be impossible, for nothing can reach it or influence it in any way. In its absolute freedom from all external influence it would have to be completely self-sufficient, a law unto itself, condemned to perpetual solitude.

Why waste time on such a ridiculous position, especially since no one can be cited who would defend this libertarian doctrine to the limit? This description will not have been in vain if it has helped to underline the grave difficulties encountered by all those who seek to offer a rational defense of human freedom and responsibility. We can now at least be sure that the attempt to ascribe absolute freedom to finite man (where freedom is defined as freedom from all external influence) is doomed to failure. For better or for worse, we have not created ourselves, nor are we ever immune to the many natural and social forces playing upon us, nor (if our religious heritage has any validity at all) can we ever escape the prevenient Grace of Deity. Whatever freedom we may have must be interpretable, if at all, within the context of man's inescapable dependence upon forces not of his making and beyond his control.

Taken in conjunction, determinism and libertarianism confront us with a curious problem—one that partly resembles and partly differs from the problem raised by the initial conflict between the relativistic and the authoritarian interpretations of value. There we found that at its constructive best each of the two interpretations contained a kernel of truth. We also found it possible to outline a third position that seemed to do full justice to the element of truth in each of the two positions and at the same time avoided the illiberal implications of each in its most extreme form. We could claim greater reasonableness and plausibility for "critical realism" than we could for either of the positions it sought to mediate. Our present problem resembles the earlier problem in that, once again, both the extreme alternatives thus far described contain an element of truth we must cling to unless we are prepared to ignore certain inescapable facts and do violence to one of man's deepest convictions. We dare not shut our eyes to the hereditary and environmental influences upon the self insisted on by the determinist, nor dare we close our hearts to man's profound sense of genuine moral responsibility. The problem of freedom differs from the problem of values in one crucial respect: all relevant knowledge and all reflective analysis seem to support the deterministic thesis, whereas our moral sensitivity impels us irresistibly to believe that, despite all arguments to the contrary, we are "somehow" free and responsible moral agents.

The dilemma here confronting us is one that Pascal might well have described in terms of an apparently irreconcilable conflict between the "head" and the "heart." Our minds point us compellingly in the direction of determinism; our hearts command us as insistently to acknowledge our moral responsibilities and to believe, however blindly, in whatever freedom they presuppose. To my knowledge, no philosopher or theologian has ever worked out a mediating position that is more plausible than determinism and at the same time really does justice to our sense of moral responsibility—a position, in short, that fully satisfies both heart and mind. We therefore seem destined, if we are really honest, to cling to two apparently irreconcilable beliefs. Our moral and intellectual integrity forbids our taking the easy way out by canceling out one of the two factors. It seems to be our fate to live and act as though we were free and responsible moral agents, despite all rational evidence to the contrary.

Having stated our human predicament as honestly and bluntly as possible, we can now suggest the direction in which a more satisfactory solution of our problem may perhaps someday be found. We can also attempt some further distinctions that may help clarify the problem.

TOWARD A DEFENSE OF CREATIVE SPONTANEITY

Any account of freedom, to be at all promising, must somehow come to grips with the highly controversial issue of the nature of an "influence," or "force," on the one hand and, on the other, of the nature of the "laws" or "regularities" science seeks to explore. The deterministic theory we have briefly outlined rests on a triple assumption—first, that dynamic forces actually exist and are in fact operative, making spatio-temporal events take place as they do; second, that these forces operate without exception in obedience to pre-established laws or patterns of order that have somehow been imposed upon our universe; and third, that every individual entity, including man, is absolutely subject to, or determined by, the dynamic forces that function in this preordained orderly way. Hence the impossibility of genuine spontaneity anywhere in the universe. What confronts us and constrains us is an all-inclusive, all-controlling cosmic order to which all entities and all events, human and subhuman, are equally and absolutely subject. This is the familiar traditional picture of universal determinism, which excludes the very possibility of genuine human spontaneity, creativity, freedom, or responsibility.

We can, however, envisage a very different interpretation of reality and our place in it. We can suppose that the source and locus of all finite forces in our universe is the individual finite entity and that each such entity is therefore endowed to some degree (large or small, depending on its nature) with a capacity for genuine creative spontaneity. We can further suppose that the forces thus generated play upon one another either in discord or in harmony, so that each individual entity is in fact influenced by all the other entities it directly or indirectly encounters. But we can also suppose that no entity need be wholly deter-

81

mined by these external forces because it possesses the capacity to resist them at least to some extent and to control the effect of these influences upon itself. We can suppose, finally, that our universe is not under the domination of any preordained laws which have been imposed upon it and to which all its constituent entities, forces, and events must automatically conform but, rather, that what we call the "laws of nature" are merely discoverable parts or aspects of that over-all pattern of order which *emerges as a statistical result* of all the interactions of all the spontaneous entities constituting the spatiotemporal universe.

These are, admittedly, no more than philosophical speculations whose truth it would be exceedingly difficult, if not impossible, to verify. Yet they have the merit of being intelligible and logical and of not overtly contradicting any assured scientific findings or current scientific hypotheses. They also have the great merit of suggesting a new conceptual account of reality that might perhaps make human freedom more intelligible. For the self could now be conceived of as possessing a genuine creative spontaneity of its own while continuing to be open to external influences—natural, social, and divine. A real, though limited, freedom could thus be attributed to the self, and with it a real though limited moral responsibility for its actions. In order to be free the self would not have to function in a vacuum; it would be deeply involved in its total environment and able to profit from beneficent influences playing upon it. Yet it would not be deterministically coerced by any of these environmental forces because it could in some measure control its own responses to them and even resist them on its own responsibility.

We must beware of concluding that any such philosophical position could completely resolve the ultimate mystery of human freedom and responsibility. To work out all the implications of such an approach would first of all necessitate a major metaphysical effort comparable to that of the late Alfred North Whitehead, and even Whitehead's account of reality, for all its profundity and brilliance, bristles with contradictions and enigmas. Here we find ourselves squarely in the center of continuing controversy. Our chief concern must be to safeguard the two vital considerations already noted: our knowledge of man's creaturely dependence and our moral faith in his freedom and responsibility. Neglect of either consideration is bound to jeopardize our effort to understand man's true nature and to impair the dignity and value we ascribe to him. Any philosophy that leads to this derogative conclusion is unworthy of our acceptance.

VOLUNTARISTIC AND NORMATIVE FREEDOM

We have thus far discussed only one type of freedom—freedom from external influence. We were justified in doing so because it is this "voluntaristic" freedom which is the essential prerequisite for genuine moral responsibility. There is another type of freedom, however, which can be entitled "normative" freedom. This is not freedom from coercion but freedom for the good life. It is man's positive ability to know and do whatever is beneficial to his own highest nature and thus to realize his own proper destiny. Any systematic account of freedom must do as full justice to man's normative capacities as it does to his voluntaristic powers.

A man can be said to be normatively free when he is actually able (by whatever means or powers) to achieve knowledge and wisdom and to escape from the shackles of ignorance, to be virtuous and to eschew vice, to create and enjoy beauty and to escape aesthetic uncreativeness and insensitivity, to find and serve the Deity and to avoid idolatry. This is the freedom of affirmative self-realization: the ability not only to apprehend objective values but really to make them one's own, to actualize them in one's own character and conduct. It is the freedom, not of independence from, but of fruitful *dependence upon and response to,* whatever in man's total environment can enhance his stature and make him a more nearly complete person. Voluntaristic freedom is man's ability to do whatever he wishes, good or evil; it includes the power to accept salvation or go to the devil. Normative freedom *is* salvation, the conversion to and acceptance of the good; it is escape from the devil and all his evil ways.

It should be noted that these two types of freedom are not in any way antithetical. Neither excludes the other; indeed, the total freedom we crave includes both. Both types have been repeatedly stressed and explored in our western culture—normative freedom primarily, but not solely, by the ancient Greeks and their spiritual descendants, voluntaristic freedom primarily, but again not solely, by the Jews and the Christians. It is only extreme positions such as complete determinism and radical libertarianism that emphasize the one freedom at the expense of the other. Determinism can do full justice to normative freedom since, even if our actions are wholly determined, they may if we are fortunate be beneficially determined by our heredity and environment; but, as we have seen, it wholly excludes the voluntaristic freedom of a really free will. Libertarianism exactly reverses the picture. It seeks to safeguard man's voluntaristic freedom but in the process succeeds in depriving him of all the beneficent contacts with reality without which he is doomed to the utter frustration of solitude.

The more we ponder this antithesis, the more we are impelled to seek a total freedom that is both voluntaristic and normative—a freedom that enables us to learn from nature and from our fellow-men and still do our own responsible thinking, to learn how to create and enjoy beauty and still appreciate beauty and create our art as we see fit, to open ourselves to divine redemption and still be free to accept or reject the divine initiative. We want to be helped but not coerced to be wiser and better than we are; we want to be voluntaristically free, yet able to use this freedom wisely and justly. Our continued exploration of freedom will be fruitful if we keep both types of freedom steadily in mind—freedom from all coercion, which stultifies the free will, and freedom for the good, which the enlightened will strives to find and actualize.

THE "FORM" AND "CONTENT" OF CONSCIENCE

The distinction between voluntaristic and normative freedom enables us to clarify a widespread confusion regarding the nature and significance of man's moral conscience. It is commonly assumed that conscience is a basic characteristic of all human beings; to say that man is a responsible moral agent is to say that he possesses a conscience. It is also assumed that conscience is man's moral guide, telling him reliably what is right, just as the magnetic needle of a compass consistently points to the north. How, then, can we interpret the indubitable fact that men's consciences direct them in very different ways, some branding as evil precisely what others designate as good? That these divergences exist, among civilized peoples and even among famous moralists, must be admitted in the light of available historical and anthropological evidence.[1] Conscience undoubtedly speaks to men in many different and conflicting voices. Does it follow, as the extreme relativist is inclined to argue, that conscience is therefore not a guide to the objectively right and good at all, that it has no transcultural moral significance, and that it merely reflects the vast, discordant variety of arbitrary social mores around the globe?

This conclusion is hard to avoid unless we distinguish between the form of conscience and its content, that is, between what all consciences have in common as their generic nature and the specific moral injunctions that so markedly differ from man to man and culture to culture. Conscience as such has at least these two universal characteristics: it witnesses to the disparity between the ideal and the actual, and it insists on man's obligation to do everything in his power to actualize the ideal. It not only makes man aware of the gap between what is and what ought to be; it also commands him to try to close this gap as best he can. It arouses in all men, however variously they may conceive of the right and the good, a sense of obligation to do the right and realize the good. In short, it is the way in which man's voluntaristic freedom expresses itself at the conscious level. Man's sense of moral "ought" is the existential expression of his moral nature as a free and responsible moral agent.

Immanuel Kant makes clear this relationship between man's sense of duty and his voluntaristic freedom. All men, he insists, feel some sense of duty or obligation. But duty is meaningless without freedom—how can I really be morally obligated to do what I am not free, that is, able, to do? We must take man's universal sense of duty seriously, as valid and not illusory; we must therefore assert his "voluntaristic" freedom. As Kant puts it, freedom (what we have called "voluntaristic freedom") is the essential prerequisite (the *ratio essendi*) of duty; our sense of duty is the crucial evidence (the *ratio cognoscendi*) for freedom. We experience a sense of duty directly, and we are unable to dismiss it as illusory; it, in turn, tells us that we are free because without freedom duty would be illusory. What man's sense of duty, or con-

---

[1] Might not anthropologists and historians find more significant areas of moral agreement if they were to hunt as assiduously for such agreement as they do for ways in which men's consciences differ?

science, prescribes may well differ from man to man and culture to culture; but there can be no question that all men feel morally obligated to do something, that is, that they have a conscience. Hence the greatest variations in "content," in what conscience prescribes, in no way contradict the profound moral significance of the universality of duty in its generic form of obligation.

If a sense of duty is the conscious expression of man's voluntaristic freedom, his persistent search for the right and the good reflects his hunger for normative freedom. Since the days of Socrates, the great moralists in the western tradition have sought to determine what is objectively right and good. This search persists today and will no doubt continue to the end of history. Here once again we find ourselves in an area of perennial controversy.

We cannot here explore this fascinating problem, but two large generalizations are in order: first, that the uniqueness of each individual person must express itself in a corresponding uniqueness of moral prescription; second, that man's common nature and common needs must imply a good that is valid for all men. If we were all identical, one common good would suffice; if we differed in all respects and were wholly ideosyncratic, the very notion of a common good would be meaningless. In fact, we both differ from and resemble one another. Our search, then, must be for that good which all men can value equally because of their common human nature and common needs; but we must also try to find whatever principle or guide can best enable each individual to take full cognizance of his own uniqueness and thus determine for himself what he, being what he is, ought to do. Aristotle's famous doctrine of the mean is his dual solution of this dual problem. He argues that, because of their common human nature, all men are equally obligated to be temperate and courageous, friendly and just; but within this embracing moral prescription each man must on each occasion decide for himself what specifically is right for him— he must learn how to do the right thing, to the right person, in the right way, with the right motive, and so on. Similarly, Christianity prescribes righteous love as a universal requirement, since all men, as sons of God, are brothers who should love one another; but how this love is to be expressed by any specific person in any specific situation is left to the morally enlightened individual.

We can conclude that differences of opinion about what is right and wrong need not in themselves jeopardize the profound significance of man's moral conscience. Let us not be misled by the "reductionistic" tendency so evident today in those sciences which devote themselves to the study of human nature. When psychology and other allied sciences come to examine man's conscience they tend to interpret it, quite naturally, in nonmoral terms, in terms of childhood experiences, social conditioning, glandular disturbance, and so on. What here concerns us is not the attempt to explain conscience in these terms but the attempt to explain it away, that is, to insist that it is merely the disturbing echo of childhood frustration, social maladjustment, or glandular deficiency and that it is therefore devoid of any real moral significance. It is precisely this "reductionism" which we must resist on every front. We must remind ourselves that no genetic, neurological, psychological, or social analysis can ever destroy either the intrinsic nature or the value of what is being analyzed. No physiological or psychological analysis of a child need lessen his intrinsic value as a person or his unique lovableness. No analysis of a work of art need destroy its intrinsic aesthetic value. That man evolved from the lower animals in no way diminishes his present dignity as man. That modern science and modern religion both had their historical origins in myth, rite, superstition, and magic does not impugn their present validity and value. By the same token, no scientific analysis of conscience, however illuminating, should ever lead us to conclude that it lacks the profound moral significance morally sensitive men and women have attributed to it since time immemorial.

MORALITY AND PRUDENCE

The fact of moral obligation raises another issue that merits our attention because it too is the source of considerable confusion. This issue can be stated in either of two ways, either in terms of morality and prudence or, alternatively, in terms of Kant's distinction between what he calls the "categorical" and the "hypothetical" imperatives. Let us start with the latter distinction.

It is Kant's firm conviction that the imperative of duty is an absolute or categorical imperative, never to be confused with the contingent or hypothetical imperative. The former, he believes, is "necessary," or morally inescapable; the latter, in contrast, is optional and not morally coercive. A hypothetical imperative takes this form: *If* you wish to attain some goal, you must do so and so, *but* you are morally free to seek this goal or not to seek it—you are not morally obligated to accept or reject it as your goal. The categorical imperative, in contrast, confronts us with an absolute and inescapable "ought": You *ought* to do so and so, and there is no way in which you can escape this obligation with moral impunity. Kant concludes that only the categorical imperative is truly moral; the hypothetical imperative is merely prudential.

Kant then proceeds to correlate this distinction between morality and prudence with the further distinction between concern for others and concern for self. The goal of prudence is, he believes, the individual's own welfare, whereas morality is characterized by a concern for others. This is the familiar distinction between selfishness and unselfishness, egoism and altruism. To follow Kant's analysis one step further, the categorical imperative expresses itself in the dual injunction to respect all persons as persons (in Kant's significant phrase, "as rational beings") and never to make an exception of yourself. Morality is thus interpreted by Kant essentially in terms of justice—not legalistic justice, but profound regard for human dignity. Prudence, in contrast, is long-range selfishness, an informed concern for one's own welfare. As such, it is for Kant of real but secondary importance; he gives unquestioned priority to duty and to the categorical imperative in terms of which duty expresses itself.

Is this eulogy of the categorical imperative valid? This issue is frequently obscured by those who insist that because man can derive great satisfaction from doing his duty and serving others, even at the cost of self-sacrifice, all human acts are therefore basically prudential. We not only derive satisfaction from helping others and respecting their intrinsic worth; we also act toward them in this "unselfish" way in order, consciously or unconsciously, to have this satisfaction. This is what actually occurs, they would argue, even when men obey what Kant calls the "categorical imperative," for they are well aware that such obedience carries with it its own unique reward, the deeply satisfying feeling of having done one's duty for duty's sake; this feeling, whether they realize it or not, actually motivates their conduct.

Kant's answer would be that men do indeed often make the attainment of pleasure or happiness their conscious motive but that they *need* not do so and, further, that they will not do so if they would be truly moral. Men can and should, he insists, make duty for duty's sake their one and only motive; only thus, he is convinced, can man achieve authentic moral goodness. To reduce all human motivation to prudence is, according to Kant's philosophy, to destroy the very essence of morality.

Here once again we find ourselves in an area of enduring controversy. It is not our task to resolve this complex issue. We must restrict ourselves to those aspects of the problem which most directly concern our understanding of man as a responsible moral agent.

First of all it seems clear that, as Kant and countless other moralists have insisted, morality does essentially concern man's relations with his fellow-men and, no less essentially, that it involves a profound concern for men for their own sake. There seems to be no question that man is so made that he is able to forget himself, lose himself in others, and thus devote himself completely and single-mindedly to their welfare. Man is capable of genuine altruism, however rarely, partially, and intermittently. It is also clear that man does, perhaps more often than not, consciously seek his own welfare, and often at the expense of others. In short, the old distinction between altruism and egoism is valid. However mixed our motives may be, it does make sense to distinguish, at least in principle, between an act of conscious altruism and one of conscious and deliberate egoism or prudence. Only obfuscation results from declaring that all human behavior is selfish because real altruism is admittedly accompanied by its own distinctive feeling of satisfaction. Even if human behavior is analyzed in terms of satisfaction alone, it is still possible and important to distinguish clearly between the satisfaction that accompanies prudential motivation and behavior and the very different satisfaction that accompanies altruistic concern and conduct.

It is also clear that men not only have made this distinction but have given priority to altruism in proportion to their moral sensitivity. The advice not infrequently heard to "take care of yourself," that is, to be as prudential as possible without regard to the needs of others, reflects a cynical underestimate of human nature. With few exceptions, profound concern for others has awakened men's admiration, respect, and gratitude. However much they may differ in other respects, the higher religions have consistently endorsed the verdict of the most profound moralists and of the common man that man is at his best when he forgets himself and devotes himself unselfishly to others. In the language of Kant, the price we pay when we repudiate the categorical imperative is the renunciation of our essential humanity; we condemn ourselves to the status of prudential animals.

It need not follow, however, that because deliberate prudence excludes authentic moral concern morality is therefore hostile to prudence or inconsistent with it. Everything we know about human nature supports the opposite conclusion. This can be demonstrated in terms of man's practical involvement with his fellow-men and also in terms of his spiritual satisfactions. Objectively, our dependence upon one another is so extensive and ramified that no individual can prosper indefinitely at the expense of others; we benefit from the welfare of others as they benefit from our welfare. The true welfare of each is inextricably bound up in the welfare of all. Hence, really intelligent concern for others tends, at least in the long run, to coincide with long-range prudence. Honesty is, despite all cynicism, the best policy. Subjectively, our deepest satisfactions are those that accompany our most altruistic efforts. The joys of helping others clearly outweigh pleasures consciously pursued. Man is not only objectively a social animal; he is also so constituted that concern for others can be his greatest delight.

We can conclude that morality and prudence do differ profoundly in basic motivation and that it is the considered verdict of mankind that a moral concern for others is a sure sign of moral maturity and responsibility. But we need not assume that a truly moral concern is harmful to the moral agent or devoid of its own intrinsic satisfactions. All superficial appearances to the contrary, the best way open to man to realize himself and enrich his life is to forget himself in intelligent and wholehearted devotion to his fellow-men. Prudence as such is not moral; but nothing is more prudent in the long run than sincere moral commitment.

MORAL JUDGMENT

One further problem urgently calls for consideration. We are aware of it whenever we feel ourselves obligated to make a moral judgment but simultaneously feel repelled by the very thought of sitting in judgment upon others. We find ourselves repeatedly in this predicament. We not only keep making moral judgments; we feel impelled to do so as our moral duty. Yet nothing is more offensive to our moral sensitivity than presuming to act as judge. We realize that failure to make moral decisions bespeaks a weakening of the moral fiber and that a society which takes no resolute moral stand and condones every type of behavior is a society well on its way to moral decadence. Yet the spontaneous tendency of decent people is to feel a profound repugnance for all moralizing in general and for self-appointed moralists in particular. Witness our dislike and scorn for moralistic puritanism.

This paradox makes its appearance at every level of moral judgment. We are aware of the value of a social ethos that reflects the basic values of a society; yet we have little respect for the censorious talk that expresses this ethos in most communities. We appreciate the necessity for the legal restraint of vice, but most of us feel profoundly uneasy when a human judge sits in judgment upon a fellow human being and with or without the backing of a jury solemnly condemns him to prison or death in the name of retributive justice. We encounter this same paradox in the Bible, which repeatedly exhorts us to shun vice and condemn it but which also contains the stern injunction, "Judge not that ye be not judged." Our response to moral approbation is no less ambivalent. We praise the good and often feel impelled to commend the man of unusual virtue, but we may also find such praise very distasteful. The more genuinely a man merits our admiration and approval, the more sincerely will he himself disclaim any such merit and be embarrassed by its public recognition. In short, it seems impossible for us either to make a moral judgment or to refrain from doing so with a good conscience. How can we account for this paradox?

First of all, we must distinguish between the agent and the act, the liar and the lie, the man of courage and the act of courage. Difficult as it may be to differentiate good from bad and right from wrong, we feel no scruples in undertaking this task, nor do we hesitate to praise what we judge to be virtue or to condemn what we find to be vicious. It is only when we presume to sit in judgment on our fellow-men as responsible moral agents that our scruples are aroused. And these scruples are surely justified, for how can a sinful human being take it upon himself to judge his fellow-men without self-righteousness? The command of Jesus, "Let him who is without sin cast the first stone," leaves us silent and conscience-stricken; we are too aware of our own unworthiness.

Will it suffice to praise abstract good and condemn evil as such but to refrain from judging persons? This is too easy a solution because it implies that man himself is not responsible for the good and evil that he does, that he is not himself a responsible moral agent. This claim, as we have seen, is precisely that of the extreme determinists, and it is a claim that does too great violence to our moral sense to be tolerable. We cannot in honesty repudiate our conviction that we are somehow free and responsible moral agents; we cannot absolve ourselves of a profound sense of guilt, which differs in kind from mere regret. We regret an unhappy or even a tragic occurrence for which we do not feel any personal responsibility; we feel guilty when we believe that we could and should have acted otherwise. And when we feel such guilt we also feel that we deserve moral condemnation; we judge ourselves to merit punishment. Moreover, we ascribe the same freedom and the same responsibility to our fellows. They too, we are convinced, are guilty; they too should feel a sense of guilt; they too should be judged and punished. Yet who can judge and punish without self-righteousness?

Here I believe the Bible gives us the answer we are looking for. For in it we also read the words, "Vengeance is mine, saith the Lord." The assertion is clear—that not only men's acts but they themselves as agents deserve moral judgment, but that only God, who "knows the heart," is qualified thus to sit in judgment upon persons. Men are not qualified to judge one another as persons; but such moral judgment is nevertheless called for and available because we are living in a just universe that will see to it that we are indeed appropriately judged. We ought to be judged, and we shall be judged, yet not by ourselves or our fellow-men but by God or by a just and orderly universe.

This insight brings us to the very heart of our problem because a human judgment of people implies a far greater knowledge of the precise degree of their freedom and responsibility than any mortal can possibly have. Hence our moral repugnance for sitting in judgment upon one another; who are we that we should presume to assess another's guilt or freedom from guilt? We have already seen how inscrutable is the voluntaristic freedom we feel morally bound to ascribe to ourselves and to others. But if this freedom is for us mortals such an enigma, how ironic is our pretense to be able to assess its actual operations and to determine the precise measure of a person's guilt or merit.

Three conclusions follow from this consideration. The first is the iniquitousness of all humanly administered retributive punishment. No parent can know his child well enough to assess his actual responsibility and personal guilt. No court, judge, or jury should presume to play God. The only type of reward or punishment that is morally defensible is the reward designed to encourage well-doing and the punishment designed to discourage vice. It would be a blessing if we could get rid of the very notion of man-administered retributive punishment, if we could direct our moral judgments entirely to good and evil actions, and if our exclusive concern for one another could be a desire not to judge but to help one another to know and seek the good, to recognize evil and shun it.

The second implication concerns man's individual sense of guilt. Men have long known what psychiatrists are emphasizing today: man's proclivity to "morbid guilt," to a sense of guilt that we are convinced is wholly incommensurate with the individual's actual responsibility. Some psychiatrists are so impressed by the pathology of morbid guilt that they are tempted to deplore all sense of guilt and to try to relieve their patients of it entirely. Other psychiatrists are wiser; they too recognize the symptoms of morbidity and seek to rectify its cause, but unlike their "reductionistic" colleagues they realize that most psychiatric patients, like those of us who are called normal and healthy, do have moral responsibilities they too must face and that they too are morally entitled to share in man's universal sense of guilt. What such a patient needs is not a naturalistic escape from all sense of guilt into a subhuman status of animal irresponsibility but rather a release from the compulsion, so often morbid and masochistic, to sit in savage judgment on himself, playing the role of an avenging Deity. No greater relief could be afforded such a patient than to convince him that he, like all of us, can safely leave it to the Lord, or to the universe, to sit in final judgment upon him—that he is not morally obligated to do what he is not qualified to do, that is, assess his own measure of responsibility for his misdoings.

It is interesting to speculate on what a human society would be like if all its members scrupulously adhered to the Biblical injunction not to judge persons. Such a society would in no way be prevented from distinguishing between good and evil or from approving the one and condemning the other. Nor would it hesitate to promote virtue and restrain vice with appropriate rewards and corrective penalties in the interest of greater normative freedom. It would, however, scrupulously refrain from all retributive punishment on the ground that such punishment would involve man's attributing to himself the knowledge of omniscience and the righteousness of God. Its members would advance confidently in their ever deepening understanding of good and evil, but all would realize that no human being can ever know any other human being, or even himself, well enough to assess his voluntaristic freedom and his exact degree of moral responsibility. What such a society would realize more clearly than we commonly do today is that we are all profoundly dependent upon one another, that no one can escape his share in our common guilt for our corporate sins of omission and commission, that the welfare of each depends essentially upon the welfare of all, and that our human task is therefore not to judge one another but to help one another in every conceivable way.

A third conclusion relates to our conception of cosmic justice. The Biblical text quoted above refers us to the Deity as righteous Judge. Those who are able to subscribe to the Biblical faith in such a Deity can be confident that God, unlike men, is indeed able to judge men with righteousness and mercy, love and justice; they can be assured that they are in just and loving hands. But what about those who find themselves unable to believe in such a Deity? Does their agnosticism or atheism necessarily preclude belief in cosmic justice? By no means, for there are many ways in which ultimate justice can be conceived of. For example, it can be conceived of in terms of cosmic laws that are applicable to man as a moral agent—laws for which there is indeed abundant evidence here and now. We can discern the operation of such laws in our daily experience—for instance, in the inescapable effects of honesty and dishonesty, human concern and callousness, love and hate. Everything we know about human life powerfully suggests that we are being judged continually, day by day, and that we are forever living in a heaven and hell partly of our own making.

In any case, the problem of how we are ultimately judged can safely be added to the list of controversial problems that men of moral sensitivity can debate without jeopardizing their common faith in some sort of authentic cosmic justice. This need not imply that all interpretations of cosmic justice are equally satisfactory or equally true; religious believers and nonbelievers alike must insist on the crucial importance of what men accept as their ultimate faith. It does imply, however, acknowledgment of our finite ignorance, of our need for faith, and of the supreme value of humility. In true humility, and with such faith as we can muster, we can continue to live with one another and help one another as men, and we can at least refrain from arrogating to ourselves blasphemously the role of divine Judge.

This discussion must suffice to indicate the complexities of the problem of human freedom. I have made no pretense to solve it. My only concern has been to stress its importance and to suggest ways in which certain widespread confusions might perhaps be clarified and avoided. The point I have chiefly labored is the supreme importance of recognizing and honoring man's freedom and responsibility. All controversy regarding the nature and implications of this freedom and this responsibility will be fruitful if it confirms and clarifies our faith in man as a moral agent. With this proviso, we can differ not only with impunity but even to our mutual advantage.

Chapter 7

Man as a Being Capable of Reverence

𝓜 AN IS CAPABLE of reverence. This assertion will displease some confirmed secularists because of its religious overtones; it will be too reminiscent of a religious faith to which they cannot subscribe. It will also displease some resolute believers because it will seem to them to fall far short of such ringing spiritual affirmations as Paul's, in the Epistle to the Romans: "For I am persuaded, that neither death, nor life, nor angels, nor principalities, nor powers, nor things present, nor things to come, nor height, nor depth, nor any other creature, shall be able to separate us from the love of God, which is in Christ Jesus our Lord." In our schizophrenic culture, half-secular and half-religious, any attempt to find and formulate what is valid for *all* men of imagination and humility is likely to be branded by both sides as an equivocal compromise that asserts both too much and too little.

I am offering this proposition as the third article of our liberal creed with no such evasive intent. Liberalism asks no one to water down or compromise his basic beliefs. The assertion can, I believe, be accepted with complete sincerity by believers and nonbelievers alike because it epitomizes another human capacity of crucial importance— one that, even more than the two already considered, justifies our faith in man's intrinsic dignity and value. Man's "quality of greatness" is above all his ability to respond to ultimate mystery with genuine awe. Men have indeed differed greatly in their interpretations of this mystery and in their responses to it, and these differences do constitute a very baffling problem that we must presently consider with care. However, let us first try to analyze the nature and preconditions of the basic experience here involved.

96

The statement that we are capable of awe points not only to our finitude but also to our ability to transcend it sufficiently to be aware of it. All living creatures are finite, but only man, so far as we can tell, is conscious of his finitude. This consciousness in turn contributes to our torment, for the more we reflect upon our finitude the more are we impressed by our lack of self-sufficiency and our inescapable mortality. Hence our profound anxiety. How, we ask ourselves, can we discover any meaning in life? What is our final destiny? It is questions such as these, and the deep anxiety they reflect, that impel us to search for an Infinite that can complement our finitude, for an objective source of strength that can make good our weakness. In short, it is man's poignant sense of finitude that renders him capable of awe by making him "open" and sensitive to whatever ultimate mystery reality may vouchsafe.

Our assertion goes further. It claims, at least by implication, that reality itself, as we most sensitively and imaginatively encounter it, actually does confront us with a dimension or quality of mystery that can evoke in us wonder and awe. It calls our attention to the fact that whenever we probe reality as deeply as we can at any point we come upon some aspect of what has been described as the *mysterium tremendum*—not just another teasing problem challenging our scientific ingenuity, but a mysterious quality of ultimate and un-fathomable significance, a quality of "holiness" to which no human response is adequate save a feeling of reverence.

The other two articles of our liberal creed dealt with distinctive and basic human aptitudes. This article cuts even deeper; it forces us to plumb the very depths of human experience. It seeks to undercut the creedal differences that today so sharply divide us into two great hostile camps, the religious and the secular. It directs us to a level of experience that underlies and preconditions our deviant metaphysical beliefs; it indicates the common source not only of the faith and "religious piety" of the man of God but also of the faith and "nat-ural piety" of the sensitive and humble secularist. Here we really face the engima of man's mortality and his mortal anguish, his ultimate spiritual quest and his perennial hope. Here we confront reality itself in all its awesome and final mystery. Only at this level can we begin to sense the overtones and grasp the implications of Pascal's inspired description of man as a "thinking reed"—a fragile and pliable reed, susceptible to all the winds of human fortune, yet self-transcendingly aware of his plight and therefore open to redemption from above. Here too we get a glimpse of what Spinoza, the "God-intoxicated" philosopher, meant when he described reality as "God-or-Nature."

That man is indeed finite and that he craves and searches for whatever in reality can make good his finitude would seem to be indubitable. When we take thought, we know that our knowledge is limited and that it will always be limited; yet we stubbornly try to envisage what we as men can never fully comprehend—absolute truth, complete justice, pure beauty, perfect love. We know that we are mortal and that our bodies are destined to die and rot; but we persist in our search for what might give our lives some ultimate meaning, and we continue to hope that death may not mean our total extinction. In our heart of hearts we crave a God whom we can worship with utter loyalty, and we continue to search for him, however blindly, amid our various idolatries. All men are, at their thoughtful best, hagridden by their finitude and "God-intoxicated" in their hunger for the Absolute.

But most of us are very seldom at our thoughtful best. "Human kind," says T. S. Eliot,[1] "cannot bear very much reality."

> . . . the enchainment of past and future
> Woven in the weakness of the changing body,
> Protects mankind from heaven and damnation
> Which flesh cannot endure.

We seem to do everything in our power to deceive ourselves and forget our mortal predicament. We immerse ourselves in the pleasures of the passing moment and try to pretend that our sensuous experiences and our ability to enjoy them will last forever. We busy ourselves with our daily tasks and try to push aside the disturbing query whether they are really worth a lifetime of absorbing effort. We bask in the reflected glory of scientific advance and technological achievement but make small effort to master ourselves as we are progressively mastering nature. Even in an atomic age we cannot really convince ourselves

[1] T. S. Eliot, *Four Quartets* (Harcourt Brace and Company, Inc., New York, 1943), pp. 4–5.

that we may actually use our vaunted science to destroy the human race. We find it easy to rest content in a modicum of justice and kindliness and to take pride in our national might, forgetful of the misery we might relieve and callous to the suffering our power may produce. We hide from ourselves the knowledge that we must die, and we try to live our daily lives as though we were destined to live forever.

This self-deception in which we all indulge is itself an indirect expression of the deep-seated anxiety our ineradicable sense of finitude generates in us.[2] Anxiety is inevitable because life itself perpetually threatens everything that we most value. We know how precarious are our private lives and fortunes, how insecure our most treasured physical and cultural possessions. We know that in our corporate life justice and injustice, kindness and cruelty, order and disorder, health and disease always go hand in hand. We know that entire civilizations have arisen, prospered, decayed, and disappeared and that ours may follow the same course. We see death on every side and know that sooner or later our own turn must come. In our more thoughtful moments, or when we are momentarily off guard, or particularly in a period of history like the present, these bitter realizations flood in on us and quicken our latent anxiety into conscious anguish. We then ask ourselves in desperation: "What purpose can life have? What is our human lot? How can we find and hold the security we crave? And if no such security is available to us, how can we face such ultimate insecurity and such final frustration?"

There seem to be only three ways of dealing with this universal human predicament. The first is the one already described—escapism, the unconscious or the deliberate attempt to suppress our deep anxiety, to forget it in the routine of daily living and in whatever happiness the present may afford. The more impulsive and thoughtless we are, or the more we become mere creatures of habit, the easier is this policy of evasion, particularly if things are temporarily going well with us. While we enjoy good health, while our business prospers and our comforts multiply, while family love endures and our community thinks well of us and the world is at peace, we find it relatively easy

[2] See Paul Tillich, *The Courage to Be* (Yale University Press, New Haven, Conn., 1952), for a brilliant analysis of this anxiety.

99

to postpone ultimate problems and to lapse into a complacency we well know is quite unjustified. There are many men and women in our society who manage to maintain this feeling of complacency and assurance for many years, some, for an entire lifetime. But is this a philosophy of life worthy of man? Is it one we could really wish to make our own?

A second possible response is that of the skeptical and courageous secularist who decides that life has no ultimate meaning, that reality is indifferent to man's deepest needs, and that our only valid option is therefore to face life and its vicissitudes and frustrations with all the human creativeness and courage we can muster. Men and women of this persuasion will waste no time or effort in useless speculation and will resolutely repudiate the spurious comfort of an illicit religious faith. Finding no God whom they can worship with integrity, they apply themselves with a good conscience to the task of building human shrines, that is, of finding human causes to which they can give their highest loyalties. They deny the charge that all such loyalties are idolatrous because, as they point out, the very notion of an idol presupposes the reality of a Deity who alone is worthy of man's ultimate loyalty. It is this very presupposition which they reject as groundless. They therefore spend their lives making the most of life while it lasts. They accept the hazards of existence as inescapable and endure life's sorrows with stoical fortitude. The more self-centered they are, the more effort will they make to be intelligently prudential; the greater their capacity for genuine human concern, the more self-sacrificially will they devote themselves to the welfare and happiness of others. Here we have secularism at its honest, intelligent, and courageous best. Our society would certainly be infinitely impoverished without the gallantry, the enthusiasm, the creativity, and the devotion of countless men and women of this secular persuasion.

But this approach does not exhaust the alternatives, even for those who must dissociate themselves from religion in any of its traditional and orthodox forms. The third way of facing life and reality is no less honest than that of the positivistically minded secularist, no less affirmative or courageous. What chiefly distinguishes it is its greater humility, its greater hope, and its greater openness and sensitivity to the mysterious depths of reality itself. Let us, for convenience, entitle this the way of trust, as opposed to the way of escape and the way of fortitude.

The man of trust combats the strong impulse to escape, which he finds even in himself, because escapism seems to him, as it does to the man of fortitude, to be unworthy of man's high calling. He differs from both the secularist and the religious believer in so far as either is dogmatic, for complacent certainty, whether negative or affirmative, seems to him utterly intolerable. He therefore distrusts equally all "proofs" and "disproofs" of God's existence. He differs from the more cautious secular agnostic in his persistent hope that reality may after all prove to be responsive to human need and in his disciplined efforts to make himself as receptive as possible to whatever reality may reveal in support of his hope. He is thus genuinely humble, both with respect to his own powers and, in anticipation, with respect to whatever reality may have to offer him in consolation or rebuke.

It is in this spirit of hopeful humility that the man of trust turns to reality to find out what it may have to offer. He does so at first with an initial faith that is, of necessity, largely blind. He simply assumes that more awaits his further probings and his greater knowledge; he makes this assumption, which most agnostics are unwilling to risk, because without it he would be unable to undertake his search. He presses his inquiry through every facet of reality men are able to encounter and explore. Starting with whatever initial understanding he may have of nature, he pursues his scientific inquiries in the faith that ever more truth will become available to him. In the same spirit, he continues his quest for ever greater justice, ever more satisfying beauty, ever purer and more unselfish love. As his efforts are progressively rewarded, his initially blind faith is gradually transformed into a better and better founded assurance, for reality itself seems to reward his faith and to provide him with an ever increasing body of supporting evidence. All these enterprises of his, taken conjointly, thus tend to confirm his initial faith that reality is indeed responsive to at least some of his needs and that it is in basic harmony with his own inquiring faculties.

This approach to reality is not only hopeful, it is also profoundly respectful. In his study of nature, the characteristic attitude of the

man of trust is neither patronizing nor exploitative. He cherishes everything in nature for what is it—its earth and stone, its trees and flowers, its multitude of swimming and crawling, flying and walking creatures. He marvels at the intricacy of their structure, their endless uniqueness, their infinitely subtle relations to one another, their unbelievable beauty. He thus approaches nature in a state of wonder and a mood of respect. As he continues his explorations and multiplies his encounters, his respect is gradually transformed into a feeling of awe —an awe akin to that of primitive man but enlightened, not blind and superstitious.

It is important to note that this feeling of awe does not diminish but steadily increases as man's knowledge grows. This curious fact will be confirmed by all scientists who have the imagination and the humility requisite for wonder and awe. Nature becomes more interesting, more intricately and wondrously fashioned, the deeper man delves into her secrets; her ultimate mysteries grow in mystery as man's knowledge increases. Why a world of nature at all? Whence the miracle of life? Why the beauty of nature? Whence natural order and why the unreduplicable uniqueness of every finite thing? These age-old queries are as pertinent today as they were thousands of years ago, and we are not one whit nearer their answer. It is as though nature beckoned us with one hand and held us off with the other, forever yielding to, and forever resisting, our attempts to know her for what she is. When man finally ceases to rebel at the apparently unknowable and summons the humility to accept nature for what she is in all her order and vagueness, grandeur and mystery, he has in some measure attained that "natural piety" which imaginative naturalists have long extolled.

All these mysteries are multiplied when we shift our attention from nature to man, for in him we encounter not only all that subhuman nature tantalizingly reveals and hides but also such new phenomena as consciousness and will, conscience and human creativity—man at impressive heights, depressing depths, and all the infinite stages in between. Here our enigmas take on added poignancy because they touch so closely our own lives and hopes. In the preceding pages we have attempted to understand some of man's most distinctive capacities, which, in conjunction, might explain in some degree why we so sharply differentiate him from other living creatures and ascribe to him such unique dignity and worth. This effort is, indeed, well worth making, but let us not delude ourselves in assessing its results. For at the end of all our search we are still left with an inscrutable mystery—the mystery of man himself—how he comes to have the endowments he has and why he is able at times to use them so effectively while more often leaving them undeveloped or putting them to evil use. If nature is a mystery to man, he is a double mystery to himself. As Kant remarked, "The starry heavens above" awaken in us a sense of awe that is excelled only by our wonder and reverence in the presence of "the Moral Law within."

But this still leaves unmentioned one human capacity and impulse, which issues in a distinctive type of experience that more than any other has moved man to reverence. I refer, of course, to what can only be called man's "religious experiences." Here the generic term "religious" must include all the varieties of religious experience described by William James and others and all the stages of progressive religious enlightenment from the most primitive and superstitious to the most mature and informed. As has already been noted, what these varieties and stages have in common is a belief in some sort of supernatural spirits or divine beings, multiple or singular, with a dynamic power of their own and with a dimension, aura, or quality that Otto [3] and his followers have entitled "holiness."

When it is used in this very basic sense, the "holy" does not necessarily connote righteousness; the holy, as primitive man tended to conceive of it, fell far short of righteousness and frequently lacked for him any association with the good. The awe aroused by the holy in our primitive ancestors was, by the same token, very different from mature religious reverence. It would be more accurate to say that man's earliest religious experience, so far as we can reconstruct it, was more akin to a shuddering sense of the eerie—more like what we, despite ourselves, still experience when a strange sound in a dark forest sends an involuntary tingling down our spine. It was from the beginning a feeling of being in the presence of the uncanny, the unknown, the disturbingly "other," and therefore the mysteriously threatening; and

[3] See Rudolf Otto, *The Idea of the Holy,* trans. John W. Harvey (Oxford University Press, New York, 1926).

the awe it awakened was more like fear than awe, yet fear of a distinctive type—a foreboding dread of the unfamiliar and unknown rather than the more manageable fear of the known, the familiar, and the foreseeable. Only very slowly and with many false starts and retrogressions did man's religious experience develop from these crude beginnings into a rich and disciplined encounter with a God of righteousness and love.

What here concerns us is not the slow evolution of man's religious experience or, for the moment, the validity or invalidity of his faith in the Divinity thus allegedly encountered but rather the historical fact that it was in and through this ever changing and deepening religious experience that the ultimate mystery of things gradually assumed a shape and character of its own. What first presented itself to primitive man as a blank but fearsome "something" and what to the spiritually sensitive disbeliever today must still remain little more than sheer mystery has become, for those who have been able to make some major religious faith their experiential own, a God whose righteousness shines through the darkness of his mysterious depths and whose love partly, if only partly, resolves the enigma of his ways that are not our ways. To quote Eliot again: [4]

> Who then devised the torment? Love.
> Love is the unfamiliar Name
> Behind the hands that wove
> The intolerable shirt of flame
> Which human power cannot remove.

I am not forgetting that Eliot here asserts, as a man of mature and reflective Christian faith, what other men no less reflective and mature must either deny or at best accept as a mere unproved and unprovable hypothesis. What is so notable in our present context is not merely man's capacity for this kind of experience and emergent faith but above all the widespread disposition of humble and spiritually minded agnostics and even atheists to honor man's religious venture rather than to view it with contempt. It is only the petty disbeliever and the brash secularist who smugly dismiss man's religious hunger and religious assurance as primitive or infantile or superstitious. All humanists of

[4] Eliot, *op. cit.*, p. 38.

stature and humility pay homage to the faith they cannot share, just as religious believers of stature and humility, unlike their petty and arrogant cobelievers, honor the sincere disbeliever and respect honest religious skepticism.

We can safely conclude that man is indeed a being endowed with the capacity to feel a sense of awe in the presence of ultimate mystery, whether this mystery reveals itself in nature to the man of "natural piety," or in mankind to the man of humane piety, or, finally, as a divine holiness that both transcends and is immanent in our finite universe—a dynamic holiness the man of religious piety entitles "God." What we have sought to stress as so important is man's awareness of his finitude, whether or not there is an answering Infinite; his capacity for profound anxiety, whether or not reality can relieve him of it; his ability to ask crucial ultimate questions, however diverse his answers to these questions may be.

Aristotle declared centuries ago that philosophy has its origin in wonder, and we have pointed out that religion has its source in man's capacity for awe. Man cannot, of course, rest content with either awe or wonder; both drive him on to further search. He must try to find answers to the questions engendered by them. Man inevitably attaches greater importance to his answers to these questions than he does to the questions themselves. Indeed, it is because the answers are of such crucial human import that men of all persuasions are so inclined to dogmatism and bitterness in the areas of ultimate belief. Nevertheless, it is the fact that man is able to ask these questions with humility and respect and in the asking to sense the mysterious depths of reality itself and to respond to those ultimate mysteries with an awe akin to reverence—it is this fact that above all justifies our ascription of intrinsic value and dignity to man.

THE VALIDITY OF ULTIMATE BELIEF

There is fortunately no need to explore the great variety of ultimate beliefs, secular and religious, ephemeral and enduring, to which men have subscribed through the ages. We can restrict ourselves here to two crucial problems. One of these concerns the criteria with which a liberal can test the validity of any ultimate faith. The other concerns the liberal's reaction to the apparently inevitable conflict of man's ultimate beliefs.

But first a word about our audience. Who in our society is likely to take a vital interest in these problems? We have already noted how greatly people differ not only in what they believe but also in how they gain their beliefs and the spirit in which they hold them. Most people seem to acquire their basic convictions from their families and their immediate social environment, to hold to them virtually unchanged, and to pass them on in practically the same form to the next generation. Beliefs that can be passed around with such ease are stereotypes— stock ideas and stock responses. This does not prevent their being held sincerely and defended loudly. But, like unaltered ready-made clothes, they never really fit their owners, nor do they do justice to the concrete situations to which they are applied. They are passed from mind to mind like counters, largely unexamined and unchanged, and are therefore of less value than they might be.

There are also those in every society whose ultimate beliefs are held without critical sophistication but with personal and enduring intensity. In religious circles, these may well be the deeply devout; in secular circles, the impassioned supporters of some humane cause. In either case, the men and women who conform to this type exhibit a sincerity and a devotion that is very moving and must elicit our respect, however naïve their belief and however dangerous their resultant fanaticism. These simple-minded believers lack the education that would enable them to transcend their naïveté; they lack the requisite curiosity and training to test the validity of their faith. Their resultant dogmatism, however deplorable, is understandable; their fanaticism, however indefensible and harmful, reflects a state of ignorance for which they often cannot be held responsible. If their beliefs are challenged, their option is either dogmatic reiteration or else a naïve appeal to some higher "authority." Only the very unusual naïve believer is able to combine passionate belief with humility and a liberal tolerance for the contrary beliefs of others.

Every society is also likely to have its quota of argumentative authoritarians, who again may be either secular or religious in orientation. They need not concern us here because their authoritarianism is by definition above (or below) the level of reflective analysis and criticism.

This leaves a small but gallant band of men and women who are liberal in their attitude toward others and also self-critical enough to want to test and correct their convictions. Some of these liberals are already expert at putting their beliefs to the test; there may be others who will welcome a brief analysis of the preconditions and criteria of a valid faith.

PRECONDITIONS OF A VALID FAITH

I. CREEDAL TRADITION

No significant faith has ever come into being in a creedal vacuum, that is, in total independence of some creedal tradition. The most imaginative genius would be unable to invent a brand-new faith single-handed. The faiths men live by are the cumulative product of generations of funded experience and reflection. The greatest reformers have generally purified and revitalized an older tradition, enriching and deepening it but working within and upon a well-established inheritance. Even the founders of new faiths have stemmed from older faiths and have given them radical reorientation. Nothing could be more naïve than to suppose that any energetic individual can, by taking thought, create an entirely new faith of his own.

2. INDIVIDUAL APPLICATION

On the other hand, no faith, secular or religious, can achieve real significance for any individual unless he really does make it his own. It is indeed imperative that he first submit himself to it for appropriate instruction and that he master its doctrines, participate in its communal activities, and accept its disciplines. But it is no less imperative that he do so as receptively and critically as possible, learning what he can but testing everything he learns by his own reflection and in the light of his own firsthand experience. If the faith in question is itself rich he can be sure that in a single lifetime he will be able to experience only a fragment of what his cobelievers have experienced in the aggregate and to test reflectively only a portion of his doctrinal inheritance. Nevertheless, his own primary experiences and his own reflection must be of crucial importance to him, for without both in happy balance he will never really assimilate the faith of his spiritual fathers. What he is after is a pattern of belief and practice that he can make his own way of life, and no faith can serve this function that is not in the fullest sense *our* faith and *my* faith simultaneously.

3. ALERT PASSIVITY AND CRITICAL HUMILITY

The attitude in which this search is undertaken and pursued is also of great moment. Faith is both a gift and an achievement. It must therefore be sought and at the same time gratefully received. So far as he is able, the searcher must open himself without initial blinding prejudice to whatever may present itself to him; in this sense he should be utterly passive and receptive. But this passivity must differ in kind from the passivity of indifference or sleepiness; what is required is an alert passivity akin to the intense listening of a bird-lover in the woods, or to the eager watchfulness of a doctor at a patient's bedside. Such alert eagerness bespeaks an initial sense of need—a definitely felt want for something, though he knows not what. He must therefore beware lest he impulsively discard what he is looking for because it comes to him in a form that is strange and unexpected. Hence the need for constant humility. But once again this humility must not be lacking in moral and intellectual integrity. For what is humbly received *must* be submitted to the searcher's mind and conscience; no faith is worthy of his complete acceptance that does violence to his reason or his deepest moral convictions. In short, the proper creedal attitude is highly paradoxical. It is both passive and alert, credulous and critical; it is simultaneously an asking and a demanding; it is humble but never servile, respectful but not lacking in self-respect.

4. THE PERSISTING EFFORT OF THE WHOLE MAN

If the faith of which we are in search is a faith to live by, it must be powerful enough to mold and guide every aspect of our life. What we are here concerned with is no mere scientific hypothesis whose merits can be tested objectively in the study or the laboratory, no mere financial gamble whose success or failure will automatically record itself on the ticker tape, no simple business venture whose results will show themselves in a tabulation of profit and loss. It is a faith by which, if we can find it, we intend to live twenty-four hours a day for our entire lives. It must accordingly have a transforming and redeeming effect upon everything we think and hope, do and suffer, upon our work, our amusements, our activities in the community, our family life, our hours of solitude, our sickness and health, our entire pattern of life, and at last, the way we face death. To do all this, a faith must be hardy. It must be able to survive all the temptations of pleasure and pain, all the excitement of man's multiple pursuits and all intervening periods of boredom and emptiness. The search for such a faith must be correspondingly sturdy and persistent. It cannot be pursued merely in moments of special need or in response to evangelical appeal and then complacently abandoned or postponed. There is no point at which the search for a living faith can be said to end because it has been perfectly achieved, as there is no moment of the search in which the search itself is not in some measure sustained by faith. Without some initial faith, the search would never have been started; as the search continues, faith grows stronger. Both search and faith continue to the end, two faces of the same shield.

These are some of the presuppositions of a worthy way of life as the liberal conceives of it. What can we now offer as usable criteria by which a liberal can test his faith and that of others?

CRITERIA OF A VALID FAITH

In formulating these criteria we must remember that faith is meaningless unless it is faith in *something* we accept as real in its own right. Since the faith here in question concerns the whole of life, to really serve us it must be a faith in what we judge to be ultimate reality. Of course, men can put their ultimate faith in almost anything; it is easy to accept as final and self-sufficient some attitude, method, satisfaction, activity, or gadget that is, in fact, incapable of supporting the whole weight of a man's life. A notable example of this tragic error would be the assumption that a faith in liberalism is a sufficient faith to live by. *The faith of a liberal must be more than faith in liberalism alone.* However crucial a liberal attitude may be—and we have argued hard for its unique importance—it must fail in and of itself to provide a man with the spiritual nourishment that only a faith in something independent of him and real in its own right can possibly provide. The articles of our liberal creed are important because they enumerate the distinctive human capacities with whose aid man can transcend himself and actually encounter and believe in aspects of the reality that objectively confront him—objective values, authentic freedom, and reality's ultimate mysteries. *It is because man can have faith in these aspects of reality itself that he is worthy of respect; only as man actually achieves such an affirmative faith in reality, and as he lives by this faith, can he be said to have realized his proper destiny on earth.*

It is not surprising, then, that the three great generic faiths of mankind have been focused, respectively, upon nature, man, and God. The naturalist at his spiritual best has derived his strength and comfort from his faith in nature as he conceived of it; the humanist, by the same token, from his faith in human nature and its unlimited potentialities; the supernaturalist, from his faith in a living God. In all their many variants these major faiths are alone worthy of being entitled mature ways of life and alone deserve serious consideration. Our task is to attempt to find criteria broad enough to apply to any of these faiths and precise enough to be of real use to us in testing their comparative validity or truth. Let us list three such criteria with a minimum of technicality.

I. THE THREEFOLD CRITERION OF THE REAL

Our first question is bound to be: "Is what we believe in, or wish to believe in, actually real, that is, real in its own right?" The test that is relevant here is the triple test of coerciveness, coherence, and publicity.

a. Coerciveness. Other things being equal, we can accept as real in its own right whatever presents itself to us in our actual experience with a coercive character of its own. This test, which is the chief corrective for wishful thinking, is easier to apply when the character reality reveals itself to have is unwelcome than when it is welcome. In the latter case, it is still hard to know whether we may perhaps be unconsciously molding our beliefs in the direction of our wishes. When, on the other hand, we dislike what we coercively encounter we feel assured that what so unpleasantly obtrudes itself upon us must be real.

b. Coherence. The existence of what we accept as real must also be consistent with other objects of experience whose reality we accept. This is the test of coherence. Our rationality not only makes it impossible to believe in a flat contradiction but also powerfully impels us to render our many fragmentary beliefs regarding reality as coherent as possible. Therefore, no single experience, however coercive, can ever be rationally accepted by us as self-authenticating; no isolated belief can demonstrate its own validity. It is only as we relate different coercive experiences and our several interpretations of them that we begin to develop a coherent pattern of beliefs, and only by reference to such a pattern can we rationally accept or reject any single belief. For example, we may well be convinced during a vivid dream that the objects we encounter in that dream are real, yet on waking we find it impossible to credit their reality. We can accept our dream experience and our waking experiences only by relegating the former to a special status, in this case to the status of dreams. Illusions and hallucinations are detected and accounted for in similar ways, as are all the normal errors of everyday experience and belief. The more rational we are, the more must we rely on the criterion of coherence.

c. Publicity. The two tests coerciveness and coherence should ideally suffice to enable a solitary individual to test his encounters with reality and his interpretations of them. Actually, however, we are here as elsewhere tremendously dependent upon our fellows for the confirmation, correction and extension of our knowledge of the real. So heavily do we rely on them that it has become axiomatic among us that whatever is real for any reflective observer must in principle be equally real and equally available to all other *qualified* observers. Our request for help expresses itself in these typical questions: "Have you experienced what I have? If not, will you try to do so? If you succeed, do you interpret what we have both experienced as I do? If not, how can we explain and reconcile our differences?" It is with questions such as these that we explore our own and our neighbors' experiences and ideas in the hope that together we may be able to avoid the errors to which any single individual is prone. We also lean on others for experiential evidence that we, for lack of time or talent, may not be able to duplicate in our own experience, and, in addition, for those complex interpretations of the evidence that, in a highly sophisticated culture such as ours, are the joint product of experts in all the major areas of human inquiry.

It is by using these three tests in intimate correlation, then, that we can hope to move progressively toward an ever richer experiential encounter with reality and to an ever more accurate and embracing pattern of interpretative theory. I hasten to add that this triple test of the objectively real applies to *everything* that man can actually experience, reflectively interpret, and discuss with his fellow-men. It is the multiple test that scientists use in all their explorations of natural phenomena. Humanists use the same test in their study of man and of the values that so deeply concern him. Enlightened and liberal theologians must, of necessity, use the selfsame test in their analysis of man's religious experiences and in their interpretations of what man actually encounters in such experiences.

A further word of clarification must be added to avoid a possible serious misconception. The further we go in any of our cognitive enquiries, the further interpretation outruns our actual experience and that of all men, despite the continuing dependence of all interpretation upon such experience. Thought moves inevitably and properly from the seen to the unseen. We start with immediate experience and initially accept as real what such experience seems directly to reveal— that and nothing more. But the more we multiply and compare our experiences, the more are we compelled to *reconstruct* an *underlying* reality as their objective source—a reality to which our most luminous primary experiences can only give us clues but which alone, so far as we can tell, will suffice to explain the occurrence and the nature of the experiences we actually have.

Thus the scientist is continually reconstructing the inner form and behavior of the physical world—a form and behavior not immediately apparent to sensory observation, even with the aid of powerful instruments. He believes in the inner world of nature that underlies the visible face of nature because it alone, as he theoretically reconstructs it, can explain or make sense of his actual laboratory observations. The scientist therefore comes to believe in far more than he can directly experience or make available to the sensuous experience of others. The naturalist pushes this process one step further by identifying this inner and invisible world of nature, together with its sensuous appearances, with reality as a whole and then by venturing to describe the essential character of reality itself in primarily scientific terms. The humanist, *mutatis mutandis,* does likewise. He starts with man's immediate encounters with his fellow-men and with his introspective observations of himself as an evaluator, as moral agent, and so on; on the basis of all these primary experiences, and always with respectful attention to the findings of science, he then reconstructs what he conceives to be man's essential nature and potentialities and what he also conceives to be the necessary objective conditions of man's characteristic normative activities. Hence his emergent account of reality itself, including man's pre-eminent place in it and whatever status in it he ascribes to objective values. The theologian employs the same methods in his interpretation of man as a being capable of religious response to Deity and of God as the source of divine initiative. The God of the enlightened believer is indeed the God he encounters in direct religious experience; yet no such experience and no aggregate of such experiences can, he believes, adequately reveal God as he is in himself, nor can such experience, however inspired, ever measure up to what he can know about God by this method of theological reconstruction. In short, the triple test of reality, judiciously applied, enables us to push behind all appearances, sensuous, normative, and divine, to an ever clearer intellectual and imaginative apprehension of reality itself.

2. THE CRITERION OF THE MEANINGFUL

Our effort to believe only in what is actually real in its own right is always coupled with an effort to discover what meaning, significance, or value reality actually possesses. Here too we must be perpetually on guard against positive and negative wishful thinking. There are those who desperately want to believe in a loving and righteous God, in objective values, and in man's moral responsibility; there are others who are as eager to be relieved of a faith in God, who prefer man-made values to discovered values, and who would welcome release from a sense of moral responsibility and guilt. In other words, wishful thinking can lead us astray in many different directions, and all such illusory belief is equally repugnant to man's intellectual and moral integrity.

The criterion of valid normative belief is partly pragmatic and partly idealistic. It is pragmatic in that one of the chief ways in which we can test the validity of our belief or disbelief in the objectively valuable or meaningful is to live by these beliefs or disbeliefs and then observe and face up to the experiential results as honestly as we can. What actually happens to our aesthetic experiences of nature and art if, on the one hand, we believe in natural and man-made beauty and if, on the other hand, we do not? What actual results can we detect in the character and behavior of a man who really believes himself to be morally responsible and who takes this responsibility seriously, and how does the contrary belief actually affect a man's private life and his relations with his fellows? What are the evident consequences of a sincere belief in a righteous and loving God and in the power of objective love and justice, and how does an equally sincere disbelief in such a God and in such love and justice really work? It would seem reasonable to conclude that those beliefs which pay dividends—which enrich life instead of impoverishing it, which lead to creativity and joy rather than to frustration and suffering, which promote understanding and harmony rather than loneliness and strife, which issue not in cynical bitterness but in "the peace that passeth all understanding" —that such beliefs must be more valid in their assessment of objective meaning and value than their opposites. Our universe would indeed be a strange place if our most erroneous beliefs proved to be experientially the most rewarding and if that faith which best enabled us to realize our fullest human potentialities were the most illusory!

The pragmatic test must be supplemented by a second test which, for lack of a better term, I have labeled the "idealistic test." As we have noted repeatedly, man has a strong proclivity to be satisfied with the second best, to be complacent with mediocrity, and to close his eyes to life's major challenges. It is accordingly easy for him to settle for what "works well enough" and to reconcile himself to half-hearted effort and passable performance. But there is also that in man, call it what we will—his conscience, or his capacity for idealism, or his craving for and sensitivity to the Infinite—which, unless he wholly stifles it, keeps prodding him out of his complacency and keeps directing his unwilling attention to his own unrealized potentialities and to untapped depths of objective meaning, unscaled heights of normative perfection. It is the special vocation of the inspired reformers and prophets of every age and in every society to quicken our sluggish conscience, freshen our idealism, and intensify that sense of guilt which is not morbid but corrective and potentially redemptive. Only as this higher challenge is heeded can the criterion of what "works" be transformed into the far more reliable criterion of what "works as well as it might and should work." In short, it is only under the sharp spur of this ideal demand upon us, whether it be secular or religious, that we can hope to shake off the lethargies of humdrum experience and become judiciously dissatisfied with low standards and tawdry values. Just because the fair-to-middling good is the chief enemy of the best, we dare not rely exclusively upon the pragmatic test as it in fact tends to be envisaged and applied by the average man in an average sort of way. We must test the pragmatic test itself against the loftiest vision available to us of perfect truth, beauty, justice, love, and holiness.

3. THE CRITERION OF HUMILITY

In a sense this is not a third criterion but an aspect of the idealistic test, since nothing is better calculated to bow our heads in genuine humility than a bright vision of a perfection beyond our reach, which, nonetheless, judges us and convicts us of our mortal insufficiencies. We will do well, however, to include the criterion of humility in our list because we are so prone to a kind of arrogance that blinds us to visions of perfection and makes us unaware of, or indifferent to, the judgment such visions might pronounce upon us. Here again we are in the presence of a paradox, for without this vision we lack the incentive to humility, yet without humility we are unlikely to glimpse the redeeming vision. This is why reformers have again and again resorted to a kind of shock treatment. They have often despaired of man's stubborn stiff-neckedness and deafness to all reasonable appeal and persuasion and have therefore tried to startle him out of his complacency and into some initial realization of his own culpable insensitivity to the voice of conscience or the voice of God.

Whatever the cure—and the cure must presumably fit the disease and differ as one patient differs from another—there can be no question about the tragic prevalence of the disease. Witness, for example, the dogmatic self-assurance of the rationalist who uncritically assumes that reality as a whole must conform to his rationalistic preconceptions of it and who therefore rejects out of hand as impossible all intimations of reality's mysterious depths. Or witness the smug assurance of the complacent atheist who dogmatically denies God's existence because he has had no "experience" of him, utterly neglectful of the fact that his own lack of religious experience may be his own fault and failure. Or witness the no less patent exemplification of arrogance among religious dogmatists who insist that their own conception of the Deity is the one and only and, forsooth, the truly adequate conception, and that their righteousness is the quintessence of all righteousness. Or, finally, witness the lack of humility of the dogmatic humanist who, without a quiver of anxiety, turns his back on man's long religious tradition and dogmatically insists that man is on his own and that his "progress" is inevitable. These are but some of the more glaring examples of an arrogance that contradicts everything we know of the limits and penalties of human fortitude. If we would really test our ultimate faith we must approach our task with all the humility we can summon; only a humble searcher can escape the worst pitfalls of wishful thinking and relate himself to the reality he would know, believe in, and obey with realistic sensitivity.

This summary must suffice to indicate some of the chief preconditions of a fruitful search for a vital way of life and the chief criteria that conjointly enable us to test the adequacy and validity of our own and other ultimate faiths. Our concluding account of the attitude of a true liberal to the bewildering multiplicity of rival faiths can be brief.

A liberal will not minimize the importance of these creedal discords. He will realize that to live at all man must have some ultimate faith; that it is of the utmost importance that his faith be as well-founded and adequate and as near true as he can make it; that no two faiths that flatly contradict each other can both be true, though both may be false; that some faiths are bound to be superior to others, that is, more adequate to reality itself; and that, in fact, one of man's great traditional faiths may indeed be the faith nearest to truth. What he will steadfastly insist, however, is that no finite being can possibly know with absolute certainty which faith, if any, is the most adequate. In the face of this predicament he will not fall back on mere tolerance and try to live in sole reliance upon the liberal attitude. He will acknowledge his own need and the need of others to go beyond mere avoidance of dogmatism, mere humility, mere tolerance. He will do what he can to search for ever more truth, to enrich and deepen his own understanding of reality, and to live up to the best faith that he himself is able to come by. He will urge all his fellow-men to do the same. But he will try never to forget man's finitude, never to lapse into dogmatic arrogance, never to lose that humility which finitude dictates and which his imperfect vision of the Infinite commands.

The liberal will thus seek to exemplify the liberal attitude most conscientiously where it is most needed, in the area of ultimate faith and bitter human strife. He will do so not merely in the spirit of tolerance but because his faith in the liberal attitude itself is rooted in his even more basic respect for man as man. He will be tolerant of others because of man's unique ability as a responsible moral agent to evaluate and to choose good in preference to evil and, above all, because man can transcend his finitude and respond with awe and reverence to whatever mysterious depths of reality seem to him to merit such response. He will thus be able to escape the sentimentality to which historical liberalism has been prone because he sees a way of justifying his faith in the liberal attitude in terms of a meaningful and positive liberal creed.

The thoughtful liberal will always be aware of the basic limitations of this creed. Any liberal creed, he will realize, can do little more than spell out the meaning of man's faith in man. If the liberal is a humanist, this faith will of course tend to coincide with his own ultimate faith. But if humanism, however noble, seems to him to be on the whole inferior to a faith that is primarily focused on objective reality—upon a reality permeated or undergirded by divine Holiness —a liberal creed must seem to him to fall far short of what can be a satisfactory total philosophy of life. This is bound to be the reaction of all sincere religious believers to our foregoing analysis. Must they then conclude that from the first our effort has been doomed to failure?

The overtones of the preceding pages have, no doubt, made it clear where I myself stand—squarely and without equivocation in the Christian tradition. This is, as I interpret it, my own faith; it is the faith to which I myself must give my ultimate allegiance. But I submit that very much can be gained and that nothing need be lost if we who openly confess the Christian faith band ourselves together with all those men and women of other religious faiths and, no less closely, with sincere humanists and naturalists, in common allegiance to a creed that not only proclaims but makes explicit our common faith in human dignity and value. No one need dishonestly pretend that this common faith in man suffices, that it exhausts all that some of us are honestly able to believe. But no dishonesty is involved in asserting in a given context and for good and sufficient reason only a part of all that one believes, provided that this partial assertion does not by implication distort or misrepresent one's more inclusive faith. It is on these grounds that I, for one, am eager to declare my wholehearted allegiance to some such liberal creed. As a professing Christian, I must go much further. But nothing I would wish to add concerning my own faith in God and my resultant understanding of man, including his sinfulness, in any way contradicts what I would be asserting by subscribing to the foregoing creed of liberalism. If other liberals, whatever their ultimate persuasion, can accept this creed or some variant thereof, I would urge them to do so. What might we not accomplish in our sick society if enough of us could band together on this affirmative platform for the common good?

One final word before we address ourselves to the problem of how to implement such a liberal creed in our own society and culture. In an earlier chapter I urged our common need for a liberal creed that would serve us as effectively as the creed of Marxism served the Communist cause. I trust that no reader expected me to produce *the* creed of liberalism, for such an expectation would indeed have betrayed his complete misapprehension of the very nature of the liberal venture. Dictators can devise an authoritarian creed and force it upon their enslaved subjects. No such procedure is available to a free people. All we can do is let anyone who will devise the best liberal creed he can and then offer it to his fellow citizens for comment and criticism and for whatever measure of agreement it can elicit. In short, my task has not been to formulate a final and definitive statement for legal enactment or compulsory acceptance. It has been the very different task of exploring a vexed problem and of attempting to help crystallize whatever common beliefs we free men and women already have and can acquire. If the foregoing discussion has contributed anything significant to this catalytic task it has accomplished its purpose.

PART III

The Practice of Liberalism

Introduction

Like all other vital human issues, liberalism challenges not only our minds but also our wills. It not only invites analysis, it also calls for decision and action. We have thus far been primarily concerned with the theory of liberalism—with the definition of the liberal attitude, the formulation of a liberal creed, and the exploration of some of the vexed philosophical problems it raises. Such an inquiry has its own intrinsic value, but this book is not merely a philosophical exercise. It is also an essay in applied social ethics, in practical politics, to give the term "politics" its older generic meaning. We cannot practice liberalism intelligently if we do not know what it is and comprehend its implications, but liberal theory will be fruitful only as we put it to work in our society. The time has come for us to ask: "How liberal are we today as a nation? How well do our social institutions exemplify and promote the cause of liberalism? What can we do, individually and collectively, to revitalize our liberal heritage and more adequately realize our cherished ideals of a free society?"

The liberalism that had its origin in a complex European culture and is so essential a part of our own American heritage has been woven into the very structure of our social institutions. It is today, however unevenly and distortedly, a vital part of our national ethos. Thus we need not invent a brand-new ideal; we need merely revitalize what is already a living force in our community. The movement we would initiate is not a revolution but a reformation—the reclarification of liberalism at the level of theory, the revivification of liberalism as a persuasive social ideal, and the more perfect actualization of liberalism in our institutions and in our daily lives.

121

The Practice of Liberalism

This goal calls for both individual and collective effort. We must reform ourselves, and we must also transform our social institutions into more effective vehicles of reform. We are in part what our institutions have made us; they are in part what we make of them. We as individuals and our institutions as vehicles of social co-operation mutually influence and depend upon one another. We must therefore try to promote the cause of liberalism simultaneously on both fronts —in ourselves and in all our institutions. Our personal liberalism will be largely conditioned by the multiple impacts upon us of our institutions, and they in turn will reflect the pervasive ethos of our nation and our entire culture. We must become better liberals individually if we would liberalize our institutions; we must band together to purge our institutions of illiberalism if they are more successfully to infuse oncoming generations with the spirit of liberalism.

Our chief concern in the remainder of this book is the problem of institutional reform. It must be left to each individual to decide for himself how he, as a unique person in a series of unique social situations, can best exemplify the liberalism he professes. Our corporate task is the assessment and reform of the institutions upon which we all vitally depend.

Chapter 8

Our Five Basic Institutions

$\mathscr{A}$N "INSTITUTION" can be defined, most simply, as a habitual pattern of social behavior, a more or less established way of doing things together. It is the social analogue of a habit or pattern of habits in an individual. If people are to live together in a society, they must have corporate habits, accepted ways of working together for common objectives. An "institution" is an evolving structure of social relations whose function it is to make possible co-operative advances toward common goals.

All human beings have certain basic needs, and all human societies have institutional ways of satisfying these needs. Every society makes some institutional provision for law and order and for its corporate safety. Sexual activity is somehow controlled, and the nurture of children is provided for. Food, shelter, and other physical necessities are made available on some sort of co-operative basis. In short, every society has some kind of political, familial, and economic institutional structure. Every society also provides some sort of institutional outlet for man's higher or more spiritual needs—for his religious aspirations, his aesthetic sense, his capacity for civic virtue and corporate loyalty. In these respects all societies are alike. They differ radically in the specific manner in which they meet these corporate requirements. What distinguishes one society from another is above all the distinctive "configuration" of its more or less unique institutional devices, its characteristic traditions and beliefs, mores and rituals.

Anthropologists find it difficult to describe the basic institutions of the simplest and most primitive societies, for even here the pattern of institutional relationships is subtle and ramified. The task of describing the institutional structure of a society as vast and complex as our own is even more difficult. We can offer only a very brief analysis of the five basic institutions that are the most influential in our society in molding our cultural values and giving our national ethos its distinctive character.

These five institutions are the state, the family, the school, the church, and that amalgam of organized activities which we call "business and industry." Each has its unique contribution to make to the corporate welfare, yet each, as we shall see, depends essentially upon the contributions of the rest. None can perform its proper task well unless all the others are performing theirs; the health of each depends upon the health of all, and our society as a whole is, in a real sense, as healthy as its major institutions make it.

The main purpose of the *state* is to protect its citizens against external aggression and internal anarchy and to provide a framework of law and order for all types of social co-operation. By its very nature it is the most inclusive of all our institutions in scope. Its power is all-pervasive; its prime vehicle is the law it enacts and enforces for the common weal; its final recourse is force. Its proper virtues are a scrupulous respect for all who live under its sway and the impartial administration of justice.

The chief purpose of the *family* is to provide an institutional framework for procreation, for protection and nurture of children, and for privacy of the home. It is by nature as exclusive as the state is inclusive; the human relations it cultivates are as intensive and personal as those cultivated by the state are extensive and impersonal. The prime virtue of the family is warm personal affection rather than impersonal respect; the attitude it characteristically fosters is love. It provides as no other institution can a "home" where man and wife, parents and children, brothers and sisters can live together in intimacy and affection.

The polar relationship of these two institutions is obvious. Each has what the other lacks; each is the foil to the other; neither can do what the other is specially qualified to do. We know what happened in China when family loyalty was emphasized at the expense of loyalty to a central government and when the family system was relied on almost exclusively for civic order and social stability. The result was civic anarchy, with irresponsible war lords exploiting the people openly and without restraint. We also know that the best-run public orphanages are a very poor substitute for the home and that children who fail to find in their families the love and security they crave are likely to exhibit throughout their lives the stigmata of these grave childhood frustrations. We need the civil defense, order, and justice that only the state can provide, and we need the personal intimacies and affection of the home. No two institutions could be more unlike, or more irreplaceable. Together they constitute our bulwark and our haven, the institutional guarantees of our public freedoms and our private liberties.

The school and the church can also be paired, but for a different reason. They belong together because we entrust to them the chief responsibility for our intellectual and spiritual well-being. They are the institutional guardians of our "higher" freedoms; it is their joint task to safeguard our intellectual and spiritual heritage, to revitalize and enrich it, and to disseminate it as widely as possible. It is to them that we should look primarily for intellectual and spiritual leadership, for imaginative creativity, intellectual exploration, and prophetic utterance.

The prime function of the *school,* in its widest generic sense, is the cultivation of the mind. Its task is education of every type and at every level—the education of the growing child and youth and also the continuing self-education of the mature citizen and the professional scholar. Such education should quicken man's natural curiosity and cultivate his intellectual powers. But education should also prepare man for effective participation in the many social activities his society makes available to him and, especially in a free society, for responsible citizenship and wise leadership. The school is our chief institutional vehicle for individual improvement and social advance. Its goal is knowledge in the widest sense—knowledge of fact and value for its own sake and as our most reliable guide to enlightened and responsible conduct. The prime virtue of the school is eager and honest critical inquiry and an ultimate loyalty to truth.

Of all our institutions the *church* is the hardest to describe objectively

125

and fairly because it is conceived of so variously in our society. Those who repudiate all religious faith regard it as the institutional home of reaction and superstition. They deny its claim to spiritual leadership and refuse to list it among our vital institutions. Others acknowledge the church's past contributions to our culture but are pessimistic regarding its continuing vitality and value. They are impressed by its present failure to elicit the wide support of "intellectuals" and even more by its frequent lack of courageous social concern for underprivileged minorities. Faithful church members, on the other hand, regard the church as the natural institutional vehicle for man's deepseated religious aspirations and as the irreplaceable institutional channel for God's revelation of himself to man and man's corporate response to God. They therefore judge the church to be the most important of our institutions. We shall return to these claims and counterclaims when we consider the proper role of organized religion in a liberal community. Let us for the moment accept the church as one of our major institutions today and describe its functions as an enlightened religious believer would describe them.

Such a believer would say that the primary function of the church is to promote the worship of God and his service. Its chief purpose is to foster direct communion with God rather than self-improvement or social welfare, even though individual salvation and brotherly love are the prescribed products of such communion. Here man's sense of his own finitude and his search for the Infinite receive unique institutional recognition. Here man discovers, as he can discover nowhere else, that God makes himself known to man and makes available the light and the power requisite for his salvation. Divinely initiated revelation, in some meaningful sense, is thus as basic for the church as is humanly initiated intellectual inquiry for the school. The believer's faith in God and his submission to God's will are as important for the life of the church as is the scholar's critical inquiry for the institutional life of the school. The prime virtue of the church is therefore reverence and awe—awe in the presence of ultimate mystery and reverence for the revealed God of righteous love.

The school and the church are also, in their own way, polar opposites. The school is man-oriented, the church, God-oriented; the school is dedicated to human initiative, the church, to the divine initiative; the school is engaged in co-operative research, the church, to corporate worship. These differences are real and should not be minimized, but they should not be allowed to obscure important similarities. For the church too, at its most enlightened fosters honest human inquiry and man's co-operative search for the highest truth; the school, at its most enlightened seeks to embrace all truth from whatever source, to encourage man's highest spiritual aspirations, and to lead the learner from wonder to awe and from awe to informed reverence. Both school and church, in so far as they respectively transcend the artificial chasm between the merely "secular" and the purely "religious" that so tragically disrupts our society today, are dedicated to man's highest total welfare—to the richest and fullest development of his mind and soul, his imagination and will, in total response to everything in our universe capable of eliciting his wonder and delight and worthy of his reverence. Different though they are in specific orientation and ultimate emphasis, the school and the church should be natural allies, each complementing the other's strength without losing its own distinctive character or failing to perform its unique functions. There is certainly no other institution in our society qualified to assume the major responsibilities of either school or church, and neither could perform the function of the other without grave distortion and neglect of its own duties.

The awkward phrase *business and industry* [1] is here used to designate that infinitely complicated web of processes and activities which provide us with our physical necessities and comforts and the physical setting for all our cultural efforts. "Industry" here includes all the practical applications of modern science, in mine, factory, farm and forest, whereby marketable goods are produced for consumption; "business" covers all the operations, including financial and promotional, whereby these goods are distributed to the consumer. The minimal function of this many-sided institution is to satisfy our basic economic needs. But we are also indebted to business and industry for our high standard of living, our health and longevity, and our technological and military strength. It is our workers and managers, financiers and businessmen who have made us economically the envy of the world.

In the context of the good life of the whole man all these goods and

[1] Often condensed to "business" in the following pages.

services must be reckoned not ends in themselves but means to higher ends. We eat to live, even though we enjoy tasty food; only the gourmand lives to eat. We may enjoy our technological gadgets—we may even become their slaves and worship them—but we know in our hearts that such slavery is idolatrous and unworthy of human dignity. The entire enterprise of business and industry must be assessed accordingly. Physical goods and all that pertain thereto are means to higher ends and should be valued in proportion to the efficiency with which they perform this mediating function. The prime virtue of business and industry, so conceived, is practical short- and long-range efficiency. They serve us well if they skillfully and economically provide us with all the physical goods and allied services we need for our economic security and well-being. Their prime virtue is integrity—the "aesthetic" integrity of good craftsmanship and the "moral" integrity that reflects a lively sense of social responsibility.

I have stressed the special responsibilities of this great institution because they are so easily forgotten in a predominantly business and industrial culture such as ours. Our tendency is to cast business and industry in a very different role—as primarily the source of the profit, the power, and the prestige that attend financial success. This is too often the spirit in which young people go into business and the spirit in which business is conducted. The many men and women in every phase of business and industry who exhibit a lively sense of social responsibility and a keen appreciation for craftsmanship prove, if proof is needed, that financial gain need not be the only or even the dominant motive in this vast area of human activity. Business can and should be a profession as honored and as honorable, as socially beneficial and as intrinsically satisfying as any of the so-called "higher" professions of medicine, law, teaching, and the ministry. The intrinsic satisfactions can be as great for those who are well qualified for the job in hand, and the opportunities it offers for genuine social usefulness are as notable as are the satisfactions and opportunities of any other profession. Its responsibilities are as real and should be as compelling as those of the doctor, lawyer, teacher, or minister. As human activities business and industry are not intrinsically inferior to the "higher" professions just because the latter seek to promote directly those values to which business and industry can contribute only indirectly. To feed, clothe, and house human beings efficiently and to contribute to their economic security and comfort is as worthy an activity as healing their bodies, administering justice, training their minds, or offering them spiritual guidance.

This brief sketch of our five basic institutions can be diagrammatically summarized as follows:

STATE

Purpose: Protection, maintenance of law and order, appropriate support of other institutions
Nature: Inclusive, impersonal
Prime virtue: Justice

FAMILY

Purpose: Procreation, nurture, intimate companionship
Nature: Exclusive, personal
Prime virtue: Love

SCHOOL

Purpose: Education
Nature: Humanly initiated self-improvement
Prime virtue: Truth

CHURCH

Purpose: Worship
Nature: Response to divine initiative, faith
Prime virtue: Reverence

BUSINESS AND INDUSTRY

Purpose: Subsistence, economic security
Nature: Production and distribution of economic goods
Prime virtues: Efficiency and integrity

It should be apparent that these five institutions are by no means mutually exclusive in nature and function. Government cannot maintain law and order without the active support of the great mass of citizens. Love must extend beyond the family circle if our society is to function justly and humanely. Education is not exclusively the responsibility of the school; each of the other institutions must play its minor but essential role in the total venture of education. Religion entrusted solely to the churches and deprived of secular support and criticism

129

would lack the spiritual power and influence it should have. All our institutions are "in business" in their respective ways, and business and industry can exemplify many of the virtues primarily associated with other institutional activities.

It is equally apparent that our society would suffer greatly if any one of these institutions were to be supplanted by any one of the others. Consider the probable results if the state were to take over all business, if business were to seize complete control of government, if the family were to be abolished, or if the state or the school were to attempt to function as a church. The five institutions (if we credit the claims of religion and include the church) are all clearly indispensable and irreplaceable; each has its essential role in our society.

This account of our institutional structure should no doubt be extended to include such important institutionalized activities as medicine, law, the press, the vast amusement industry, and the countless fraternal and philanthropic organizations that bulk so large in the lives of many of our citizens. Some of these might be included in the loose category of business and industry; for example, medicine might be defined as the therapeutic branch of technology and therefore as that "business" activity which, in a free society, provides for the social application of scientific discoveries relevant to health. But such institutions tend to cut across these boundaries. For example, medical research is an essential part of the total program of research for which the school assumes primary responsibility; the press and the amusement industry function, for better and for worse, as very powerful educational agencies. The multitude of clubs, fraternities, and other civic organizations defy classification under our rubrics; they are a notable expression of the healthy tendency in a free society for people to band together spontaneously for amusement, philanthropy, or civic reform. Moreover, these and other types of organizations and activities can exemplify liberalism and illiberalism as definitely as can the five major institutions. Indeed, it might be argued that they are the most sensitive institutional indexes of significant change in our prevailing ethos. The great importance of their actual and potential contributions to the cause of liberalism must certainly not be forgotten.

It is the five major institutions, however, that will chiefly determine the extent to which we as a nation will manifest the spirit of liberalism in the coming years. If we allow them to fail us in the defense, nurture, direction, and practical implementation of liberalism, our cause is lost, however courageous may be the continuing efforts of stanch solitary liberals and groups of liberals. They must be our chief institutional vehicles for effective co-operation in the defense of our present freedoms and in any long-range campaign to purify and intensify the spirit of liberalism in our society.

We have noted the polar relationship of the state and the family, the broad similarity of the objectives of the school and the church, and the major role of business and industry in providing the economic basis for the other four institutions. We address ourselves now to the problem of how a vital liberalism can express itself in each of these institutions and, more particularly, how we as individuals might help to make each of them more effectively liberal than it is at present. As we proceed, we shall do well to relate these five institutions in a somewhat different way. The democratic state is our political and legal *bulwark* of liberalism. The family, the school, and the church are the institutions on which we must primarily depend to nurture, strengthen, purify, and direct the *spirit* of liberalism. Business and industry are our chief institutional vehicle for the *implementation* of liberalism in the world of practical affairs. Let us briefly examine these five institutions in this order, keeping before us throughout one central question: "What should each contribute to the cause of liberalism, and how efficiently is each at present performing its special task?"

Chapter 9

The Bulwark of Liberalism:
Political Democracy

$\mathscr{O}$UR DEMOCRATIC FORM of government is our political expression and defense of the basic liberties that we as a nation have cherished since the founding of the Republic. It would never have come into being had not our Founding Fathers been animated by a passion for freedom and a resolve to protect their liberties with all the political and legal safeguards their wisdom could devise. They borrowed much from the religious and secular strands of western culture—from earlier philosophers, prophets, statesmen, and writers. They were particularly aware of the long struggle for political liberty in England and of the treatises on liberty in contemporary France. Only we, from our mid-twentieth-century perspective, can fully appreciate what they achieved —a political philosophy and a form of government that have triumphantly survived internal tensions and foreign threats whose gravity the most keenly prophetic eighteenth-century eye could not possibly have foreseen.

Alfred North Whitehead has pointed out that it took about two thousand years for the ideas of freedom and persuasion to prevail over the older ideas of slavery and force. These ideas first had to germinate in a few brilliant philosophic and prophetic minds; then to disseminate themselves and gradually gain social momentum in ancient and medieval times; then to receive a fresh impetus from the industrial revolution, when at last machines could be substituted for slaves; then to stir the popular conscience with the help of various evangelical movements; and finally to be tested in political struggle and bloody conflict—all this before they were able to achieve modern political and

132

legal expression. This is our costly heritage of political liberty, the fruit of the spirit of liberalism and today its chief institutional bulwark. It is this bulwark which we must renovate and strengthen generation after generation if we would protect ourselves and our children against a recrudescence of political and social tyranny.

Our experiment in political democracy rests squarely on the assumption, or faith, that man is able to co-operate voluntarily with his fellow-men at the political, social, and legal levels of corporate life. Man is here conceived of as a particular kind of social and political being—one who possesses not only the capacity for responsible evaluation and decision but also the ability to put this capacity to responsible social use in a free society. What do we mean by a free society, and what are the prerequisites for full participating membership in it?

Man is a social being because, like many other living species, he is dependent upon his fellows for his physical needs, indeed for his very life. Ants and bees are also social in this primitive sense because of their mutual dependence within the nest and the hive. Even the most primitive human societies also possess some type of social organization upon which they consciously depend for peace and order. This ability consciously to recognize and abide by whatever type of social authority the group happens to have distinguishes man from insects and other social creatures who achieve similar ends entirely by instinct. Political awareness distinguishes man from even the best-organized animal species.

For our present purpose, human societies can be classified into three distinctive types, each type including a multitude of variations. Two of these, which we shall label the "libertarian" and the "authoritarian" types, are human extrapolations from two analogous forms of social organization at the subhuman level. The third type, which we shall designate as "free," has no animal analogue. It alone is distinctively human because only human beings possess the prerequisite capacities for the creation of and participation in this type of organization.

LIBERTARIANISM AND AUTHORITARIANISM

A human society conforms to the "libertarian" type of social and political organization when the individuals composing it are able to lead their own lives with a minimum regard for other members of the group. The ideal of such a society is complete laissez faire with no coercive social controls whatever and no felt responsibility for others. So defined, no completely libertarian society has ever existed or could exist because no human beings could live under such chaotic social conditions. For survival even the higher animals require some social device for the care of their young, for protection against common enemies, and, it may be, for some primitive type of companionship. Male and female co-operate sufficiently to safeguard their progeny; many living species group together in flocks and herds. The nomad comes closest to the libertarian at the human level, for he acknowledges only two areas of social responsibility, the family and the loosely organized tribe.

For a few decades in our own country, the adventurous Western pioneer was able to live an exceptionally free life, often without family responsibilities and with a minimum of group restraint. He was as completely on his own as a human being can be; he relied primarily on his own initiative and ingenuity for food and shelter; he ventured on or settled as he chose. Yet even he had to band together with others for the great trek westward; he had to join forces with others for protection against hostile tribes of Indians and against the elements. As the West gradually became settled, some limits had to be set to individual initiative; some sense of justice and some machinery for its enforcement, however crude and informal, became imperative. Similarly, extreme individualists like Thoreau have been able to survive in more stable communities only because their friends were willing to protect them from legal pressure and social censure. Throughout human history, solitary ascetics have survived only because the society from which they fled was willing to feed and clothe them.

In our own day, it is primarily the economically successful and secure who still preach the gospel of rugged individualism. They find it convenient to forget the many political safeguards and the complicated social machinery that provided the necessary setting for their own initiative and made their success possible. Yet when their profitable activities or their investments are threatened they are often the first to demand governmental interference on their own behalf. Today the motto of rugged individualism tends to be: "Let others be controlled so that I may be free to do as I like." The rugged individualist is iron-ically forced to become what he officially most hates, a social parasite; the more ruthlessly individualistic he is, the more dependent he becomes upon those whom he exploits.

An authoritarian society is the extreme opposite of a libertarian society. It too resembles a type of organization in the animal kingdom that is best exemplified by ants and bees. Since men are capable of independent reflection and action as insects are not, no human society is ever likely to become as perfectly regimented as the ant nest or the beehive; instinct lends itself far better to regimentation than does in-telligence. Cunning and ruthless as were Hitler and Mussolini in their attempts to quell opposition, silence criticism, block private initiative, and enforce robot conformity, they were only partially successful. There is a limit to how far Communist totalitarianism can go, even with the aid of intensive propaganda, the iron curtain, and such diabolical de-vices as brain-washing, to force millions of people into complete con-formity. This very effort, indeed, is likely to sow the seeds of its own destruction, for a society loses its corporate strength and vitality when it loses free initiative and independent thought.

Libertarianism and authoritarianism are thus opposite poles toward either of which a society can move and which all human societies exemplify in some degree. What are their respective presuppositions?

Libertarianism gives priority to what we have previously called "voluntaristic" freedom. It honors man's sense of autonomy as a free agent. At its most unbalanced, it reflects man's passion for freedom from all restraint and his repudiation of all social responsibility to others. It expresses the individual's preoccupation with his rights and the neglect of his corresponding duties; it bespeaks a one-sided insistence on my rights at the expense of yours, your duties without regard to mine. It is thus in essence unco-operative and predatory. The libertarian spirit can transform itself into the liberal spirit of a free society only when rights and duties, my welfare and yours, are cherished in co-operative harmony.

Authoritarianism gives priority to what we have called "normative" freedom. It recognizes man's dependence on his fellows and stresses his need for social order and stability. Here welfare is conceived of in social rather than individual terms, and social welfare is believed to be possible only if it is imposed upon men from above. At its best, as in Plato's *Republic*, it entrusts ultimate authority to a wise and beneficent philosopher-king (or some aristocratic equivalent). Such a ruler is expected to use his power to "compel" the citizens of the state to be normatively free. They are not exploited but are nurtured and protected for their own good; they are carefully trained to be docile participants in a regimented society in which voluntaristic freedom is feared and therefore restrained.

Even at its ideal best, such a state differs radically from a free community in its systematic repudiation of man's higher freedoms of speech and worship and in its indifference to man's basic civic rights. It is humane but inhuman; it cherishes the normative content of the good life at the expense of man's voluntaristic freedom as a responsible moral agent. At its worst, authoritarian regimentation loses all concern for man's cultural welfare and focuses its attention exclusively upon the physical well-being and the economic and political security of the state. It ceases to be even humane; it treats men as though they were animals, destroying the unprofitable and caring for the useful only in order to derive greater benefit from them. It holds in contempt not only man's voluntaristic freedom but his normative freedom as well. It degenerates into a ruthless and exploitative dictatorship, the dictator doing everything in his power to control and use the masses for his own benefit. Unlike the regimentation of insects, human authoritarianism tends, at its worst, to approximate more and more closely rugged individualism at its worst, differing finally only in its greater efficiency. In the end the only rights it honors are the rights of the dictator, secured by force; the only duty it acknowledges is the enforced duty of the masses and of the dictator's underlings.

No human society, we must repeat, has ever perfectly exemplified either libertarianism or authoritarian regimentation; man cannot exist in a state of either complete anarchy or complete slavery. But every society is continually threatened by those who incline toward one extreme or the other, and some societies, to their sorrow, have traveled far along one or other of these roads—toward wolfish predatory individualism or toward bovine regimented docility. These are the opposite yet converging dangers against which a free society must be on its guard.

LIBERALISM AND ITS PREREQUISITES

The basic philosophy of a "free" society seeks to combine the partial insights and the one-sided merits of both these extreme positions. It values equally and sets in harmonious balance man's voluntaristic and normative freedoms. It cherishes private initiative but, no less, the social good and man's duties to his fellows. It defends man's freedom from restraint, but only to the degree that he exercises it responsibly, with lively concern for the freedom of others. It cultivates man's normative apprehension and realization of values, but by persuasion rather than by covert or overt force. It is equally opposed to anarchy and regimentation, to absence of order and to forcefully compelled order. Its social ideal is neither an aggregate of rugged individualists nor a subhuman regimented nest or hive, but a free community of self-disciplined men and women who respect each other's rights as much as they do their own and who perform their own corresponding duties without external compulsion. A society is therefore free when its members do in fact voluntarily co-operate with one another as equals. It is liberal when its members exhibit what we have defined as the liberal attitude, respecting one another as intelligent evaluators, responsible moral agents, and beings capable of awe. A free society is a community in which liberalism really prevails. No perfect free society has ever existed or ever will exist, but a society like ours can make this freedom its social ideal and can assess its own health and vitality by reference to this ideal.

A free liberal community, as distinguished from its illiberal opposites, has two basic prerequisites: prudence coupled with altruism and faith in law and justice.

VOLUNTARY PRUDENCE AND ALTRUISM

The first distinctive condition of membership in such a community is the dual ability to be voluntarily prudent and voluntarily unselfish. A liberal believes that men are capable of both and also that real prudence and real unselfishness, though differing radically in attitude, need not conflict in the long-range results they produce. Libertarians and authoritarians conceive of human nature very differently.

137

The libertarian may or may not himself exhibit prudence. He may be deliberately imprudent—the hobo prefers the carefree life of the "road" and declines to worry about the future; or he may be prudent to the point of masochism—some men choose to forfeit all present enjoyment of life in the grim determination to pile up worldly treasure against a rainy day or heavenly insurance against the day of judgment. The more single-mindedly and rigorously prudent the libertarian is the less faith he is likely to have in the ability of other people to be prudent at all. He is inclined to trace all human misfortune to the individual's culpable sloth and dissipation and therefore in the name of cold-hearted justice to let him suffer for his earlier imprudence. This decision echoes the libertarian's dominant selfishness, his basic unconcern for others. He is willing to fight his own battles and appeals to government for remedial measures only when he feels that the cards are stacked against him by an unfair society; he insists that others fight their battles and take the consequences. He stifles his own altruistic impulses and never experiences the deep satisfaction of a sincere concern for his fellow-men; he therefore has no faith in the alleged altruism of others. Lacking all genuine interest in or respect for other men, he ascribes the same attitude to them and interprets all protestations of social concern as hypocritical, all apparent generosity as a prudential maneuver. Only a successful fellow-individualist can elicit his grudging respect as an opponent against whom he can match his own strength and wits.

This is not a pretty picture of the ruthless libertarian. But liberalism is sentimentally unrealistic if it ignores its enemies or fails to recognize their typical profile and characteristic attitude. A liberal should realize that our society, dedicated to bitter economic competition, produces many such predatory individuals—not only the racketeers of the underworld but men and women in positions of trust and high social esteem. No society as a whole can travel the road of rugged individualism all the way without disaster, but many individuals in our society can and do closely approximate the state of completely callous selfishness. In the aggregate they are one of the greatest threats to a liberal community.

The authoritarian, in turn, whether he is benign or exploitative, has faith in his own prudence but little or no faith in the ability of others to look ahead and to work and sacrifice for their own future welfare. If he is benevolent he will try to make good this widespread deficiency by forcing or cajoling the masses to do whatever may be necessary today to insure them against unhappiness tomorrow. Some of our current utopian proposals for sweeping old-age benefits for all regardless of need, or for social insurance on a scale that would upset the stability of our present economy, are "democratic" expressions of the patronizing authoritarian attitude. Russia provides another, more dramatic, expression of this attitude, if we credit the claims of the Politburo that the proletariat is being forced to slave and starve now for the benefit of future generations. In both cases, the major assumption is the same— that most people are unable or unwilling to plan and live prudently on their own initiative and that they must therefore have prudence thrust upon them for their own good.

Such authoritarian benevolence always tends to transform itself sooner or later into authoritarian tyranny. This shift is understandable, for if we start with little or no respect for people as responsible moral agents we are very apt to lose whatever initial concern we may once have felt for their welfare. Most people are not likable enough to elicit our lively concern; a spontaneous impulse of generosity can easily change into a feeling of dislike and contempt. Moreover, power always tends to corrupt. The benevolence of a dictatorship is likely to be short-lived and to be succeeded by tyrannical despotism. When this happens, greed and cruelty quickly spread throughout the body politic. Greed nurtures greed, and cruelty breeds reciprocal cruelty and hatred. The dreadful story of the moral disintegration first of the guards and then of most of the prisoners in the German concentration camps provides an unforgettable lesson in practical pathology—a lesson we can also learn in this country if we probe deeply enough into areas polluted by tyrannical power.

The true liberal, in contrast to both the libertarian and the authoritarian, is a resolute optimist about human nature; indeed, his besetting sin is an inclination to overrate people's intelligence and goodness and to expect of them the humanly impossible. He has great faith in the common man's innate capacity for prudence, his native intelligence, his ability and willingness to learn, his basic integrity, and his capacity for self-discipline. If he is a "Jacksonian" liberal, he will tend to trust the ordinary voter as he is and will go far toward an egalitarianism in which the people's representatives make no pretense to lead but conceive it to be their sole political duty to reflect the present wishes, however unenlightened, of the electorate. If he is a Jeffersonian liberal, he will put his faith rather in the ability of the people to elect wise leaders, if given a chance to do so, and to follow their leadership with cautious loyalty. That is, he will have more faith in the common man's political and economic potentialities than in his present state of political wisdom or economic sagacity. He will be realistically aware of man's shortsighted follies, but he will also believe that, given time and the requisite education, people can learn how to become more prudent and more intelligently co-operative for their own and the common good. He will agree that you cannot fool all the people all the time; he will also hope that, for all its shortsightedness and provincialism, the citizenry can be more safely trusted with political power in the long run, particularly under wise and persuasive leadership, than can any individual or dynasty or self-elected clique, however benevolent its momentary or average attitude may be.

Nineteenth-century "liberalism," better named "libertarianism," must be sharply distinguished from the "liberalism" defended in this book. It believed that everyone would benefit in the long run if man's economic activities were left uncontrolled in the spirit of complete laissez faire. This policy seemed to work reasonably well during an era of expanding markets, but at the close of the era its utopianism became apparent. It left out of account man's all too frequent lack of long-range prudence; it also entirely ignored man's perennial impulse to predatory exploitation. Shrewd and ruthless individuals and groups are quite right in believing that the quick returns from clever exploitation of the public may well benefit them more in the short run than the evil effects of their raids on society will harm them. So long as a laissez-faire social policy permits such lucrative raids at the public expense, there will always be individuals ready and eager to feather their own nests. The failure of nineteenth-century libertarianism to take account of these grim aspects of human nature makes it a good example of the sentimentality a realistic liberalism should avoid. Libertarian utopianism was no *more* unrealistic, however, than is the cynical disbelief still frequently encountered in the common man's ability, under wise leadership, to correct the shortcomings of a laissez-faire economy and, by popular consent, to set up the necessary safeguards against such predatory exploitation.

The true liberal, then, believes in man's ability to grow in prudence and to learn, however slowly, to co-operate with his fellows for his own good and theirs. He also believes in man's innate capacity for unselfish concern for others. If he is as clear-eyed as he should be, he realizes that man's innate tendency to take care of himself is probably stronger than his impulse to cherish the welfare of others. He will also be aware that on the whole our competitive society tends to reinforce man's native egoism more than his native altruism. But this knowledge will not lead him to the cynical conclusion that man is incapable of genuine unselfishness. He will take seriously the impressive evidence of instinctive "unselfishness" in the animal kingdom, for example, the untaught impulse of many higher animals to risk their lives for their young and of many insects to behave in a manner best calculated to promote the common good. He will take no less seriously the many instances of notable self-sacrifice in every human society and culture. He will attach particular importance to man's demonstrated ability to strive wholeheartedly for goals that simultaneously afford him profound satisfaction and conduce to the common good—goals such as the conquering of disease, the discovery of new truths, the creation of beauty, and the promotion of justice. He will acknowledge that men's motives are often mixed, but he will insist on the frequent presence and the significance in this mixture of genuine and sincere altruism. Above all, he will be acutely aware of how much can be done in a society like ours to strengthen and intensify man's native altruism, to minimize the importance of nonsharable goods like property, and to maximize the value, both to the individual and to his society, of such sharable goods as truth, beauty, justice, and mercy.

This liberal faith in man will seem most unrealistic to the skeptic whose reading of human nature resembles that of Hobbes and other self-styled "realists." It will also seem unrealistic and utopian to theologians who attach greater importance to man's universal depravity than to man's essential goodness as a "creature" and "child" of God. There is, I believe, a profound truth in the Christian doctrine that man cannot save himself without God's redemptive help, but this very doctrine becomes nonsense if one denies the equally Christian doctrine that man has been made in the image of God and that however sinful he may be he never loses the capacity to respond to God's redemptive love and, with God's help, really to love his fellow-men. Which of these readings of human nature is correct—that of the cynical secularist, that of the cynical theologian who has lost all faith in man, that of the secular humanist who believes that man's innate goodness can and must suffice to ensure human progress, or that of the religiously oriented humanist who has faith in both God and man and is therefore confident that divine grace and man's essential goodness can together counteract man's egoisms and idolatries? This question brings us once again into an area of perennial controversy and in the last analysis forces us to take sides as best we can.

It is certainly the profound conviction of the liberal that man does have his "better"—that is, more altruistic—nature, that this side of him can be cultivated and strengthened, and that the absolute prerequisite for a truly liberal community is widespread and authentic concern for one's fellow-men in addition to and in harmony with long-range, intelligent prudence. He admits that sincere unselfishness is often uninformed and therefore harmful in its actual results, even as selfishness may inadvertently benefit certain individuals or groups. Hence his deep concern for knowledge and intelligence as well as for motive, and his effort to promote intelligent altruism as well as intelligent prudence. Hence his insistence on social reform and on education designed to strengthen our socially oriented motives and to make their translation into concrete behavior more enlightened and beneficial. In short, the realistic liberal is persuaded that man is capable of both selfishness and unselfishness; that man can derive at least as much joy from his altruistic efforts as he can from his egoistic striving; that both selfish and unselfish motives may in fact produce both socially beneficial and socially harmful results; and that the prime purposes of education in a liberal society should therefore be to cultivate man's unselfish impulses and to help him acquire the knowledge he must have to be not only intelligently prudent but intelligently unselfish as well.

FAITH IN LAW AND JUSTICE

The second prerequisite of a free society, as distinguished from liber-

tarianism and authoritarian regimentation, is a faith in objective justice
and a respect for legality and law. The justice in which the liberal puts
his ultimate faith is ideal and perfect justice, the justice all righteous
men seek to apprehend and actualize, so far as they can, in their own
behavior and in the laws and legal procedures of their society. He believes that the only proper purpose of a law is to express and implement true justice so far as possible. A liberal therefore respects law as
such and approves of recourse to law for the settling of stubborn disputes and for the orderly furtherance of human justice. A liberal community is one that believes in ideal justice, that has faith in law as
man's best device for actualizing such justice as he can grasp, and that
insists on the use of and obedience to the laws and legal procedures of
the community even when they fail, as they must, to embody ideal
justice.

How does this liberal respect for law and justice differ from the
libertarian and authoritarian conceptions? When we say that a rugged
individualist is or tries to be a "law unto himself" we are using the
word "law" very loosely. What we actually mean is that such an individual recognizes no "higher" justice and that he feels no respect for
law and legality as such. He wants to be his own "lawmaker," that is,
he wants to do what he wants to do when he wants to do it. He toler-
ates public law as a necessary evil; he actively supports only those laws
that favor his own interest; he ignores or evades the rest when he can
do so with impunity. This attitude clearly betrays his lack of faith in
any kind of objective justice.

The benevolent authoritarian, in contrast, may believe in objective
justice, either in religious or in secular terms. But if he does so he will
also insist on the absolute authority of some privileged interpretation
of it, and he will use this interpretation as his criterion in his assessment
of all public laws. He will normally favor obedience to the laws of the
land, either because he believes on religious grounds in rendering to
Caesar the things that are Caesar's, or because he believes as a secularist
in law and order as such. What chiefly distinguishes him from the
liberal is his supreme confidence in his source of legal wisdom and his
belief that the state should impose the laws dictated by this wisdom
upon a people who must be less informed and less wise.

The authoritarian who has become arbitrary dictator repudiates the very notion of objective justice as brusquely as does the libertarian. If his control of the state is absolute, the "laws" of the state are merely his arbitrary decrees, which he rescinds or reverses as easily as he proclaims them. He differs from the ruthless libertarian chiefly in his more ambitious determination to force his own will, in the form of edicts backed by force, upon all the members of the state. He is thus a Napoleonic individualist who liquidates his rivals and suppresses opposition instead of competing with his rivals in a laissez-faire society.

A liberal can have no respect for "laws" that are merely arbitrary decrees arbitrarily enforced. He believes that laws are worthy of respect only if they reflect man's honest attempt to apprehend and actualize objective justice. He realizes that in the absence of faith in and loyalty to objective justice law can be nothing but the expression of the selfish interest of some individual or group. This holds true even if the group in question is a large majority of the population, for without the possibility of appeal to a higher justice no minority could have any rights the majority was morally bound to honor. In short, his concern for all men as intrinsically valuable and worthy of respect compels the liberal to believe in objective justice and in its morally inescapable claim to man's highest social allegiance. It is this assumption which enables him to be simultaneously law-abiding and critical of all existing man-made laws. He feels not only free but morally obligated to scrutinize all actual laws on the statute books with an eye to their justice or injustice and to fight openly for the repeal of unjust laws and the enactment of laws that seem to him to embody greater justice. But since—until the reign of universal love—man can make justice, as he understands it, prevail in a society only with the aid of laws and legal procedure, the true liberal will be scrupulously law-abiding, however inadequate the laws may be. His motto is: "Obey the law, but improve it whenever possible!" This will not, of course, preclude his open disobedience of laws that violate his conscience and his willing acceptance of the legal penalty for such disobedience.

In summary, a liberal community is essentially a law-abiding and law-respecting community that relies on orderly legal procedures to resolve otherwise unresolvable disputes and yet never ceases to improve its laws in the direction of a more sensitive and impartial justice. Our society can be said to be libertarian when it allows individuals and groups to flout the laws and to be a law unto themselves and when a spirit of disrespect for law as such commonly prevails. It is authoritarian when certain individuals and groups have acquired such political and economic power that they can force their wishes upon the people, either benevolently or in a spirit of exploitation. It is liberal when its prevailing ethos reflects a deep concern for justice and when its laws elicit the critical respect and the responsible obedience of most of its citizens. Human nature being what it is, some degree of compulsion will be necessary in the most liberal of communities because there will always be those who will try in petty ways or on a large scale to take the law into their own hands. It is sheer utopianism to suppose that all the members of any actual human society will be ideally law-abiding or that evil, left unchecked, will not flourish. A realistically liberal community will therefore take all necessary steps to restrain evil, humanely but firmly. It will avoid both sentimental softness and vindictive cruelty; it will seek to prevent crime and to reform the criminal primarily by suitable education and appropriate legislation.

Such a law-abiding community might be described as the secular equivalent of a religious community whose members are dedicated to the worship of a God of righteous love and are animated by a sincere love for one another. Compared with such love, justice is cold and impersonal. Righteous love, in contrast to sentimental love, includes justice and transcends it, whereas mere justice lacks the outgoing warmth and mercy of righteous love. But such love is rare; no human society can today or in the foreseeable future rely solely on man's love for his fellow-men to assure the requisite law and order, just as no society can expect of all men a sense of justice and fair play or escape the necessity of using force to quell occasional lawlessness and to curtail predatory exploitation.

Love, justice, and force are related to one another in a scale of descending excellence. Perfect love tempers justice with mercy and empties force of all hatred for the individual upon whom force must be used. Justice resembles love in its equal concern for all men and in its fair, nonarbitrary, and humane use of force. Without the transforming compassion of love and the restraints of justice, force exhibits itself in all its untrammeled brutality. Considered in reverse, force is necessary in extreme cases and as a weapon of last resort for the effective administration of justice; justice is a necessary ingredient in righteous love. Force is thus a necessary but not sufficient condition of justice; justice, a necessary but insufficient condition of righteous love.

A society like ours, part secular and part religious, must depend primarily upon man's varying and unpredictable love for his fellow-men for whatever unselfish motivation and genuine altruism may in fact be forthcoming. Justice is more readily within our grasp, yet in every human society even justice remains only partly apprehended by the most just of men and only imperfectly implemented in law and social behavior. Some implicit and explicit recourse to force seems inescapable. Nonetheless, the goal of a liberal community will ever remain the minimum and most humane use of force, the continuing extension of justice, and the steady growth of that love all of us so profoundly crave.

These two prerequisites of a free society constitute the faith of the liberal that man is a being who has the latent ability to co-operate voluntarily with his fellow-men as equals. The "equality" here in question is not the superficial equality of social status cherished by the egalitarian. It is the profound equality of men as men, that is, as human beings of intrinsic dignity and worth, whatever their race or creed, their innate and acquired ability, their social background and present social status. The co-operation here postulated is that willing co-operation which differs in kind from compulsory servitude and reflects man's awareness of common needs, the prudential value of collaboration, and, above all, a genuine concern for the welfare of his fellows. The "ability" for such co-operation here ascribed to all men is, indeed, a latent capacity which must be cultivated and nourished and which, in fact, manifests itself very unevenly in men as we know them. Liberalism, confident that its faith in man's potentiality for free co-operation is well founded, but also aware of how often and to what extent this potentiality fails to ripen into overt co-operative behavior, must address itself to the unending task of helping all men in every possible way to realize this precious potentiality more fully. Only as it progressively succeeds in this effort will men be able to put to social use their ability to evaluate and to decide and act as responsible moral agents.

ADDITIONAL PRESUPPOSITIONS

The more specific presuppositions of our political democracy are all

146

corollaries of our basic faith that men can and should respect one another and learn to co-operate with one another freely and without compulsion. The following are all political articulations of the liberal creed.

1. The state is not a mystical entity more valuable than its members and is not entitled to regard any of them as expendable.

2. The people must keep ultimate political power in their own hands for two reasons: negatively, because no individuals or groups can safely be entrusted with absolute power; positively, because it is right for responsible moral agents to assume the duties of self-government.

3. Such self-government is possible only under the "rule of law," that is, in a society dedicated to the principle of legality as opposed to rule by arbitrary wish and whim.

4. All governmental machinery is merely a political and legal means for the furtherance of social ends.

5. The ends government should seek to realize are partly negative—to prevent external aggression and internal disorder—and partly positive—to foster our social well-being, that is, to protect our life and liberty and to promote our pursuit of happiness.

All these presuppositions of our political democracy are not only consistent with liberalism but are implicit in the very spirit of liberalism. Of course, more specific political and legal devices whereby we attempt to translate these basic principles into viable procedures raise new problems. The task of practical implementation is always hazardous and controversial. These details and controversies do not here concern us. What does concern us is the fact that certain aspects of the contemporary scene constitute a special challenge to political liberalism. There are four areas in which enlightened liberal leadership is particularly needed today.

FOUR CONTEMPORARY THREATS TO POLITICAL LIBERALISM

THE SOLITARY VOTER

The first threat relates to the predicament of the individual citizen in a nation as huge and complex as ours has now become. How can the solitary individual, with just one vote and just one voice to raise amid the crashing din of our democratic technological jungle, keep from becoming lost, bewildered, and so frustrated by a sense of his own impotence that he presently gives up the fight and ceases to function as a responsible citizen? How can he get from the press a fair picture of what is really happening around him—abroad, in Washington, and in his own community? How can he wisely interpret the news and assess the reports of news commentators who bombard him with their mutually contradictory oracular pronouncements? How can he understand the complex issues confronting him well enough to form a responsible opinion about them? How can he have any significant voice in the selection of his own governmental representatives when the final candidates for office are selected for him by men and forces working behind the scenes with a secrecy he is quite unable to break through? How can he escape a sense of utter futility when he considers the ineffectiveness of one solitary vote in the bewildering anonymity of a general election? How can he avoid the conclusion that liberalism is doomed in a technological society like ours—that in our age the political freedom and responsibility of the individual have become an anachronism?

The general direction in which the stouthearted liberal must look for an answer is obvious. He must start with the insistent reminder to himself and others that the whole of our free society, for all its bewildering complexity, is created and run by individuals like himself. He must remember that he is living in one of the few societies today with a government that does, in however devious and obfuscating ways, submit itself periodically at the polls to popular approval or censure and that it is still his vote, coupled with those of all his fellow-citizens, that delegates and abrogates political power. Those who today are politically enslaved and who enjoy none of our political freedoms would not thus minimize the significance of these powers.

A well-informed liberal will also realize that individuals have always been relatively ineffective when they persisted in playing a lone hand, and that in the past they have been able to acquire political influence only when they banded themselves together. If we would escape political ineptitude and futility we must put to use our freedoms of speech and assembly, our right to consult with one another and formulate common ends and common policies. Functioning as pressure groups, we must work for the goals that seem to us most beneficial for our society and our world. Every Rotary Club and industrial union, every *ad hoc* group organized to achieve some specific end is a potential training ground for civic leaders who can proclaim their beliefs and further their common policies. Such groups as these can and should serve as rallying points and phalanxes effective in pressing for change in governmental policy. They can enable solitary individuals to pool their resources, develop corporate strength, and give voice to opinions that would otherwise not be heard, or, if heard, would be largely disregarded. From his point of view, Hitler did well to suppress all such local groupings as possible centers of resistance. What he suppressed and feared we should welcome and encourage.

The danger of such groupings and of the power they can easily come to exert is obvious. They, like powerful predatory individuals and like many existing pressure groups, can do us great harm if they press only for their own prejudicial advantage in indifference or hostility to the welfare of other groups and of our nation as a whole. The vice of lobbies intent on plunder is today common knowledge; more harm than good would issue from the further extension of such vicious group egoism and selfishness. Only when those who thus band together and make their corporate pressure felt are themselves responsible liberals, truly concerned for the welfare of all, will their influence be beneficial. But it is only through such co-operative efforts, as well as along the more conventional political channels, that a civic-minded liberal can cease to be a political cipher and gradually become an affirmative force in our great, sprawling, technological, free community.

PUBLIC AND PRIVATE CORRUPTION

A second focal point for liberal effort is the corruption that, despite all our safeguards and efforts at reform, still infects our vast political machine with the knowledge and even connivance of the public. This is an insidious cancer sapping the vitality of our political democracy, the cause of much inefficiency and injustice and, worst of all, the source of disillusionment and cynicism in the general public, whose respect for and confidence in its own representatives and public servants is so essential a condition of political health. Where lies the blame for the perpetual "mess," not only in Washington but in every state capital, county, borough, and township, and under both parties alike? The blame cannot be localized. Much of it must be laid at the door of the corrupt politician and civil servant, since nothing could corrupt them if they themselves were incorruptible. But we, the public, are no less to blame, for there would be little or no public corruption were it not for widespread private inducement to corruption, and were we private citizens not so apathetic toward open chicanery and venality in high places and in humble posts throughout the nation. Our corporate easygoing indifference to political corruption is our own contribution to this persisting scandal. We get, in the long run, what we deserve.

This situation is particularly serious because it involves us all in a vicious circle. Widespread corruption breeds disgust and contempt for politics. This disgust discourages able young men and women from entering public life and makes it easy for unscrupulous politicians to capture and hold political power. They complete the circle by perpetuating political corruption. The more firmly this vicious circle establishes itself and acquires the inertia of tradition, the more disillusioned and apathetic the average citizen becomes, until finally his chief concern is to avoid trouble with the powers that be and to advise all those he cares for and respects to "keep out of that dirty game."

We have thus far been saved from destruction by the many able and loyal public officials at every level who despite all temptation have maintained their integrity and have combated the corruption around them as best they could. We are also indebted to many private individuals and organizations, such as the League of Women Voters and the Civil Liberties Union, whose persistent efforts to give the public much-needed information about candidates and issues, to protest the miscarriages of justice, and, in general, to work boldly and unselfishly for public decency and social justice have done much to purify our public life and give us a renewed self-respect as citizens in a free democratic society. All such efforts reflect the spirit of liberalism and go far toward giving it effective political and social implementation.

CONTROVERSIAL ISSUES

The spirit of liberalism can also express itself in clear thinking and outspoken speech on such explosive issues as that of our national sovereignty in a world of sovereign states struggling against gigantic odds to resolve our world-wide conflicts and to lay an enduring foundation for world peace. Here again liberalism must beware of identifying itself dogmatically with one side of this raging dispute and of declaring that all who sincerely defend the other side are therefore necessarily illiberal. Here, as elsewhere, our chief concern is the liberal attitude and the liberal's abiding respect for the dignity and value of all human beings of every race, nationality, and creed. What is so profoundly illiberal in the current discussion of our proper role in the international scene is the frequent expression of contempt for other peoples, the self-righteous claim to our essential superiority to other nations, and, above all, the apparent determination of some of us to put and keep America first in power and prosperity, at whatever cost to other nations and at whatever risk of further war. It would, indeed, be suicidal for us to disarm before we were assured that such an act would not leave us utterly defenseless against foreign aggression. We must safeguard our shores with our own military might until, if ever, the nations of the world are so organized that individual nations need no longer depend entirely upon their own resources and the help of their allies. Such safeguards are certainly not illiberal. Nor need we minimize the great difficulty our statesmen are bound to have in deciding from day to day just how to act in order to assure our short-range security and simultaneously to contribute what we as a nation can and should contribute toward the long-range security that only some sort of international co-operation not yet clearly envisaged can possibly provide. These are indeed controversial issues on which liberals are bound to disagree. Liberals can, however, unite in their efforts to promote a national *attitude* that is essentially liberal. They can express a lively concern for world peace rooted in justice and maintained by the joint efforts of all nations. They can give voice to a profound respect for the rights of other nations and for the intrinsic value of all their citizens as human beings. Above all, they can loudly protest every self-centered defense of our national sovereignty as sacrosanct.

THE LIBERAL AND THE ILLIBERAL

The spirit of liberalism must manifest itself in the attitude we adopt toward those who are sincerely hostile to liberalism in general and to our political democracy in particular.

Some people argue that if it is to be genuine, freedom must include the right to undermine and destroy the very framework of human

151

liberty. They insist that the tolerance liberalism espouses must include the tolerance of intolerance and that those who truly believe in progress by evolution must permit those who believe in revolution to plan for and execute a revolution that, if successful, would put an end to all peaceful and law-abiding evolutionary progress. How should we assess this argument?

If we are truly liberal, we must demand for each of us as much personal freedom as is consistent with the freedom of all. This certainly includes the freedom to be critical. Honest scrutiny of all the political devices set up to safeguard our freedoms must be encouraged and so must all honest re-examination and reappraisal of the nature and value of freedom itself. If we really believe in intellectual inquiry and moral integrity we dare not set any limits whatever on what a man may examine and critize and believe. Any attempt at censorship of thought and speech would deny the very freedoms we most cherish and would hamper the search for that greater truth, that greater efficiency, and that evolutionary advance to which liberalism is committed. We would indeed destroy the liberalism we profess and we would reveal a dangerous weakness in our liberal society if we declined to listen to the sharpest criticisms any critic can formulate of our cherished freedoms, of our Constitution and form of government, and of our political theories and practices. We would in effect be declaring the bankruptcy of our liberalism if we muzzled such critics. To enforce silence instead of inviting open debate is in a liberal society a sign of weakness, not strength.

However, a liberal society can hope to preserve its freedoms only if it maintains and defends the necessary legal framework for orderly change. It need not tolerate the exercise of freedom for the abolition of freedom, the use of democratic privilege to end democracy and all its privileges. We should point out to our revolutionary critics that they are seeking by persuasion or force to discredit the very freedoms they are presently enjoying and using and that they are invoking a right in order to repudiate the right invoked. We should clearly distinguish between legitimate criticism, constructive or destructive, from within the framework of our democratic government and the kind of agitation and activity that is democratically intolerable because it is designed to *undermine and destroy* the framework itself and the government it supports.

So long as the vast majority of us subscribe to the basic tenets of our political democracy we have every right to protect ourselves against any attempt of a minority group to overthrow the government by treason and force. If, having listened to this minority (for it too is entitled to be heard), we are still of the same mind, if we still believe in the rule of law, the sanctity of human life, and man's inalienable rights—if this is still our corporate conviction, we should be culpably stupid not to do everything in our power that is consistent with our own basic principles to defend ourselves against every threat to our political health and strength.

We shall not be defending ourselves consistently with our own principles if we resort to legally irresponsible witch hunts, to "trial by slander," to suppression of academic freedom, or to any acts that violate our basic rights as citizens of the United States. Any governmental act of this nature is unconstitutional, undemocratic, illiberal and un-American. No attempt to uncover un-Americanism by un-American Fascist methods can strengthen the liberal position or safeguard the American way of life. All acts that tend to engender in us the suspicions and fears with which the citizens of totalitarian countries are so tragically familiar are a travesty of all that we hold most precious. Particularly in times of international tension such as the present, it is of the utmost importance that all to whom power has been delegated act with exemplary democratic legality and restraint. It is no less imperative that individual citizens and our own free press exercise their right to publicize instances of undemocratic behavior and to demand justice and fair play. In short, we dare not be sentimentally tolerant of intolerance; we must resist it with all our power when it makes its appearance—whether in ecclesiastical or in secular dress, whether in the name of communism, big business, labor, or self-styled 100 per cent Americanism. But we must be sure to resist it in a truly liberal and democratic manner, that is, openly, legally, within the framework of the Constitution, and not by resorting to any of the devices that are employed by those against whom we would defend ourselves. We dare not use Fascist or totalitarian means to combat fascism or totalitarianism; to do so would be to throw away the chance of victory before the fight had begun.

If we accept the presupposition of our political democracy, that what we, the people, want should ultimately prevail, we must also admit

153

the possibility that we may at some future date freely choose to abdicate—to give up our basic political rights and turn over the power we now reserve to ourselves to an autocratic individual or group. There is no legitimate democratic way of preventing a democratic society from taking this fatal step if it is determined to do so. So long as the will of the people is to prevail this will cannot be coerced, even if it threatens to issue in a final suicidal act. The only safeguard against this possibility is the continual and effective revitalization of the true democratic spirit.

When the Germans elected Hitler they acted as they did partly because their experience of democracy had been too brief. They had not had time to learn from experience the responsibilities and privileges of democracy. They had not become sufficiently impregnated with the spirit of liberalism. They were also bedeviled by internal dissension, grave economic want, and acute insecurity and fear. No wonder that under these circumstances they made the choice they did, preferring the promise of national strength and economic security to the preservation of freedoms they were unable to understand or exercise. But we need not follow their example, for we in this country are more fortunate. We have a well-established democratic tradition. We have seen our democracy work, not perfectly, but, all things considered, amazingly well. We have every reason to know what freedom is, how precious it is, and what it entails politically and legally. We shall never repudiate our democratic heritage and commit political suicide as long as an enlightened liberal spirit is alive in us.

Such are some of the contemporary political challenges to liberalism in our nation and in our day. Barring the utter disaster of an atomic war, no other nation or group of nations can rob us of our political freedoms and our civil liberties; if we ever lose them, we shall lose them by default, by our own indifference. It is therefore imperative that we do everything in our power, individually and collectively, to promote an ever livelier sense of individual responsibility and social consciousness. Our freedoms *can* be preserved by a crusading liberal spirit, by the dynamism of an awakened and pioneering liberal community.

Ours is indeed a glorious democratic experiment, a magnificent achievement unique in the history of mankind. It should evoke in us not complacency but confidence, not self-righteousness but hope, not fear but assurance that we are on the right track, and that, if only we bestir ourselves to the limit, we can preserve our precious heritage in the face of any foreign foes and internal threats.

Chapter 10

The Spirit of Liberalism:
Family, School, and Church

W<small>E HAVE SEEN</small> that liberalism expresses itself in the liberal attitude but that it is more than merely an attitude. We have argued that it can and should be rooted in the affirmative belief in certain basic human traits—in man's ability to evaluate, to decide and act with moral responsibility, and to search for whatever dimension of infinity there may be that can complement his incurable finitude. This creed is important because it gives meaning to the claim that man has intrinsic dignity and value.

But liberalism is also more than an intellectual creed. It is a spirit, a dynamic force capable of molding men's minds, kindling their hearts, strengthening their wills, and girding their individual and corporate activities. In the words of a great liberal, Leonard Trelawney Hobhouse, "The heart of Liberalism . . . is not a matter of mechanical contrivance, but of the liberation of living spiritual energy." [1] This "living spiritual energy" expresses itself in the liberal attitude and articulates itself in a liberal creed. It is this spirit of liberalism which demands political defense. But the attitude, the creed, and the political bulwark of liberalism cannot, in and of themselves, generate or nourish the living spirit of liberalism. If it is to operate as a vital force, this spirit must be instilled in childhood generation after generation and, through the cycle of each adult life, be tested and strengthened in the atmosphere of the loving home. If it is to escape sentimentality, it must be informed and disciplined by an educational process that is itself liberal and liberating. If it is to escape dogmatic rigidity and idolatry, it must be quickened and

[1] Leonard T. Hobhouse, *Liberalism* (Henry Holt and Company, Inc., New York), p. 137.

oriented by a lifelong dedication to whatever in the universe transcends all actual human achievements and all human evaluations. In short, the liberalism we have inherited from our ancestors, the liberalism we profess, and the only liberalism worth fighting for is a living spirit implanted in infancy, warmed by family affection, informed by education and, so far as possible, oriented in some worthy ultimate dedication.

The family, the school, and the church are, of course, the institutions in our society specifically responsible for this complex task. However, they can perform their proper liberal function only in so far as they themselves are impregnated with the dynamic spirit of liberalism. Their strength is a fair index of the vitality of our corporate liberalism. Their weaknesses are correspondingly ominous, for if the salt hath lost its savor, wherewith shall it be salted? Weak or strong, the family, the school, and the church must be relied on to nourish, discipline, and orient the spirit of liberalism.

LIBERALISM IN THE HOME

The real estate business, aided and abetted by the manufacturers of various household appliances and furnishings, has persuaded the American public to use the word "home" to signify what was once known as a "house." "Buy your home from . . . ," "Furnish your home with . . . ," "Warm your home with . . ."—these are the familiar slogans that have robbed the word "home" of much of its original meaning by reducing it to its mere physical components. Family life does, of course, have its physical aspects and requirements. A warmed and furnished house or apartment provides a family unit with requisite living quarters. It can also contribute greatly to the comforts and joys of a real home, conceived of as a haven of affectionate intimacy and understanding from which to sally forth into the relatively impersonal and competitive world (in the words of T. S. Eliot, "Home is where we start from") and to which to return for comfort, refreshment, and love. But this kind of home can be neither bought nor sold. It is only superficially dependent upon household furnishings, though its inner life can be warped and stained by ugliness and squalor. The warmth that brings joy and comfort to its members cannot be produced by the costliest of heaters or the most efficient of fuels. The home is a

157

co-operative and creative achievement of husband and wife and, as they grow up, their children.

Like society itself, the family can be predominantly anarchistic, absolutistic, or co-operative and liberal. It is anarchistic when each member is neglectful of or hostile to the other members of the family and goes his own way, resentful of all demands upon him and quick to escape from uncongenial family bonds. This is the family headed for separation or divorce. When no actual break occurs, it is the household of the unlit hearth and the lonely heart. No loneliness can equal that of a loveless family—of isolation where the heart cries out for intimacy, of cold indifference where above all man needs and expects love. Nowhere is the fruit of a callous rugged individualism so bitter.

The absolutistic family is the opposite extreme. It is the family whose distinguishing characteristic is authority and dominance. In our society this is a somewhat old-fashioned but by no means extinct family pattern. It is as often matriarchal as patriarchal, since in our culture the mother can be as tyrannical as the father. The dominant parent commands and the other obeys; the parents control the children by threats of punishment and elicit obedience through fear. The same pattern is copied by the older children in their relation to their younger brothers and sisters. This reliance on authority can produce considerable family solidarity and even loyalty, particularly in the face of external criticism. It is often conducive to economy and thrift. It is also an appropriate training ground for life in a regimented society where governmental or ecclesiastical authority takes the place of the authoritative parent. The domineering paternalistic or maternalistic family is the familial analogue of the paternalistic state and church, and these institutions tend to regard it as the natural and proper type of family.

From the point of view of liberalism its defect is its failure to recognize the value of maturity and to promote such maturity. It maintains itself by catering, on the one hand, to man's deep-seated infantilism—his natural disinclination to grow up and assume the moral responsibilities of the mature adult—and, on the other hand, to man's complementary craving for unchallenged power. In his childhood phase man craves protection and the security of absolute authority. But even as a child he also wants to have his own way and hates to be criticized and frustrated. Authoritarian parents have achieved no more maturity than their young children. They have merely lived long enough to escape the domination of their parents and have acquired children whom they can subjugate in turn. Just as in a regimented society the same individual bullies his social inferiors and toadies to his superiors, so in the autocratic family the bullied child becomes the bullying parent of the next generation.

The pattern of liberal growth from childhood to adolescence to real maturity is very different. That a small child, ignorant and defenseless, should crave security and authority is natural. We call this attitude of trustful dependence "childlike," and we do everything in our power to respond to it with an appropriate sheltering love and care. It is only when it persists longer than it should, into the life of the adult, that we refer to it in a derogatory way as "childish."

It is no less inevitable that the growing child should presently exhibit the familiar traits of rebellious adolescence. This should be the period of gradual emancipation from blind obedience to parental authority and of more and more open resistance to parental and social restraints. The adolescent's natural reaction is negative. At this stage he resents orders and even suggestions; he doubts everything he hears; he breaks as many rules and regulations as he dares, experimentally and defiantly; he tries prematurely to act as though he were mature; he affects a sophistication he does not in fact possess. This is a painful period for all concerned—for the adolescent boy and girl no less than for their parents, teachers, and older friends. But it is a normal and healthy stage that cannot be bypassed; it must somehow be lived through if youth is ever to graduate into maturity. It becomes tragic only if it perpetuates itself in the chronic adolescence of the adult skeptic or cynic who is old enough to be mature but who still indulges in the irresponsible, rebellious moods of puberty.

What, then, is the hallmark of maturity? It is at once a fusion and a transformation of childlike faith and adolescent doubt. It expresses itself in the ability to realize that life requires of us decision and action at every moment, that decision can never be made on the basis of complete information and with absolute certainty about the outcome, but that reflective and informed conduct is superior to blind, impulsive behavior. The mark and measure of maturity is reflective commitment—the ability and determination to reflect as much as possible on all controversial issues and then in the light of this reflection to decide boldly and act with steadfastness and courage. In the terms of our liberal creed, man is mature when he evaluates wisely and acts responsibly as a finite being capable of reverence.

According to the criterion of liberalism, the ideal family is the family in which husband and wife are mature in their dealings with one another and with the outer world and in which they make every effort to help their children pass from childhood through adolescence to maturity in a normal and healthy way. The liberalism of mature parents will express itself in the following four complementary ways.

HUSBAND AND WIFE

A mature relationship between husband and wife is one of mutual respect, unsentimental love, and genuine co-operation. It must be rooted in sincere respect for the inevitable differences of temperament, taste, and opinion, even on matters of great importance to both parties. Since in our society marriages are not, for the most part, arranged by the older generation, a young person can and often does pick a wife or husband with a very different temperament from his or her own. This may be nature's way of strengthening the human stock, but it calls for difficult adjustments. What is required is not only the frank recognition by both parties of differences between them in outlook, habit, taste, and conviction but, in addition, a deep-seated desire on the part of each that his or her partner in marriage will be himself or herself so far as possible and not consciously or unconsciously a shadow or imitation of the other.

Such mutual respect is a prerequisite to mature conjugal love. Sentimental or romantic love is not only notoriously blind but is essentially selfish and possessive, and this selfish possessiveness, even if it is unconscious, may eventually lead to various forms of physical and mental cruelty. Mature love will express itself in growing mutual understanding and the desire of each partner to promote in every way possible the happiness and welfare of the other. Such love is in essence undemanding and unpossessive; its abhors any form of coercion or constraint; rather, its impulse is to yield whenever there is a clash of interests and desires. This impulse to yield, if it is reciprocated, may lead to occasional disputes, but they will be happy, not bitter, disputes since each will be championing the other's welfare, not his own.

Love such as this, rooted in respect, is the ideal basis for mature co-operation, husband and wife each recognizing the special aptitudes and inclinations of the other. In such a setting, similar or dissimilar tastes and needs in food, sex, play, and work can be explored and satisfied or compromised with tenderness and joy. Major and minor problems can be discussed without restraint, and decisions can be made jointly. Differences of opinion can become a source of mutual interest and benefit rather than of irritation, frustration, and anger.

Simply because of its unique intimacy, married life is thus the ideal training ground of liberalism. Here if anywhere mutual respect is crucially important; here more than in any other human situation love can reach its fullest fruition. Here comfort for disappointment, failure, and tragic loss can be found; here joys and successes can be shared. The mature marriage is the perfect human setting for the progressive liberation of the human spirit.

PARENTS AND CHILDREN

The family is also the most powerful formative influence upon the growing child. It can do more than any other institution in our society to start children on the road to mature liberalism. We are told by psychologists that our enduring character traits are established in us by the time we are six years old or even earlier. If there is any truth in this generalization, the family is the chief conveyer of our basic cultural values to impressionable children.

The difficult—and fascinating—parental problem in the training of very young children is how to get them to acquire those personal habits and attitudes of acceptance and rejection which are the necessary foundation for reflective evaluation in later life; how to encourage all those tentative ventures which will eventually issue in responsible decision and action; how to discipline the child in such a way as to develop in him the capacity for self-discipline and self-control; how to evoke and cultivate the child's innate capacity for love and friendliness so that this precious human trait may in time develop into mature love and willing cooperation.

This is indeed a baffling problem as it presents itself day after day, always concretely and always in new and unexpected ways. Some parents are more harassed than fascinated by it, more bothered than intrigued. As a result, they lose much of the joy of parenthood and deal with their recurrent perplexities in a heavy, unimaginative, and moralistic way. Others are more fortunate; they are sufficiently at peace with one another and the world to enjoy their children and to preside over their early lives in a gay, experimental spirit, with a sense of humor tempered by solicitude.

As the child grows older, other inherited traits ripen and invite encouragement and guidance. With speech comes a quickening of curiosity and that flood of questions that torment the tired parent but will be welcomed by the teacher in him with endless patience, in the knowledge that if this curiosity is discouraged now the child's intellectual development will be permanently retarded and his later capacity for independent thinking weakened or destroyed. Even at this early stage, the foundations of a critical or a submissive attitude can be laid. Discouragement and censure now may give the child a lasting authoritarian cast of mind, whereas encouragement and help may sow the seeds of a later mature liberalism. Similarly, the child's aesthetic capacities invite recognition and approval as they begin to unfold. His potential creativity first shows itself in a preoccupation with color, form, shape, song, and dance. Here is the chance to introduce him to the excitement of original creation and self-expression and, as he grows older, to the profound satisfactions of aesthetic response to the expressive creativity of others.

The growing child explores, at first timidly and crudely and then with greater self-reliance, an ever enlarging web of social relationships—with his parents, brothers and sisters, other children and adults, with animals and their distinctive traits and needs, and with the things he comes to know as possessions, his own and others'. These are his first encounters with persons as persons, whose interests now conform, now conflict, with his own. Now begins the lifetime struggle to get along with people cooperatively—to learn when to yield and when to stand fast, how to receive and how to give, how to forgive and how to be forgiven. Now the child first learns the price of love and hate, of exploitation and sharing, of respect and contempt. Now is the parent's golden opportunity to help him understand the meaning and the value of humility, tolerance, gratitude, and praise.

As discussed earlier, the hardest period for both child and parent is probably the period of adolescence and postadolescence, when the boy or girl is striving to throw off the shackles of childhood and take on the responsibilities of maturity. The postadolescents' crucial need is for radical readjustment within the family circle. After years of parental authority and supervision, parents must learn to accept their boys and girls for what they are now, youthful adults eager to enjoy the privileges of adulthood without as yet a full realization of the corresponding responsibilities. It is not easy for the parent to abandon voluntarily the habits of parental control, nor is it easy to know how fast to relinquish this control. It is difficult to stand by and let youth make its own mistakes and learn the hard way what has not been learned in the safety of the home. It is not easy to treat one's boy or girl as an equal, too old now to welcome a love that is predominantly parental but still too awkward and too lacking in self-assurance to enter fully into a mature friendship between equals. This is the acid test of parenthood, the test of the parents' own liberal maturity. Some parents lapse at this point into an authoritarianism that infuriates or baffles, breaks or alienates the adolescent at the very threshold of maturity. Other parents retire in defeat behind a mask of indifference. Only the parent whose own capacity for growth has not atrophied and whose liberalism is deeply rooted and informed can remain the friend of his offspring as they painfully graduate from adolescence to maturity. With the wise help of an understanding parent this transition can be greatly accelerated and eased; without it, youth must fight its battle alone and against heavy odds.

THE FAMILY AND THE COMMUNITY

Families are subject to both centripetal and centrifugal social forces. They tend to become either too self-centered or too dispersed. The happier the family life, the greater the temptation to enjoy the family as a comforting retreat rather than as a home base for socially useful activities in the community. Conversely, enthusiastic participation in social and civic activities invites a corresponding neglect of family life and often leads to a failure to share richly in its joys and sorrows.

Centuries ago, Plato and Aristotle gave classic expression to two contrasting analyses of the problem of family loyalty and its relation to civic loyalty. Plato was convinced that family loyalty is so strong that it will always jeopardize a wider loyalty to the state and all its members. In delineating the ideal state he therefore carefully deprived the "guardians," or rulers, of all family ties. He insisted that they must be separated from their parents in infancy and forbidden to have families of their own. It was his hope that in the case of the state's guardians the natural centripetal pull of family loyalty might thus be psychologically transformed into an equally strong centrifugal loyalty to the city-state.

Aristotle, in contrast, conceived of the family as the natural and proper training ground in childhood and youth for later mature civic responsibilities. The parents, he felt, should be best qualified to help young children acquire those basic moral virtues which are so necessary for responsible activity in a community. In short, he believed the family could best prepare children for later life in the community and that children could most effectively learn the meaning of responsibility and loyalty in the intimacy of the home.

Time seems to have supported Aristotle rather than Plato on this issue. A narrower loyalty is not necessarily hostile to a wider loyalty; on the contrary, it can be made the prelude of a wider loyalty. Children who learn the give-and-take of co-operative life in the family are thereby better equipped to participate in the give-and-take of co-operation with others in the encircling community. Moreover, parents who have a lively sense of wider social responsibilities are often in a better position to appreciate mature co-operation and are therefore better able to generate the authentic spirit of social obligation within the family circle.

According to the criteria of liberalism, the ideal parent will not put conjugal love or parental affection above all else. Husband or wife will regard each other as partners with whose help each can best discharge his larger responsibilities to the community, and both parents will try to introduce their maturing children to these wider opportunities and responsibilities.

ULTIMATE BELIEF

Families differ most in their corporate expression of man's capacity for awe and reverence. Nowhere is the problem of man's ultimate beliefs more poignant, for here another's well-being is also crucially concerned. The more casual our relations with our fellow-men, the easier it is to adopt an attitude of good-natured tolerance, of believe-what-you-like; the more deeply we love another person, the more impossible it is not to be profoundly distressed when his ultimate beliefs differ sharply from our own. How, then, can a devoted husband and wife who differ sharply in their ultimate beliefs handle this disagreement? What guidance can liberalism offer the many married couples in this country who find themselves in this state of creedal tension?

Several unsatisfactory solutions of this problem are frequently resorted to. A couple may agree that the stronger faith of the husband or the wife should be made the official faith of the family as a unit and that the children should be brought up in this faith. Here family harmony is bought at too high a price. It threatens the spiritual integrity of the parent whose faith is judged to be weaker. It is also based on the false assumption that intensity of belief, whatever its nature, is of prime importance, whereas, in fact, hesitation and doubt may reflect a much more profound sense of finitude and awe. The parent whose faith is less assertive may well have spiritual intuitions that are the deeper and more truly religious.

Some parents try to side-step the problem of their children's instruction in religious matters until they have grown up and are ready to make their own decision. This policy is sometimes favored by parents whose ultimate beliefs are in substantial agreement on the ground that it is unfair to children to indoctrinate them in any ultimate faith while they are too young to encounter rival faiths and objectively decide between them. Those who adopt this policy ignore the fact that genuine neutrality on these matters is impossible and the further fact that early education in this area is as important as it is in any other area of human experience.

What actually happens when parents taboo all discussion of ultimate belief within the family circle is that the resultant vacuum is filled by whatever cultural influences are dominant in the children's social environment. In our predominantly secular society these influences are so overwhelmingly secular and sensate that the children will probably grow up as religious barbarians with a strong secular orientation. This may be precisely the attitude secular-minded parents wish their children to develop, but it is certainly not an attitude of neutrality. In any case, parents who adopt this policy are "solving" this aspect of their children's religious education by default. Unable to agree on what they believe their children should have in the way of religious or nonreligious instruction, they leave it entirely to the prevailing ethos of their community to mold the slowly evolving ultimate beliefs of their own children.

In so doing, they also ignore the fact that, from early childhood on, children need all the help and guidance they can get in the supremely diffi-cult art of ultimate commitment and that they will later find it much more difficult to make mature and responsible decisions in this area if in their youth they have not acquired the habits and attitudes requisite for such mature commitment. Man's normal spiritual growth does not differ in this respect from his normal intellectual, moral, aesthetic, or social growth. No intelligent parents suppose that a child whose educa-tion in any of these areas has been entirely ignored can suddenly at the age of twenty exhibit a mature understanding of intellectual issues, moral problems, art, or social obligation. Nor do they assume that familial training in these areas will permanently warp the mind of the child or the adolescent and preclude his later mature reappraisal of all that he has been taught. Intelligent parents, in co-operation with the school, teach their children all they can about moral and social obligation, art and human knowledge, with a justified assurance that this training can develop the knowledge and the values they will need as adults when they assess their own education and arrive at their own mature positions.

A similar policy is no less valid in the area of ultimate belief. Children whose parents fail to teach by precept and example the significance of ultimate wonder and awe, the sense of finitude and the meaning of humility, the importance and the difficulty of responsible ultimate belief —these children have been deprived of the help their families should have given them to learn about a precious part of their cultural heritage. They must face later life without the childhood training to which they are entitled.

A third solution is somewhat less inadequate. After due reflection, some parents may decide that they are not equipped to give their chil-dren wise instruction and guidance in the area of religious faith. They therefore turn elsewhere for help—to whatever church or school, what-ever wise friends and counselors they can find to whom they can entrust this aspect of their children's education. Such a solution is, of course, second-best, but it may well be the only one available to some parents. At least it has the merit of parental honesty and humility, and it may prove beneficial to the children if the institutions or individuals entrusted with this difficult task are qualified to undertake it.

None of these solutions really arrives at the heart of the problem. The crucial issue, as seen in liberal perspective, is still this: How can liberally minded parents exhibit toward one another and toward their children a really liberal attitude when they honestly disagree with one another on questions of ultimate belief? The earlier discussion of man's essential nature as a responsible moral agent and as a finite being capable of partial, but only partial, insight into the ultimate mysteries of reality becomes relevant here.

What the truly liberal husband and wife should do, I believe, is to start with mutual respect for one another as responsible moral agents. This respect will preclude intolerance; moreover, it will strengthen in each the desire that both may achieve maximum moral and spiritual integrity. If this mutual respect is then accompanied by the humility liberalism dictates, neither will dogmatically assume that his beliefs embrace the whole truth or, indeed, that they are necessarily superior to those of the other. Each will honestly stand by whatever faith is in him; but each will no less steadfastly wish the other to do the same. Only on this basis can a man and wife discuss their creedal differences with mutual profit, each learning from the other, each widening his perspective and enriching the beliefs that are most vital to him. A husband and wife can thus transform an initial liability into a positive asset. In thus transcending their differences, they can achieve a sense of humility and genuine tolerance deeper and spiritually more significant than either could perhaps have achieved alone or with a married partner of similar persuasion.

Such parents can also direct the religious education of their children along similar lines. Of course, young children are not ready for mature controversy, but they are quick to catch the overtones of tension or harmony, of mutual disrespect or respect, of intolerance or tolerance in their parents' attitude to one another and to others. They can understand and respect parental confessions of ignorance or doubt. They can learn at an early age that their native curiosity is precious, that their religious questions are proper and important, and that the answers they receive are not infallible truths but merely the best answers their parents are able to give them. This does not solve the problem of what they should be taught by parents of sharply divergent opinions, but it does indicate the spirit and attitude in which all these issues would be dealt with according to the liberal principle. If both parents have enough humility, neither will insist on a dogmatic approach but both will approve of whatever affirmative instruction can somehow be made available to their children, even if one or the other parent hopes that, as the children grow up, they will renounce or radically modify what they have learned in their youth. For example, a sincerely agnostic parent of liberal outlook might well want his children to learn the rudiments of the Christian faith so that in maturity they will have the real option of accepting this faith or of choosing an enlightened agnosticism. In the same spirit a parent of sincere religious belief might well welcome the exposure of his children to the honest doubts with which all mature faith must somehow come to grips.

A different sort of problem arises for parents who heartily agree in their ultimate beliefs. Such parents tend to slip into an attitude of dogmatic assurance about the rightness of their own convictions and a self-righteous condescension toward all whose beliefs differ from their own. Such an attitude will permeate their entire family ethos and infect the children, sometimes with heightened virulence. Nothing could be more alien to the spirit of liberalism; nothing could do more to establish in the children a basically illiberal attitude they may never be able to outgrow. Viewed in this liberal perspective, the common conception of "the problem of religion in the home" can thus be seen to be very superficial. The real problem, as liberalism sees it, is not the orthodox question of whether or not the parents are "religious" in some traditional sense and whether or not they are seeing to it that their children receive correct religious instruction in the home or in a neighboring church. It is the profound and more truly religious question concerning the prevailing ethos of the home as this ethos is created and maintained by parents. It is the question of whether or not the parents really feel, and therefore exhibit as well as profess, a real sense of finitude and awe, a genuine capacity for mature belief, an authentic tolerance, and an open-mindedness that signalize the most enlightened religious attitude. In such an atmosphere, the spirit of true religion will be alive at its humble, critical, and hopeful best. What finer family atmosphere can we envisage for young children and adolescents who must presently face a world torn by dogmatic strife and poisoned by secular and religious self-righteousness? What better training can we conceive of in genuine wonder, awe, and reverence?

We can summarize what we have tried to say regarding the multiple challenges to and opportunities for liberalism in the family by conceiving of each member of a family as standing at the center of a series of concentric circles. The innermost circle is the family itself; the successive outer circles are the local community, the nation, humanity as a whole, and, finally, the cosmic ground of all meaning and value. Each of us is always tempted to become preoccupied with himself at the expense of family, with family in disregard of community and nation, with nation in indifference to other nations and human welfare in general, and finally with mankind apart from whatever in the universe is worthy of our highest reverence and dedication. Each of us is also liable to the opposite danger of failing to translate an ultimate spiritual dedication into the concrete terms of active concern for humanity, of failing to express loyalty to mankind in our concrete relations with our nation and our local community, or of allowing our activities in the community to encroach upon the intimacy of family life. These are complementary dangers against which we should also be on our guard.

The creation of a truly liberal family is a co-operative and creative venture. No two families will enter upon it in the same way or with identical results. Here, if anywhere, there is full scope for temperamental difference and creative originality, for patience, good will, wisdom, humor, and tact. As it actually functions in our society today, the family is often the scene of intolerance, cruelty, misery, and heartbreak. At its worst, it induces man to exhibit all the callous selfishness of which he is capable. But it can also be the source of untold happiness, comfort, inspiration, and strength.

The family is what the parents make it. They, in turn, are what they are and behave as they do partly because of their own family training plus whatever educative influences have been brought to bear upon them by other institutions in their society. The family *as an institution* is not capable of self-improvement or self-reform. It can be improved and strengthened primarily through the impact of the school and the church upon present and future parents. Each family will be as liberal or illiberal as are the parents, and they in turn will tend to be as liberal or illiberal as the molding institutions of their society have made them.

LIBERALISM IN EDUCATION

Every corporate venture must be organized, yet nothing kills the creative spirit more quickly than formal organization. This applies to the school as the institutional vehicle of formal instruction. Education cannot be left to spontaneous individual initiative; it must be institutionalized. Yet this very act tends immediately to transform a vital human activity into a regimented routine. Education becomes a business; the school becomes a factory into which malleable young people are poured for wholesale processing and from which they presently emerge duly "certified," as "educated," according to predominantly quantitative standards. Like their students, administrators and teachers tend to be enslaved by this routine. Even when they recognize its evils they usually find themselves unable to remedy them; often they feel too hopeless even to protest.

The first word about liberalism in education must therefore be a strong and persistent protest against the perversions such wholesale institutional procedures inevitably tend to generate. Four common types of perversion in our school system deserve special notice.

SPIRITUAL ENTROPY

The first and most general protest of liberalism must be against all manifestations in education of the spiritual equivalent of the law of entropy, that is, of the process of progressive spiritual stagnation. Liberalism must constantly reiterate that education is not mere formal routine. It must insist with righteous passion that it should be a living, creative process and that the school can fulfil its proper function only when it somehow initiates and nourishes this process.

"Progressive education" has been a protest against such soul-destroying and mind-stultifying academic "disciplines" and a gallant effort to revitalize education in the schools. It tried to accomplish this by encouraging the spontaneous creative impulses of the child and by eliciting his free participation in the educational process. It also sought to recapture the vision of the "whole man," the total human being, and so reconstruct the educational process that the child's imagination and will as well as his reason and memory might be brought into play. It took cognizance of John Dewey's emphasis on man's social needs and dependencies and strove to make education a social experience designed to prepare youth for active citizenship and responsible social behavior. In all these and in many other ways, "progressive" education exemplified the liberal spirit.

It did the cause of education a great service in its justified protests against academic formalism and rigidity and in its imaginative efforts to overcome the evils of academic traditionalism.

Like many another reform movement, however, "progressive" education presently became enslaved by its own virtues and began to promote a new set of academic vices in its efforts to overcome the vices of the older tradition. In the hands of its most enthusiastic exponents it largely forgot or ignored various aspects of the educational process that traditional education had too exclusively emphasized but that are, in fact, essential ingredients in any well-rounded education. The extremists were inclined to stress pupil participation at the expense of teacher guidance; they failed to realize that a "child-centered" school is as far off balance as a "teacher-centered" school. They stressed motivation at the expense of discipline, imaginative creativity rather than factual knowledge, enthusiasm instead of basic skills. They were disposed to allow the student his choice in areas where his ignorance and lack of experience made it impossible for him to make wise decisions. They gave children freedom when what they most needed was mature guidance. In their effort to free the child from harmful academic regimentation they tended to forget man's inescapable need for both mental and moral discipline. Whereas the students of earlier teachers had all too often been well-trained robots, the students of extreme progressivists presently gave signs of growing into undisciplined and uncivilized barbarians.

One of the most reassuring characteristics of the progressive-education movement has been its recent disposition to re-examine itself, reform itself, and curb its own excesses. It has itself begun to move back toward a more balanced center. In so doing it has exemplified a basic principle of liberalism in education, namely, the principle of balance and proportion.

THE MIDDLE ROAD

Mature liberalism is ever wary of extremes, of all forms of violent radicalism. The second protest of liberalism in the area of education must be against all one-sided emphases, all partial diagnoses of human need, all forms of lopsided development. Its embracing educational goal is neither spontaneity alone nor discipline in and for itself, but disciplined spontaneity, that is, significant originality—not a mind crammed with isolated facts nor a factually unfurnished mind, but a mind respectful of fact and equipped to find and use the facts man needs to live and to live well; not human rights without regard to man's corresponding duties, or duties imposed from above without concern for the rights of the individual, but rights and duties in healthy mutual dependence. The liberal in education is often wrongly identified with the revolutionary radical because he protests against all traditional abuses and always tries to reform the status quo. But he is just as concerned to preserve the achievements of the past and to cherish the wisdom of the ages. In short, he always seeks to mediate between the one-sided radical and the no less one-sided conservative by duly compensating for the excesses of both. He tries to see life steadily and whole, without utopianism and without reactionary fear. Hence his perennial desire in the field of education to progress along the little-traveled middle road of creative and inclusive synthesis.

LIBERAL EDUCATION AND VOCATIONAL TRAINING

This mediating role of liberalism should express itself in a third protest—against the stupid dichotomy at present so deeply entrenched in American education of "liberal" versus "vocational" training. There is, of course, a historical explanation for this artificial separation of the "theoretical" and "practical" emphases in education, an explanation provided by the development of our American society and, before that, by the centuries of European development from ancient Greece through the Renaissance to modern times. But we are less concerned with its historical genesis than we are with its continuing evil effects in the contemporary world. The overtones that have inevitably attached themselves to this fateful dichotomy are profoundly at variance with the spirit of liberalism. For example, there is the implication that liberal education is essentially an impractical, aristocratic, snobbish luxury, as useless and as ostentatious as the long fingernails affected by the idle rich in some cultures as a symbol of their superiority to all manual labor, and the complementary implication that, because it is designed for practical utility, vocational training can without apology be as narrow and inhumane, as purely monetary in motivation and as indifferent to social responsibility, as a narrowly practical mind can make it. Small wonder that today our liberal-arts colleges are filled with intellectually incurious young people intent primarily on social prestige and that our state universities and vocational schools are crowded with young men and women grimly resolved to improve their social status through the acquisition of financially rewarding skills.

Here again the voice of liberalism must be raised in protest against the false values behind the ivy-covered walls and within the confines of the vocational classroom and shop. Once again, liberalism pleads for man as a total human being with mind *and* body, headed for work *and* leisure, in need of cultural achievement *and* practical employment; it pleads for the whole of society, whose health depends upon a vast array of highly specialized activities to be performed by men and women as humane and as socially concerned as a truly liberal education can help them become. Of course, there is a perfectly valid distinction to be drawn between what we have come to call "liberal education" and "vocational training." What is so disastrous is the widespread belief that these are two alternative self-sufficient forms of preparation for life, neither requiring the supplementation of the other. It is this belief which has impelled many so-called "liberal" educators to look with scorn upon practical training and which has inclined the self-styled "practical" man in our society to regard liberal education as at best a harmless luxury for those who can afford it.

What, in a word, is the essence of liberal education? Its purpose is simple and eminently humane: to liberate mankind from the shackles of illiteracy and inarticulateness, ignorance and normative insensitivity, muddy thinking and blinding provincialism. A man is liberally educated to the extent that he has learned to express himself accurately and felicitously in more than one of the many "languages" of human discourse and to the extent that he is able to really understand what others communicate to him. He is liberally educated when he is factually well enough informed to understand himself and his complex environment and sufficiently respectful of fact to hate all wishful thinking; when his moral, aesthetic, and religious evaluations are sensitive, enlightened, and mature; and, finally, when he is able to escape the multiple provincialisms, racial, social, secular, religious, temporal, and spatial, that bedevil him. In short, a truly educated man is a man become fully human—alert, clearheaded, informed, imaginative, disciplined, socially concerned, and humble. He is a man of faith, but whose faith is enlightened and disciplined; a man of taste, but whose taste is sensitive and cultivated; a man of deep social concern, but whose concern is neither sentimentally utopian nor crassly "realistic"; a man of action, but whose actions are wise and courageous, efficient and humane.

This description of a liberally educated person defines an ideal to which no one can perfectly attain. Yet what is there in it that is irrelevant to any living human being? We seem to differ greatly in natural endowment; at least we differ greatly in how much we can benefit from such an education. But all of us surely need all the liberal education we can assimilate and make our own. No human life can fail to be enriched by such a process or impoverished by its absence. It is impossible to acquire too much liberal education.

What is the essence of vocational training? It is a training in specialized skills requisite for the many highly specialized activities in our complex technological society. In a society like ours everyone except the day laborer needs such skills, and even he may acquire and benefit from a few simple dexterities. No doubt many skills can be acquired as well or better by apprenticeship; it is probably a waste of good time and energy for intelligent young men and women to take formal courses in these areas. But in school or out, all of us must acquire practical skills of some sort in order to escape parasitic uselessness and to play our part in our highly specialized society. Moreover some of the most responsible and challenging careers open to us, such as medicine, law, engineering, and research, call for years of intensive, specialized, formal training. Our society must have its vocational schools; future specialists in these fields must be trained in youth for the occupations upon which we all are so dependent.

What is needed today is therefore not an educational either/or but a both/and. Young engineers and doctors stand in need not of less training in engineering or medicine but of more liberal education; liberal-arts students need not less liberal education but a balanced total education that will quicken their sense of social responsibility and instill in them a desire to use their education for the common good. Skilled doctors without compassion and social responsibility are a menace to themselves and their society; so are liberally uneducated engineers, lawyers, businessmen, and priests. But no less a menace to our social order and to themselves are the graduates of liberal-arts colleges who have acquired from their so-called "liberal" education the false value of snobbish superiority and who have largely failed to develop a lively mind, a sense of craftsmanship, and a real social conscience. What this country needs above all else today is the dynamic ideal of a truly rounded education for the whole man, qualifying him for a well-rounded life in a free community —an education that is at once theoretical and practical, scientific and humane, secular and religious.

We should not minimize the difficulty of working out the details of an educational program designed to realize this ideal. Educators must indeed struggle with such ever present stubborn facts as time and cost, individual motivation, and public support. But unless those who address themselves to this practical task keep the liberal ideal steadfastly before their eyes and refuse to be satisfied with anything less than its closest possible actualization, the present highly unsatisfactory policy of patching and tinkering, evading and compromising will continue, to the harm of the individual student as well as his society. What is called for in the liberal-arts curriculum and in the vocational school is drastic reform—a basic rethinking of the proper objectives of education in a free society, a thorough reorganization of the entire educational process from kindergarten through graduate school, not an endless series of petty changes at this or that level without any over-all guiding ideal or plan. In sum, what is needed is a *really* progressive movement in education, more sweeping and inclusive than the "progressivists" ever dreamed of.

EDUCATIONAL EGALITARIANISM

An enlightened liberalism in education must also protest against the widespread egalitarianism that is still powerfully operative in our society and is still the source of great harm in the school. I refer to the very undemocratic policy, usually defended in the name of democracy, of refusing to give abler students special educational opportunities of which the less able, because of their more limited endowments, could not avail themselves. This policy rests on the absurd assumption that it is unfair and undemocratic to help Tom develop his marked native ability because John, less well endowed, cannot benefit from such help, even though the still less able Ed is quite inconsistently judged to merit special help to compensate for his subnormal aptitudes. It is truly amazing that legislators, parents, and teachers find it so difficult to realize that real democracy is not stupidly egalitarian, requiring a mechanically equal distribution of educational services to all students however bright or stupid, but rather that it insists only on equal *opportunity* for all, regardless of race, color, or creed. Nothing could be more undemocratic and illiberal than the denial of educational facilities to a student because of his race, economic status, or social background; but nothing could be more democratic and liberal than the equal *availability* to all students of whatever educational facilities—remedial, normal, or advanced—any student may need and be able to benefit from. It is no more undemocratic to make sugar freely available to nondiabetics, even though diabetics must largely avoid it, than it is to provide diabetics with insulin, which nondiabetics do not need.

Here again the liberal policy is simple and unanswerable: to everyone according to his need, whatever this need may be. No other policy can possibly do justice to the mentally underprivileged, the normal, and the unusually gifted student. No other policy can prepare all young people as effectively as possible for the richest and most useful lives of which they are capable. No other policy can so well facilitate the training of those leaders in every walk of life upon whom the health of a democratic society so essentially depends. Egalitarianism would condemn us all to a dismal mediocrity and deprive us of the expert leadership a free society must have to survive and prosper. Why, then, define democracy in egalitarian terms and commit us to a policy that not only robs gifted individuals of the chance to realize themselves as completely as possible but is also socially suicidal?

These are some of the protests liberalism should make against current educational stupidities and iniquities. Such protests, though apparently negative, are actually affirmative; they are protests against various contemporary failures to achieve positive values in the area of education.

Liberalism must also raise its voice in explicit defense of various aspects of teaching and scholarship which our society today tends to underestimate or ignore.

THE IMPORTANCE OF EDUCATION

We Americans pride ourselves on our concern for education, but this pride is largely unjustified. The cold fact is that as a nation we spend far more on liquor, tobacco, cars, and refrigerators than we do on the education of our children. In general we hold the teaching profession in low esteem. Our teachers are notoriously ill-paid and generally regarded as timid and frustrated individuals who teach because they lack the ability and the ambition to enter a more lucrative profession with greater social prestige. I recall telling a businessman on a train some years ago that I was a teacher. His condescending response was: "Oh, an elevator boy! You take them up and then come down for another load!" I was headed toward a Western town on a speaking engagement, and I can also remember the jubilant report of my host, when he met me at the station, that his school system was in luck: the state legislature had just passed a four-million-dollar appropriation for sewers, with a beneficent million-and-a-half-dollar rider for education. That is a not unfair symbol of our national regard for education. Despite the many millions we spend annually for public and private education in this country, our attitude toward education is still pathetically unrealistic. How intelligently do we love our children when we persist in depriving them of adequate educational facilities and when we spend far more time and energy on gadgets than on their education? How culturally enlightened are we if we hold the entire teaching profession in such low regard? Here liberalism pleads for greater realistic concern for the entire educational process.

RESPECT FOR TRUTH

We also pride ourselves on our love of truth and our loyalty to free speech and untrammeled inquiry and criticism. Yet books are being censored in our schools because the opinions expressed in them are uncongenial to certain would-be reformers. In some states teachers are forbidden even to discuss with their students the work of the United Nations and UNESCO. Eminent scholars are suspect if their honest thinking runs counter to some current national prejudice or policy. The outstanding example of the current fear of truth is the virtual ban on all informed study of communism in schools and colleges. As a result the vast majority of school and college graduates are almost entirely ignorant of, and therefore naturally indifferent to, the ideology of communism—and this at a time when communism is judged to be so grave a threat to our very existence that billions of dollars are being spent in military defense. In effect our young men are being told that they must be prepared to fight an enemy without knowing what it is that makes him so dangerous and obnoxious to us. We are being heavily taxed without adequate information about the true nature of the enemy against whom these taxes are chiefly spent.

This national indifference to the truth is not restricted to the truth about communism and the creative efforts of the United Nations. It extends to all controversial issues. Not long ago I was told by the dean of a leading school of education that he felt himself morally obligated to advise the young men and women who were about to become school principals and school superintendents to forbid all classroom discussion of racial and social discrimination, sex, politics, economics, internationalism, and religion, because otherwise the prejudices rampant in their prospective communities would endanger their jobs. Is this America, the land of the free, the nation that has prided itself on its freedom of speech and devotion to truth and justice? Here liberalism's response is instant and unequivocal in support of honesty, truth, and justice, even to the point of severe personal sacrifice.

SIGNIFICANT SCHOLARSHIP

Liberalism defends no less ardently the cause of significant scholarship. I say "significant" because scholars do tend to lose perspective and lean to pedantry. There is a sense in which all truth, however trivial and inconsequential, must be valued for its own sake and for its possible though unpredictable future use. However, the first-rate scholar is notable for his awareness of values, his sense of balance and perspective, his ability to assess short-range projects in the light of long-range objectives. "It is more important," said Whitehead, in his characteristically epigrammatic way, "that a proposition be interesting than that it be true." [2] Of course, Whitehead would have been the last to set "truth" and "interest" in opposition, as this sentence seems to imply. What he was pleading for was significant truth of serious human import.

The current popular criticism of scholars that they are guilty of dangerous opinions on controversial issues could scarcely be more stupid. What we should censure our scholars for is their too frequent preoccu-

[2] Alfred North Whitehead, *Adventures of Ideas* (The Macmillan Company, New York, 1952), p. 313.

pation with relatively trivial and humanly unimportant truths (witness many Ph.D. dissertations as exemplifications of this deplorable insistence on "originality," however trivial, on "new discovery," however banal), their tendency to stress "research" for its own sake as an exercise in form at the expense of content, and their feeble and infrequent efforts to address themselves boldly and determinedly to the inevitable controversial issues it is their primary task to illumine. The eggheads whom we should scold are the timid heads cluttered with a thousand inconsequential details, not the powerful and dynamic minds whose critiques of ourselves and our society we sorely need.

CONTROVERSIAL ISSUES

In education as in the family the spirit of liberalism can show itself in its true colors where tensions are greatest and controversy most bitter. The most controversial areas today in teaching and scholarship are the economic, the political, and the religious—significantly, in that descending order of emotional intensity. It is a sad commentary on our liberal pretensions that the teacher who takes a bold and honest stand in any of the explosive areas is likely to be accused out of hand of being prejudiced and propagandistic, and that a scholar who takes a correspondingly bold stand is suspected of having betrayed the ideal of "impartial" scholarship.

What conception of teaching and scholarship do these accusations imply? They assume that the teacher or the scholar should avoid the discussion of all controversial topics (and all topics of vital human concern are inevitably controversial), that he should form no opinion on any social issues (thereby revealing his insensitivity to vital human problems and his failure to evaluate and act as maturely as possible), or that he should conceal his opinions from his students or his reading public (thereby exhibiting himself as a hypocrite or a coward). All three assumptions are in fact radically opposed to everything we should most value in the teacher and the scholar and to everything an enlightened liberalism must defend at all costs.

What could be more harmful to our students and our adult society than the systematic neglect of controversial issues by those who should be our teachers and intellectual leaders? What kind of leadership can they give us, young and old alike, if they themselves lack a sense of

179

human import and a vital interest in whatever most profoundly concerns us as human beings? And how can youth learn what it means to take sides on a controversial issue in a mature and responsible way unless our teachers and scholars tell us where they stand and what they believe and, above all, *why* they stand where they do and believe what they believe?

No institution in our society today has as great a responsibility as does the school to teach us how to distinguish between emotional propaganda, which is always essentially illiberal, and enlightened persuasive discourse; between blind prejudice and well-grounded conviction; between irresponsible dogmatism and responsible evaluation; between intolerance and the tolerance of firm belief coupled with genuine humility. It is precisely in the discussion of our most serious economic, political, and religious issues that teachers and scholars alike have their best chance to exhibit whatever liberalism is in them and to expound the gospel of liberalism by precept and example to the youthful and adult members of a society that would be free.

Here again the school, as one of our basic institutions, and society itself, as the community the school should serve, find themselves in a paradoxical state of mutual dependence. The school is bound to be very largely what society makes it; its present deficiencies and vices reflect the blindness of the society that supports it and seeks to mold it to its own immediate interests. Yet we must look to the school for leadership in the search for and dissemination of truth. The school must, therefore, defend its own proper autonomy, resisting benighted social pressures and insisting on policies that may well bring down upon it public censure. If those responsible for education and scholarship are no better informed and no wiser than their students, their students' parents, the average citizen, and the average legislator, our school system is either a fraud or a reactionary vehicle for popular egalitarian conservatism. If we teachers and scholars do not know our job or do not perform it well, we should be dismissed and others, wiser and more courageous than we, appointed in our place. So long as we still hold our positions of teaching and research it is clearly our responsibility to our students and our society to exemplify in every possible way the true meaning of liberalism in the field of knowledge and informed opinion. It is our task to lead, not follow, and to lead as imaginatively, courageously, and wisely as we can.

LIBERALISM IN RELIGION

DOCTRINAL AND ATTITUDINAL LIBERALISM

Let us distinguish once again between liberalism as an *attitude* and liberalism as a distinctive set of *doctrines*. Without this distinction any discussion of liberalism in religion will be more confusing than clarifying. My own experience has convinced me of the need for laboring this point, especially in religious circles. I have long had to contend with the widespread assumption, both inside and outside the church, that because I called myself a "liberal" in religion I must therefore disavow the "orthodox" doctrines of historical Christianity—Revelation, the Incarnation, sin, redemption, and so on. When I have protested this charge and declared my sincere belief in these and other central Christian doctrines I was then usually accused of either distorting their "orthodox" meaning in order to make them acceptable to my liberal conscience, or else of not really being a liberal at all. My professed religious liberalism has repeatedly been interpreted, and then approved or disapproved, in terms of the content of my religious faith, that is, in terms of what I believe rather than in terms of the manner, the spirit, the attitude in which I believe what I do. My liberalism has been judged by a doctrinal rather than an attitudinal standard.

The doctrinal conception of liberalism leads to hopeless obfuscation because it confuses the two radically different questions: "Is X a man of religious faith, and, if so, a Christian?" and "Is X's religious commitment, and is his Christian faith, liberal?" A refusal to distinguish these questions would force us to designate as religious "liberals" only those who were able to subscribe to certain specified doctrines, presumably of our own choosing, and to brand as illiberal all who accepted a different set of doctrines, without any reference to the spirit in which these "liberals" and their "illiberal" opponents held their respective beliefs. In effect we would be using the term "liberal" as a synonym for such terms as "radical," "leftist," "unorthodox," "latitudinarian," or

181

"heretical"; we might even find ourselves compelled to call religious liberalism the "right" or "true" position, as opposed to all "wrong" or "false" positions, or to assert the reverse, depending upon our own creedal commitment. If I approved of "liberalism," so defined, I would automatically identify liberalism with my own specific beliefs and declare all my opponents to be "illiberal" simply because they disagreed with me on very controversial issues. This would not only completely distort the meaning we have assigned to liberalism in this book; it would also place liberalism in the very position from which it has always sought to disassociate itself: it would commit us to the notion of a "liberal orthodoxy," a complete contradiction in terms.

If religious liberalism is defined not in terms of any specific set of religious doctrines but solely in terms of a distinctive attitude, what is this attitude? It is, in general, merely one of sincere open-mindedness, sincere humility, sincere tolerance. A liberal will believe what he can and disbelieve what he must with that complete tolerance for contrary beliefs and disbeliefs which reflects his abiding sense of human finitude, his awareness of the inadequacy of all human knowledge, and his real respect for the responsible deviant opinions of others.

The liberal attitude in religion will not differ in kind from the liberal attitude in any other area of human inquiry and decision. However, the liberal will attach greater importance to this attitude in religion because he will be aware that in this area of man's "ultimate concern for the Ultimate" our comprehension is necessarily most limited. Here the claim to dogmatic certainty must be most unjustified, and all self-righteous intolerance most indefensible and intolerable. To a liberal, man's living faith in the ultimate nature of things, whatever the content of this faith may be, must above all reflect his sense of his own finitude and awe in the face of ultimate mystery. It must be a *faith,* not an arrogant claim to perfect knowledge, and a moral *certitude* firm enough to live by and die for, never a spurious pretense to absolute intellectual *certainty.*

LIBERAL AGNOSTICISM AND ATHEISM

The liberal attitude may, of course, express itself in the religious skepticism of an agnostic or an atheist as well as in the religious affirmations of a contrite believer. The hallmark of liberal agnosticism or atheism will be an initial sympathetic openness to all the serious claims of thoughtful religious believers. The liberal skeptic, in sharp contrast to the dogmatic and illiberal skeptic, will not assume a priori that all religious experience must be rejected as authentic encounter with the Deity. He will not approach any affirmative religious belief with the smug presupposition that it must be invalid because, "of course," there is no God. He will, on the contrary, approach religion with genuine humility and a willingness—indeed an eagerness—to share in these experiences if he can and to accept some affirmative religious faith if he is honestly able to do so.

If, having approached religion in this spirit and having really given himself a fair chance to be persuaded by it, he still finds himself doubtful or overwhelmingly convinced that he cannot credit these claims and subscribe to these affirmative beliefs, he will then declare himself to be not a jubilant but a resigned agnostic or an unhappily convinced atheist. His humility will be genuine; he will realize that the failure may be his, that he may lack what others possess, that others may indeed have encountered and come to know the Deity or an ultimate dimension of reality from which he seems to be cut off. As a man of integrity, he will be honest and profess only what he can believe in all sincerity. He will live by whatever faith is in him. He will be as steadfast in his doubts and disbeliefs as others are in their positive assurances. But he will not delude himself with the notion that he "knows" whereas they merely profess a "blind faith"; he will acknowledge that he too is necessarily indulging in an act of faith because in this area only faith is ultimately possible. His chief concern will be to render his faith as reasonable and well grounded as he can make it.

A religious skeptic who is truly liberal not only will approach religion in general with this open-minded humility but will do his best to address himself to the distinctive beliefs and rites of this or that specific religion with a similar receptivity and understanding. He will realize that the term "religion" is a very loose generic term covering a great variety of experiences, beliefs, and practices and that the "religion" which is so vital and significant to many people is never religion in general but always some specific variant.

He will also be aware of the fact that some individuals in every society are really devout but have no explicit affiliation with any re-

ligious body or tradition and that they are members of what Paul
Tillich has called the "latent church." He will honor these sincere
seekers after God who, rightly or wrongly, feel obliged to worship
in their own solitary ways; indeed, he may find himself to be a member of this "latent church." But he will not regard this approach as
typical of man's historical religious quest. If he is really liberal he will
continue to do his best to understand what a living religion really means
by firsthand contact with at least one variant of one of the enduring
religions of mankind. He will relate himself to the specificities of this
religion with as much initial sympathy as possible, that is, with a rich
measure of initial faith, however blind it may be. Only later, after he
has actively participated in it so far as possible, will he be in a position
to decide critically and cogently what his emergent or resultant faith
really is. In short, he will do his best to keep his initial doubts from
blinding him to what might in fact present itself to him coercively and
convincingly as holy. He will try to give both himself and religion a real
chance—himself a chance to learn, and Deity a chance to speak to him.

This attitude of initial open-mindedness can be illustrated by reference
to two beliefs that have been of crucial importance in historical Christianity: the belief in Revelation and the belief in the Incarnation. For two
thousand years dogmatic skeptics have cavalierly dismissed both beliefs
as irrational and preposterous. What secular analogue to either Revelation or the Incarnation, they have asked, can possibly be cited or even
imagined? Indeed, is not the very notion preposterous of a Being, conceived of as Infinite Spirit, "revealing" himself or itself to man? And is
not the claim equally unbelievable that such a God has uniquely identified himself with one solitary human being in the whole of human history? Do not both beliefs do complete violence to everything we know
about an orderly world of nature and human nature? By what objective
criteria *could* the Christian's belief in Revelation and in the Incarnation
possibly be substantiated?

These are indeed unanswerable objections within a secular rationalistic perspective. What these two doctrines assert has no secular analogue; it is unintelligible in strictly naturalistic or humanistic terms. But
is this, the liberal skeptic will ask himself, the only possible perspective
or frame of reference? Is there not at least a possibility that there may
be more to reality than our spatiotemporal world of nature and human
nature? If so, may not this something "more" differ in kind from the

merely "natural," and may it not also perchance make itself known to man in distinctive phenomena and through experiences which themselves have a distinctive character? What compelling reason have we for dismissing out of hand the very possibility of authentic prophetic inspiration and even of a unique Incarnation?

Such open-mindedness is not, of course, identical with a positive faith in the validity of prophetic utterance or a living faith in Jesus Christ as the Son of God. Such a positive faith, if it is mature, comes late, not early, in man's religious quest if he is thoughtful and critical; it is a faith that must be rooted in painful experience and tested by reflection. But only a man capable of the requisite initial faith, blind and childlike though it is, can hope eventually to attain to the informed and tested faith of Christian maturity.

There is nothing in this situation to radically distinguish the problem of religious knowledge from man's epistemological predicament in other areas of experience and belief. No one can achieve a mature understanding of or faith in poetry who has not initially approached it with open-minded, childlike credulity. To read poetry with an initial hardened skepticism automatically prevents one from ever really "experiencing" poetry or achieving a true understanding of it. The same is true of human love and friendship and of science and morals. How can one come to "know" love and friendship for what they are without an initial faith in their possibility? How can one understand science without initiation into its mysteries, participation in its characteristic activities, initial acceptance of its basic faith? How can one learn at first hand the feeling of moral obligation without entering, with an initial trusting attitude, into those human relationships which generate in man a sense of moral obligation? Everywhere we encounter the need for an initial willingness to believe that what others have experienced we too may experience and that what others say they believe on the basis of experience and reflection we too may believe, if only we can share in these experiences and submit these beliefs to our own reflective tests. In this large and inclusive sense the claims of religion in general, and of this or that historic religious faith in particular, will therefore present themselves to the liberal mind as not initially implausible or irrational, whatever may be his eventual conclusion.

This analysis should not be construed as a plea for a blind faith or for a suppression of honesty anywhere along the line. In the end, the only religious faith worthy of our respect is a faith as informed and critical, as firmly rooted in our individual and in man's corporate experiences, as carefully tested and critically scrutinized as we can make it. In short, the true liberal honors doubt as highly as he honors sincere belief; he holds no brief for a persisting blind credulity; he knows that gullibility in an adult is not admirably childlike but culpably childish.

Adventure in the realm of religious faith is difficult; it is hard to do what is called for here—to have both faith and doubt, to believe and to be critical of our own beliefs, to indulge wholeheartedly in the commitments necessary for eventual understanding and, simultaneously, to stand aloof with all the critical objectivity we can muster. Man being what he is, blind faith and timid agnosticism are both easy; reflective commitment is painful and arduous. Moreover, the distinction between initial and resultant faith is too simple to do justice to the facts of human experience. For these two types of faith merge into one another in a continuous spectrum of belief; no state of faith is either wholly blind and credulous or completely reflective. Every initial act of faith echoes the more or less reflective beliefs that preceded it, and, while life lasts, every emergent act of faith is the beginning of new ventures in experience, reflection, and belief. But such considerations as these will not dismay the courageous liberal or dissuade him from participating in man's religious quest with confidence and hope. They will in fact reinforce his conviction that here, even more than elsewhere, dogmatism of any sort is intolerable and that humility is both the necessary seed and the precious fruit of spiritual assurance.

LIBERAL RELIGIOUS AFFIRMATION

How shall we describe the liberal who is also a man of positive religious faith? The spirit in which he clings to his affirmative faith will not differ from the spirit of the truly liberal agnostic or atheist. He will differ from them only (not a negligible "only") in what he believes and in the many ways in which this growing faith may make available to him light- and strength-giving experiences that may generate in him an ever deepening humility.

It is a very disturbing fact that the history of all the "high" religions of mankind records so much dogmatism where tolerance might have been expected, so much closed-mindedness in the presence of mysteries that should at least have elicited curiosity and awe, so much arrogance and self-righteous complacency where a repentant humility should have been sought and felt. I can explain this anomaly only on the dual supposition that, first, the urgency of man's religious need and the ultimacy of his quest combine to induce him to grasp with frantic desperation whatever faith he has, as a drowning man clutches anything within his reach and that, second, the widespread social acceptance accorded to conventional religious practice has added to the small nucleus of sincere and truly sensitive religious believers a host of conventional religionists whose religion is too superficial and stereotyped to induce in them the humility real reverence engenders. It is impossible not to regard religious arrogance, the *self*-righteousness of a *God*-seeker, as the most profound of all contradictions. Witness the testimony of saintly men and women of different religious faiths that the love of the Lord is the beginning of wisdom and also of humility. The stalwart humanist who has encountered nothing nobler than man and whose only strength is his own may understandably take pride in his own strength and virtue. But the man of God believes himself to be in the presence of a holiness that, in the hyperbole of utter contrition, makes his very virtues mere "filthy rags." On his knees he finds himself before a Judge whose righteousness probes his inmost sins, whose wisdom reveals to him the pathetic inadequacy of all his presumptive knowledge, and whose love and mercy alone give him hope and save him from despair. This surely is man's chief experiential source of humility—a humility not self-induced but evoked by the objective righteous love of God himself.

Does all this imply that the man of faith is wholly prostrate in mind and spirit in the presence of Deity? To answer this question in the affirmative would be to fail completely to distinguish between the superstition of primitive and contemporary idolatries and the self-respecting faith of a religion that has become enlightened and mature. Paul Tillich has done us a great service by differentiating so clearly between three possible contrasting positions—"heteronomy" of the enslaved heart and mind, "autonomy" of the responsible humanist, and "theonomy," that is, worship of the God whose service is perfect freedom.[3] Let us pause for a moment to consider this threefold distinction.

Tillich defines "heteronomy" as man's belief in and worship of false

[3] See Paul Tillich, chap. I in *The Christian Answer,* ed. Henry P. Van Dusen (Charles Scribners Sons, New York, 1945). See also Paul Tillich, *The Protestant Era* (University of Chicago Press, Chicago, 1948).

gods, finite "creatures" unworthy of man's reverence demanding slavish subservience when man makes them his idols. False gods, Tillich points out, may be either secular or ecclesiastical; we can become enslaved by such institutions as an authoritarian church or a totalitarian state, by our own human artifacts (for example, the Frankenstein of modern technology), by our own bodies and their appetites, in short, by anything that can intrude itself upon us and dominate us from without. Whatever our idol, it reveals its falsity by requiring of us an abject submission that is incompatible with complete moral and spiritual integrity.

"Autonomy" Tillich defines as man's ultimate reliance on himself and on his own resources, with full respect for the intrinsic dignity of his highest powers. The spirit and temper of autonomy exhibit themselves in man's respect for truth and in his wholehearted dedication to its endless pursuit; in his respect for his own creativity and for the beauty his imagination enables him to find in nature and to create out of nature; in his respect for his own capacity for justice and love and in his ceaseless effort to perfect human justice and to cherish all men in an ever deepening love. Here we have man at his self-sufficient responsible best —man acutely alive to his own rights and duties, his own failings and achievements, his own potentialities and limitations, deeply respectful of himself and others, obedient to the dictates of his own intellectual and spiritual integrity, and bowing his head in worship to no god in heaven or on earth. Responsible autonomy is placed in sharp contradistinction to all religious submission and reverence—autonomy is a humanism proud but not arrogant, assured but not defiant, a humanism with a clear-eyed self-confidence and humility of its own.[4]

"Theonomy," as Tillich conceives of it, contrasts sharply with both heteronomy and autonomy. The theonomous man believes in God and is in complete submission to His will. But theonomy differs from ecclesiastical heteronomy by virtue of the fact that the God who commands man's ultimate allegiance is not a tyrant who demands groveling submission but a "loving Father" who wants man to respect and honor all the human faculties with which God himself has endowed him. What this God asks of man is not blind subservience but enlightened obedience, not mere submission to a superior force but a free and spontaneous

[4] The writings of John Dewey, Erik Fromm, and Lewis Mumford all exemplify this humanism.

response in love to a divine self-sacrificial love. Faith in and obedience to this God cannot do violence to our intellectual integrity, if we interpret it aright, because God is the God of truth. Faith in him cannot do violence to our highest moral integrity because he is the God of justice and righteousness. Reverence for such a God is consonant with man's most inspired creative efforts because in all his human creativity he is doing no more than imitating in his limited, finite way divine creativity. Theonomy, in short, takes seriously the Christian doctrine that, despite his inescapable sinfulness, man is essentially good—as good as any humble humanist ever declared him to be—and that he has indeed been created in the "image" of God in being endowed with an ineradicable capacity for apprehending and responding to the divine initiative.

This interpretation of theonomy as a God-centered (not man-centered) faith and as faith in a God who exalts man (instead of demeaning him) to the status of being his own child and finite partner, enables us to conceive of "high" religion, that is, a mature and enlightened religious faith, as embracing all the merits and as doing full justice to all the aspirations of responsible humanism. But theonomous faith transcends humanism by putting man in contact with a Deity able and eager to help man realize himself as man is not able to do by his own unaided efforts, according to the testimony of both saints and sinners. It thus provides man with a resource that can enable him to resist the inevitable tendency of a lofty autonomy to degenerate into a kind of servile heteronomy. It does indeed insist that man is not sufficient unto himself and that he should not play God; but the God it offers man as the object of his ultimate faith and reverence is a God whose service is not slavery but perfected freedom, not abject submission but an obedience fully consonant with man's own complete self-respect.

We must be careful not to minimize the paradoxical character of theonomous faith. It is without qualification a faith in God himself and a wholehearted worship of him for his own sake, not just a surreptitious device for achieving salvation. We must not be misled by the insistence of all "high" religions that man can and does achieve his own salvation only by worshiping the Lord and obeying his commands. This is precisely the paradox of theonomy—that we fail to worship God as we should if we worship him in order to achieve salvation but that if we do worship him for himself our own salvation will be assured in the

189

process. From first to last, theonomy is theocentric; nothing could more radically distort it than the attempt to reduce it to a covert egoism, a pretense at worship masking a primary concern for personal advantage. That the religion of the preachers and the priests has so often reduced itself to such long-range prudentialism is a sorry comment on the extent to which a pious heteronomy can supplant an authentic theonomy in the church. But the church's own prophetic voice has again and again been raised in protest against this blasphemy of putting self or church in place of God. However depraved its practices, the church's deepest insights have been theonomous, not heteronomous or autonomous.

Those of us who find the theonomous interpretation of religious faith highly satisfactory must beware of identifying it with liberalism and of branding all who honestly disagree with us as illiberal. But we are surely entitled to recommend this theonomous approach to all who are eager to have faith in God but cannot believe in a God who seems to violate man's highest moral and intellectual integrity. Here, we can argue in all sincerity, is a faith not only consistent with the spirit of liberalism but ideally qualified to undergird the articles of our liberal creed. Here God is conceived of as the very Source and Ground of the values man tries to discover, assimilate, and actualize; as the Being who endows man with genuine freedom and responsibility; as the Love men can in some measure reflect in their own efforts at humane co-operation; and, finally, as the God all men consciously or unconsciously search for with awe and seek to worship with reverence. Theonomy is not identifiable with liberalism, but it is consistent with and complementary to liberalism at its most enlightened.

Meanwhile, a liberal who is honestly able to embrace the theonomous interpretation of "high" religious faith is under an obligation to explore its implications for the church and to apply them as best he can to the doctrines and rites of the church and to the social attitudes and behavior it advocates. His general attitude to the church will, once again, be paradoxical—both receptive and critical, both obedient and alertly watchful. He will respect its cumulative wisdom and humbly seek to learn what it has to teach, but he will not accept any of its teachings that seem to him, in all humility, to do violence to his own integrity. He will honor its intrinsic authority as the finite institutional vehicle of authentic inspiration and revelation, but he will openly repudiate any effort it may make to deify itself, to claim for itself an omniscience that belongs only to God, and to coerce him with a spurious extrinsic authority that in fact it does not and cannot possess. He will accept its doctrines as wise but fallible, its rites as authentic instruments of Grace only for the contrite, its precepts as worthy of respect and often worthy of obedience—but never sacrosanct. In short, he will do his best to think out and practice his theonomous faith with complete autonomous self-respect and with alert awareness of the multiple possibilities of ecclesiastical heteronomy.

More specifically, he will protest against any and every tendency to substitute worship of church or scripture, rite or ecclesiastical edict, for the worship of God himself. He will never forget how necessarily inadequate are man's most inspired theological apprehensions of God, and he will make every effort to worship, not the God of the Hindu or the Mohammedan, of the Jew or the Christian, of the Roman Catholic or the Protestant, but the one and only true God—the God who is perennially sought for in all these religions and who both hides himself and reveals himself to all in varying degrees; the God, as Tillich puts it, "behind all 'gods'," that is, behind *all human apprehensions* of him. He will, if he is a Christian, believe that the Bible and the church are indeed inspired by God, and he will accept as valid their joint account of the Incarnation. But he will refrain from absolutizing any human interpretation of what God has here revealed to man and what the Christ who became flesh is in all the length and breadth and depth of his divine nature. He will wholeheartedly participate in his church's rites, but with all the imaginative intelligence and all the contriteness of heart that he can muster. He will judiciously submit to the social injunctions of his church, but he will be ever mindful that it too can be mistaken and sinful.

Is all this possible? The extreme authoritarian on the one hand and the convinced humanist on the other will agree that it is not—that what is here called for is both too little and too much—too much institutional authority for the humanist and too little for the strict authoritarian, too much autonomy for the authoritarian and too little for the humanist. All that a liberal believer in theonomy can do, beyond this point, is to leave it to the conscience of each individual to ignore God or to seek for him and perchance find him and then worship him as he is able. Of the three positions differentiated by Tillich, the only one all liberals can agree to resist in all its manifestations is the position of heteronomy, which, by its very nature, does such violence to the spirit of liberalism and to man's precious integrity and freedom.

Meanwhile, the theonomous church is under perpetual obligation to cleanse itself of its own iniquities. It has a corresponding obligation to the society in which it finds itself. Here its task is, so far as possible, to be in the world but not of it, to serve society without capitulating to any of the social forces that run counter to its own highest principles and loyalties. It is the church's duty to identify and denounce all secular idolatries for what they are—finite goods made evil by being absolutized and worshiped. It is its duty to join hands with all humanistically oriented individuals and movements in furthering the cause of social justice and in resisting all forms of injustice and cruelty, in supporting man's search for truth, and in making the fullest use of the fruits of his creative imagination. It is also duty-bound to benefit from cogent secular criticism and to beware lest it do violence to man's responsible idealism and fall below his most enlightened secular behavior.

Above all, however, the theonomous church must beware lest it too, particularly in a historical period given to institutional giganticism, allow itself to become a tyrannical leviathan insensitive to the endlessly subtle private needs of the individual. If there is anything more offensive to human decency and to the spirit of liberalism than wholesale education it is wholesale religion. If any institution is charged with a responsibility to every individual *as* an individual person (a responsibility greater even than that of the family and the school) it is the church, dedicated to man's public *and private* communion with his God. A church that is not truly liberal in at least this sense must forfeit the respect and loyalty of all liberals, whatever their ultimate creedal commitments may be. By the same token, a church whose constant major concern is to comfort the fatherless, aid the oppressed, and in every way help every individual it can reach to find God and worship him in spirit and in truth—such a church can hardly fail to elicit the gratitude and the support of liberals of every creedal stripe, for such a church will in its own way be exemplifying and strengthening the spirit of liberalism.

Chapter 11

The Implementation of
Liberalism: Business and Industry

*I*F THE BASIC STRUCTURE of our free society is political democracy, its basic texture is our economic system of free enterprise. It too is largely indebted for its rationale to British and European thinkers; it too reflects experiments and trends in other lands. Yet, as we find it in operation in this country today, it is a thoroughly American phenomenon in its characteristic motivations and goals; in its relation to government; in its impact upon the school, the church, and even the family; and more generally in its profound influence on the mores and values of our society as a whole.

Business and industry are of vital importance in a liberal community in two ways. On the one hand, they constitute a second major bulwark of liberalism by giving economic implementation to the freedoms government seeks to safeguard politically; on the other hand, they reflect the extent to which our cultural ethos is in fact liberal by exemplifying in practice the values we really live by. Unless business and industry function in a liberal manner, political freedoms are jeopardized and large portions of the people, though politically free, remain economically enslaved. Any claim that we are really a liberal community because we profess liberalism is idle if this liberalism is not translated into liberal attitudes and practices in the business world.

Those who benefited most from our system of free economic enterprise a few years ago regarded it as an admirable expression of the traditional American love of and right to liberty. How could a man realize his right to freedom more effectively, they asked, than in the actual freedom to earn his livelihood as he wishes, to invest his capital and sell his services as he chooses, to manufacture and distribute his products to the highest bidder? Indeed, is it not the *right* of each individual, as a free moral agent in a free society, to decide what he will spend and save, how he will spend what he chooses to and how he will dispose of his savings when he dies?

These questions, which echo the spirit of mid-nineteenth-century laissez-faire economic libertarianism, still voice the sentiments of many of our economically successful citizens. They also express what most freedom-loving Americans approve of as an ideal. Freedom of economic enterprise, with a maximum of untrammeled competition and a minimum of governmental control, sounds good to all typically energetic Americans, particularly to those who foresee the possibility of a successful career for themselves under such a system. But the vast army of the unemployed and unemployable, the economically underprivileged who, try as they will, cannot escape economic fear and want and those who lack the economic resources for adequate care in illness and old age— all those who for one reason or another suffer under this system instead of flourishing under it find it a most inadequate expression of man's right to work and live in decency and safety. Their cause is championed by all of us who are sensitive to the claims of human justice. We believe, with them, that a free society does have a responsibility for the economically less fortunate. We agree with them that this responsibility should be primarily assumed by government, especially in a democratic government dedicated to the welfare of all its citizens. Hence the tension in our American society today between the haves and hope-to-haves, on the one hand, and the have-nots and those who rally to their defense, on the other.

Underlying this tension there is fortunately a growing realization that political and civic freedoms mean little when they are divorced from economic security and opportunity. A worker living in a slum on uncertain wages and unable to migrate in search of a better job derives small comfort from the fact that he still has the right to vote. Freedom of speech is seriously curtailed when forthright speech puts a man in economic jeopardy. We are pretty well agreed that those whose freedom is restricted to the freedom to starve or barely subsist are scarcely in a position to enjoy their basic political and civil liberties. We acknowledge that there is validity in the criticism often made of us that

194

we profess a measure of freedom that our actual economic practices still deny to a considerable proportion of the population. This failure of the economic system to measure up to the political ideal gives Communist agitators in our midst their strongest arguments.

It is within this area of significant agreement that major economic disputes arise today. We are at one in deploring abject poverty and economic tyranny, but we disagree sharply over the best remedies. Labor has gone far in forcing higher wages and the improvement of working conditions, but in the process it has exhibited its own penchant for monopoly and its own disposition to exploit the public. To what extent should the growing power of labor unions be tolerated or encouraged, and how can their abuses of power best be restricted? Capital and management have not only yielded to the pressures of organized labor when they had to; they have also done a good deal to improve wages and working conditions on their own initiative. But they still tend to value profits above all else, to drive a hard bargain with labor, to press for special governmental protection and support, and to exploit the public. When, to what extent, and how should their ambitions be curbed in the interest of both labor and the public? Government has increasingly been drawn into these disputes; it has done much to restrain the excesses of both capital and labor and has provided the public with services that business and industry could not, or did not, provide. But what should be the policy of a liberal government on both counts—the restraint of predatory exploitation of the public and the establishment of public works designed to promote the common good? These questions reflect a large area of contemporary dispute in which the sincere liberal has abundant chance to clarify and implement his liberal faith.

Business and industry are also a test of and a challenge to liberalism at a more basic level. Our society as a whole is not predominantly intellectually or religiously oriented, nor is it above all politically minded. We are first and foremost an economically oriented, profit-conscious, business-minded nation in which success is gauged chiefly in economic terms and in which social prestige is primarily associated with wealth and economic power. A foreigner who really wants to know us as we are in our typical daily activities and with our typical motives and goals should observe us not in school or church or political assembly or even in our private family life but in the "market place," that is, in the area where most of us spend most of our lives and find our dominant interests. It is here that most Americans are most alive; it is here that we tend to practice what we really believe. The market place provides the best pragmatic test of the sincerity of our professed ideals; it is the truest index of our real cultural ethos. Whoever wishes to know what cultural values we have actually made our own should not attend merely to what is preached at us on Sundays and what is taught our children on weekdays, or even to what is promised us by our politicians during a political campaign. He would do better to note what the members of our congregations actually carry away with them from church and act on in their daily activities, what our children really assimilate and express in their practical behavior as adults, and what our hardheaded voters really want and demand of government. The Biblical statement, "By their fruits shall ye know them," is as applicable to cultural as to spiritual values, as pertinent to man's institutional activities as to his private dealings with his fellow-men. In our society it is the market place where the actual fruits of family nurture, educational effort, and corporate religious faith are most clearly evident. It is here that whatever authentic liberalism may have worked itself into our blood stream and become a real part of us will finally reveal itself. Here is the litmus paper on which we can test the depth and power of our liberal professions. If little real liberalism exhibits itself here, we can be sure that we still have a long way to go before we can honestly call ourselves a liberal society. If genuine liberalism does show itself at this everyday practical business level, we can be assured that the spirit of liberalism is a dynamic force in our midst.

Business and industry can function more or less liberally in three areas —in their relation to government, in their internal operations, and in their relation to the public. How can they do so, and how well do they exemplify and implement the spirit of liberalism in each of these areas?

THE RELATION OF BUSINESS AND INDUSTRY TO GOVERNMENT

In a free society, government and business and industry are peculiarly dependent on each other; each has distinctive responsibilities to the other. The task of government, seen in liberal perspective, is not only to restrain all predatory raids on the public, whether by individuals or by organized groups, but also to promote the public welfare in all appropriate ways. However, it must attempt to do so without illiberal regimentation and without lapsing into a paternalism that, in the long run, discourages private initiative and is therefore hostile to the liberal concern for individual and group responsibility.

How can it best discharge this difficult obligation? There is no magic formula, no quick and easy solution. The problems a liberal government must solve are always complex and concrete; their solutions must therefore always depend upon the wisdom, sagacity, patience, good will, and sense of justice of all parties concerned—legislators, governmental officials, the courts, leaders of both management and labor, and an informed and articulate public. There are, however, two sets of familiar maxims that serve in some measure to express the spirit and intent of liberalism in this area.

The first pair of maxims might be formulated as follows:

1. Government should take all necessary steps to prevent human suffering.

2. Government should not do for its people what they can and should do for themselves.

Taken together, these maxims would dictate appropriate governmental provision for unemployment and old-age insurance, with due care that such insurance will not discourage individual thrift or lessen the responsibility of private enterprises for the welfare of their employees.

The second pair of maxims might be formulated thus:

1. Government should undertake whatever socially useful services and projects private enterprise cannot, or will not, undertake for the public good.

2. Government should avoid unnecessarily entering into competition with private economic enterprise.

That is, government should provide the public with a police force, a postal service, highways, and so on; moreover, it should undertake large projects, such as the building of gigantic dams, which business and industry cannot, or will not, undertake in a manner most advantageous to the public good. But it should avoid entering into direct competition with business and industry when such an act would entail no benefit

197

to the public; for example, it should not set up and operate its own telephone system if, with suitable governmental supervision, private enterprise can perform this service with real efficiency and at reasonable rates.

Such general maxims as these will no doubt receive the overwhelming approval of most governmental officials and businessmen. It is the application of the principles that occasions sharp differences of opinion. Here liberals should keep in mind the inevitability and the legitimacy of honest difference of opinion. Such differences usually arise when individuals and groups are intent on making a special plea for a local area or a specific enterprise. The expression of special interest, whether it is geographic, racial, social, political, or religious, may reflect a perfectly valid minority claim that government should make every effort to honor. But government must also recognize the inevitable attempts of regions and groups to benefit themselves illegitimately at the expense of other groups and regions and of the public as a whole. It is the difficult task of government to adjudicate such conflicts and to try to mediate between conflicting interests as fairly as possible, recognizing proper minority claims and at the same time cherishing the over-all needs of public welfare.

In short, a liberal government has a triple role in its relation to business and industry. It must restrain them from harming the public. It must, so far as the public good permits, refrain from competing with them and from engaging in economic activities that could and would be undertaken as well or better by private enterprise. It must also actively promote the welfare of business and industry by co-operating with it in every legitimate way. Of the three roles, the third is perhaps the hardest because government is under the obligation to be wiser than the institution it seeks to undergird and help. Its long-range responsibility to business and industry is to help it—and when necessary to force it—to organize itself and function in such a way as to promote its own greatest health and security in the long run. It must resist all tendencies on the part of business and industry to insulate themselves against new ideas and better procedures, to rigidify their present structure and perpetuate the status quo. It must resist monopolies not only for the sake of the public but also for the sake of healthy business competition; yet it must avoid making a fetish of competition, and it must seek to promote that type of competition which is most favorable to industrial creativity and advance. It must do all it can to keep business structure and policy flexible and adaptable to ever changing local and world conditions, receptive to new insight into economic law, and open to new co-operative devices that will benefit capital, labor, and the public at large. Above all, it must strive to create an environment conducive to the best possible functioning of responsible private initiative. In so far as it succeeds in this difficult task it can progressively relinquish direct control. Such controls will become unnecessary as our economy becomes wiser and more effective.

What is here advocated is in no sense a new form of statism or illiberal socialism. On the contrary, the goal envisaged is a community whose health depends upon private initiative and the relative autonomy of all our major institutions, including business and industry. A liberal government should try to strengthen, not weaken, the competitive economic system so that it can more effectively serve the public. In our day this effort may entail less rather than more governmental bureaucracy and more decentralization of power both in government and in industry. But these objectives cannot be reached by a do-nothing governmental attitude. What is needed is more, not less, governmental guidance, but guidance motivated by the desire to help business and industry to function better for their own sake as well as for the sake of the public. The crucial question of how such a policy can best be translated into legislation must, like all other practical questions, be left to those who are expert in such matters and whose responsibility it is to lead us.

Business and industry, in turn, have a grave responsibility to government. They should co-operate wholeheartedly with government in its efforts to promote their own welfare as well as the welfare of the public. They should also resist all illegitimate governmental encroachment on their proper and creative initiative and their corporate responsibilities to the public. They should not try to "capture" the government or to coerce it into giving them special privileges, nor should they try to weaken the power of government or restrict the scope of its proper responsibilities. They should not blow hot and cold, demanding governmental help and then resenting governmental supervision. An industry is not justified in saying to government, when things are going well and profits are mounting, "Leave us alone and don't supervise us at all," and then turning to government when problems arise and saying, "We are so important to the public that you should help us out of our difficulties." An industry so crucial to the public welfare that it deserves governmental support and defense in time of need may well require continuing governmental supervision in the interest of the public welfare. Such industries cease to be merely private enterprises with a right to complete autonomy.

Here again, all specific decisions about what kind of governmental help and supervision is called for, and for how long, are difficult questions that must be grappled with by government and business leaders in the context of the specific situation. It is the duty of liberalism to insist that business no less than government approach all such problems in the liberal spirit of self-respect and lively concern for the greatest welfare of all.

LIBERALISM WITHIN BUSINESS AND INDUSTRY

When we try to assess the internal functioning of business and industry according to the criterion of an informed liberalism, we encounter three basic factors that must be reckoned with. Each, in its own way, tends to impede the realization of our liberal objectives.

The first of these factors is that of motivation, the powerful drive for profit and for the prestige that money can buy. This motive is, no doubt, a major source of economic competition, and competition, in turn, tends to intensify this drive in our society. The profit motive is not in and of itself hostile to liberalism since profit can be derived from economic activities that are of great use to the public and since, in addition, the profit motive need not exclude all other motives or even dominate all others. It can be kept on a par with them or subordinated to them whenever necessary. However, its strong tendency to become dominant in our society, not only within business and industry but by contagion in other institutions and social activities as well, does present liberalism with a major challenge.

There is scarcely any activity in America in which the profit motive is not to some degree operative, but there are many in which it does not normally become dominant. Our clergy are, quite properly, paid for their work, but only a small minority allow themselves to be primarily motivated by the large salaries of wealthy city churches. Teachers are paid for their services. Some do enter the profession of teaching chiefly for the sake of the financial security, however modest, that teaching affords; some seek administrative posts primarily because of the better pay such posts carry with them. Yet most teachers, like most members of the clergy, are tempted to become money-minded only because their pay is so wretchedly inadequate to their basic needs. Most artists are bedeviled by economic anxiety, and some in desperation do prostitute their creative talent to keep alive. But the true artist, now as always, refuses to sell his soul to clothe his back. Mercenary doctors who drive a hard bargain with their patients and cater to the rich for their money are relatively rare; most doctors are so devoted to their patients that they either make only an adequate living or else, if their practice does become lucrative, devote a large percentage of their time to voluntary treatment of needy patients.

Even more noteworthy is the fact that we tend to censure persons in these and similar professions who allow the acquisitive motive to become dominant. We feel that the clergyman and the doctor are betraying their vocations if they substitute financial gain for the cure of souls or the cure of bodies. We do not begrudge them reasonable economic security and comfort, but we insist (unless we have become very cynical) that they have been disloyal to their true calling if they put money first and service to their fellow-men second. We feel the same way about artists, teachers, scholars, and lawyers. Artistic pursuits, the education of our youth, research, law, and medicine—such activities, we feel, are too intrinsically and socially valuable to be made simply means to the end of private financial gain. We are convinced that in these activities the work itself and its value to other human beings should be the worker's chief reward and constitute his primary concern. It is partly because these activities have this character that we call them "professions," or, in the older, theological meaning of the terms, "vocations" or "callings."

There is nothing in business and industry as such to prevent those who engage in them from regarding their activities in the same way a devoted clergyman, doctor, teacher, artist, or lawyer regards his professional tasks. We need food, shelter, and clothing to keep us alive. Money is essential in any advanced economy. We benefit greatly from the countless products of modern business and industry—the cars, the telephones, the kitchen appliances, the many media of communication and amusement, and so on—that make the lives of so many of us so comfortable and agreeable.

Why is it, then, that most of us assume that the dominant motive of the businessman (whether he is a small shopkeeper or the powerful owner of a great chain of stores, a manual worker or a top executive, an employee or an employer, a manufacturer or a financier) will necessarily be the making of as much money as possible as rapidly as possible? In our society the statement, "I'm in business," has become almost synonymous with, "I'm out to make all the money I can." Any lucrative activity is, on the whole, approved if it is "within the law," and the more lucrative it turns out to be the more approval it gains.

In this area a bold and unapologetic drive for economic success has come to be sanctioned both within business and by the public, whereas a similar acquisitive drive in the professions has been only tolerated and often openly condemned. Why this disparity between the professions and business? Why this approval of predatory acquisitiveness in the production and handling of commodities and the contrasting disapproval of a similar financial acquisitiveness when it makes its appearance in other walks of life? Does this distinction reflect in a secular manner a puritanical approval of "worthy" activities and contempt for "worldly" activities conducive to mere physical well-being? Or does it express a sociological trend in our society toward the "higher" professions on the part of those whose sense of values and whose social responsibility is livelier, and an opposite trend of the less "idealistic" into the more "realistic" market place? Or is it a fact that business success is dependent on a ruthless quest for financial gain and that business is essentially hostile to human rights and human values and therefore basically illiberal?

The attitude and behavior of many successful businessmen indicate that the last interpretation, that business is necessarily predatory and antisocial, is completely unsound. Many employers do have a lively social consciousness that expresses itself in genuine concern for their employees and for the public. The attitude of many employees toward their fellow-workers, their employers, and those who buy their products is friendly and just. All these socially minded men and women make a real effort to deal with one another fairly and justly. They also have a good conscience with regard to the public because they believe that the products they handle are well made, reasonably priced, and really beneficial to the purchaser. Moreover, many men and women in business and industry enjoy their work and take pride in doing it well, and some, though too few, find in it opportunities for ingenuity and creativity. Despite the strength of the acquisitive motive in our highly competitive society and despite the continual temptation to get ahead ruthlessly, there are among us many businessmen and businesswomen who elevate business to the level of a responsible, creative, co-operative, socially useful, and intrinsically satisfying form of activity.

This proves that business need not be predatory and exploitative, but it does not meet the charge that much business *is* exploitative, both internally and externally in its relation to the public. That the acquisitive motive and the exploitative attitude tend to be dominant cannot be denied. This is a sociological fact with which we must reckon in our assessment of business in America today according to the criterion of liberalism.

A second basic factor to be reckoned with is the natural tendency of business to function autocratically. Anyone who invests his capital in a business enterprise naturally tries to protect this investment and make it yield him a profit. He therefore insists on hiring those who in his judgment are most likely to fall in with his plans and obey his orders. He thus becomes the boss of his employees and it is natural for him to insist on determining the policy under which his business is run. His argument is simple and cogent. "I take the risks; why should I not reap the rewards and, to this end, run my business as I like and hire and fire my employees at will?"

This autocratic tendency expresses itself even in small businesses where an employer has only one or two helpers. It is greatly intensified in big business by various factors: by the need for capital normally borrowed from stock-and-bond-holders who demand security for and profit from their investments, by the enormous complexity of a big-business enterprise, and by the resultant need for special financial, industrial, and technological knowledge. Any attempt in our highly competitive and vastly complex society to conduct a large business by direct democratic control is doomed to failure. What would happen if the policies and crucial commitments of such an enterprise were to be decided in an open forum on the basis of a majority vote of all the employers, directors, executives, foremen, and workers? The result would be endless debate and the final substitution of ignorance for knowledge, inexperience for tested experience. How, then, can business function liberally and still be efficient and profitable?

A third factor to be reckoned with is the discontent and frustration of many employees and workers. Anyone at the mercy of an autocratic employer will chafe under regulations and resent his lack of freedom. His resentment will grow when his wages fail to provide him with economic security and reasonable comfort. It will increase still more when he finds himself further and further removed from those who have the final say, and, above all, when the work he is hired to do becomes mechanical and deadening. The cumulative impact of all these factors can be appreciated if we compare the life of the old-fashioned shoemaker, who was his own master, purchased his own materials, made his own shoes, and dealt with his own customers, with the life of a worker in a shoe factory today, who rarely meets his top-level employer, spends his entire day tending a machine that performs a single operation with tedious precision, and never sees the finished product or the customer's pleasure or displeasure on receiving it. No wonder such a worker tends to become machine-like, uninterested in his work, unconcerned with the quality of the product manufactured or sold, impersonal in his relationship with his employer, and indifferent to the public—in short, a robot-like cog in a complicated machine.

The organization of unions has done a great deal to raise wages, provide the worker with various forms of security, and give him an organization in which he can achieve a sense of belonging, of comradeship under effective leadership, of membership in a community of fellow-workers with common problems and a common policy of self-defense and self-improvement. But in order to be effective labor unions have also had to resort to autocracy. They have now become so large and powerful that their leaders are as far removed from the average worker as are most employers. The worker is under compulsion to join the union and play the union's game. He therefore now finds himself today at the mercy of two hard taskmasters, the employer and the union boss, who between them decide autocratically what he shall earn, what he shall pay in union dues, how much he shall work or how little, when he shall work and when he shall refuse to work in a strike.

Walter Wheeler, of Pitney-Bowes, has stated the situation from the point of view of management with admirable lucidity:[1]

This problem is an outgrowth of a conflict too few of us recognize . . . a conflict between the freedom of expression which all citizens enjoy in their private and political life, and the relatively autocratic life which we find in industry. . . . This is the old problem of leadership in a democratic society. . . . How do we go about directing ever greater numbers of people in such a way that they will accept our direction and not undermine it?

This statement assumes that management must continue to manage and that one of its major tasks is to discover how to "direct," or "manage," labor so as to make it efficient and productive. It assumes that the employer and his executives are the only ones who understand the firm's goals and problems and who must therefore give the orders to their employees. There is no hint here of genuine co-operation, of any real exchange of ideas, of honest give-and-take, of joint participation by many individuals with different skills and aptitudes in a common co-operative venture.

The authors of the *Fortune* article in which Wheeler's remark was quoted have given the liberal reply to this question:

The answer is plain: through *participation*. Now participation, of course, is something everybody is for, and in more instances than not, industrial "participation" programs have been little more than well-meant fictions designed to give the worker a "feeling" of belonging and very little else. But where the basic principle has been followed, where management has *wanted* the participation of the worker, the results can almost be called exciting. Whatever the mechanics—Pitney Bowes's "industrial council," the Scanlon plan (*Fortune,* January 1950)—in every case there has flowed a strong and lubricating confidence.

This brings us back to the articles of our liberal creed. If we start with the assumption that business is essentially exploitative, the result is inevitable: employer and employee, capital, and labor will all do their best to exploit the public and one another. But if we start with the opposite assumption that in a liberal society business can and should like other groups function as a humane and co-operative enterprise of potential advantage to all concerned, including the public, we create an atmosphere

[1] Quoted in "Is Anybody Listening?" *Fortune,* September, 1950, p. 176. The whole article is relevant and illuminating.

congenial to mutual respect and understanding and more efficient co-operation. In such an atmosphere it is possible for the worker to realize that management must be entrusted with certain responsibilities and must, if it is fit to manage at all, possess various types of knowledge and experience that the worker cannot possess. But, by the same token, management can come to realize that employees will make their maximum contribution to the total operation if their distinctive experiences are utilized, their ideas, good, bad or indifferent, are freely expressed and really listened to, their grievances heard and met, and their hopes taken into account and realized wherever possible.

The most effective incentive to genuine co-operation between worker and employer is a common dedication to the common public good. If both really believe in the value of their total enterprise for the public welfare, and if both make "public service" their real and dominant motive, they will find the strongest motive for mutual respect and effective co-operation. With this incentive, they will be able to devise countless ways in which to overcome the impersonality of their relationship to one another and their present failure to communicate with one another effectively. They will learn how to live and work not as rivals in a hostile world but rather as co-workers in a society dedicated to liberty and human rights and the dignity of all men as human beings.

Such a pervasive attitude would also go far to encourage a pride in craftsmanship that Americans today are in grave danger of losing. Anyone who has had a house built or repaired has encountered indifference to craftsmanship, lack of pride in doing a job as quickly and as well as it can be done. We find evidence of loss of respect for good work not only throughout business and industry but in schools and churches, in government, and in the home. One of the few places where craftsmanship is still valued by the participants and by the public as well is in the field of sports. Most amateur athletes and their coaches and many professional athletes still take pride in perfected skill, and the public is still keenly appreciative of this skill. In nearly every other activity, however, we tend to be satisfied with what is just good enough to get by. We are thus robbing ourselves of one of the great sources of human satisfaction and one of the chief components of moral integrity. Business and industry have today an unparalleled opportunity to revive in their own workers a sense of craftsmanship, respect for quality, pride in excellence for its own sake. Here business and industry have a chance to inject into our national ethos a set of values that could immeasurably enrich the lives of all of us.

THE RELATION OF BUSINESS AND INDUSTRY TO THE PUBLIC

This also is a relation of mutual dependence and reciprocal influence. The public obviously needs the services and products of business and industry. Business and industry obviously need a consumer market for what they produce and offer for sale. Furthermore, business enterprises can function and prosper only within a beneficial political and judicial framework, which, in our democracy, is the product of and ultimately controlled by the public.

More subtle but no less significant is the interaction between business and the community at large at the level of values or objectives. By and large, business must look elsewhere for whatever nonacquisitive goals it may be able to set itself in place of or in combination with its traditional acquisitive goals of wealth and economic power. It must rely upon the moral temper and standards of the entire community and particularly upon such key institutions as the school and the church, whose distinctive task it is to vitalize this temper and gradually to raise these standards. Individual businessmen will tend to behave fairly and humanely toward one another and toward the public in proportion to the extent to which the society that has molded them is itself just and humane enough to inspire them with the ideals of human welfare and justice. They will show respect for their fellow-men in their dealings with them and will make an effort really to serve them in their business activities only if the ideals of respect and service are strong and vital in the community as a whole.

Such an inculcation of values also works in the reverse direction. If business continues to be predominantly acquisitive in motivation, it tends to seduce the public at large into a complacency toward and even an active espousal of the acquisitive motive. Business preoccupied first and foremost with profit invites its consumers to give top priority to their own advantage and comfort. "You owe it to yourself"; "Be satisfied only with the best"; "Be safe, be comfortable, be beautiful!"—these

207

are the slogans with which business "educates" the public. The same motives are encouraged by dollar-minded businessmen in their own homes; their children quickly learn to value what their fathers value above all else and to cherish their own pleasures and comforts at whatever cost to others. The net effect in our society is perhaps best symbolized by the type of appeal that for some time has been appearing on government posters designed to encourage voluntary enlistment in the armed forces. Here the typical exhortations read: "Join up! Why? For travel to exotic lands, for security, for educational benefits." In such appeals government itself is imitating business by seeking to capitalize on the attitudes predominantly characteristic of business and, largely under its influence, of our whole national temper.

One gauge, though by no means the only one, of a typical attitude of business to the public is to be found in present-day high-pressure advertising. Such advertising differs from advertising designed to inform the public fully and accurately of the nature and cost of available commercial products. It is geared to create a market, to awaken new desires, and, above all, to impel the public to buy the advertised product without regard to its quality, cost, or genuine human value. If the slogan of authentic education is: "Stop! Look! Listen! Learn and reflect and then quietly make up your own mind as objectively as you can," the contrasting slogan of business propaganda, as it expresses itself in high-pressure advertising, is: "Don't stop, look, or reflect—yield, the more automatically and unconsciously the better, to our emotional and reiterated appeals to you to buy our product!" Witness, for example, the reliance on irrelevant association, as in beer advertisements featuring pretty girls. The advertiser's premise is that people like pretty girls and may therefore be induced to buy their beer if they can be made to associate their brand with a pretty face. Witness also the use of maddening reiteration, as in familiar cigarette advertisements, where the advertiser's theory is that people will buy whatever has been dinned into them long enough, blatantly enough, and insistently enough. Witness also the unctuous voice in which the sponsor's "important message" is delivered on radio or television—a voice whose saccharine hypocrisy was never equaled by the most banal religious evangelist. Witness, finally, the surreptitious appeal to family affection, national loyalty, and even to religion, notably in pre-Christmas advertising. In the whole field of high-pressure advertising it would seem that any device, however insulting to our intelligence and however indecent in its prudential exploitation of man's nonacquisitive motives, is sanctioned by business if only it results in sales.

Here we see business at its very worst—unashamedly self-adulatory and ruthlessly exploitative. Fortunately, this is not the whole story. Many commerical products are excellent in quality, fair in price, and conducive to real happiness. Many businessmen are fair, humane, decent, courteous, and genuinely interested in their customers. According to the criterion of liberalism, any concluding estimate of business and industry, regarded as a complex set of interlocking economic institutions, must be a mixture of approval and disapproval. There is much in business and industry that is genuinely liberal in attitude and performance, and there is much that is profoundly illiberal and cries aloud for recognition and correction. In extreme cases remedial steps must be taken by legislatures and courts, but ultimately only business can reform itself with the help of judicious social pressure and encouragement. The more mature and healthy American business is, according to liberal standards, the more able and willing it should be to correct its own abuses and clean its own house. The cumulative harm it has done us in helping make us the "sensate" and acquisitive people that we so largely have become cannot be denied. The cumulative good that it has done us in raising our national standard of living and in providing us so efficiently first with necessities and then with physical comforts is equally undeniable. Business and industry, we repeat, are both a bulwark of the American way of life and a proving ground for such liberalism as we possess. In our society they enjoy more power and prestige than any of our other institutions. Theirs is the corresponding opportunity and obligation to advance rather than retard the Great American Experiment in liberal democracy.

Chapter 12

Conclusion: Challenge and Response

$\mathscr{I}$N HIS BRILLIANT HISTORY of the cultures of mankind, Arnold Toynbee has pointed out that cultures have survived and prospered when they were advantageously challenged and when they had the requisite inner resources to meet this challenge. He has made it clear that cultures can be challenged in many different ways—by climate, by natural resources, by foreign aggression, and very frequently by the internal tensions to which their own inner development gives rise. Some cultures have lapsed into apathy for lack of sufficient challenge. Others have been overwhelmed by challenges to which they could not rise successfully. Those cultures were fortunate which had the requisite inner resources to meet a great challenge.[1]

The relevance of this analysis to contemporary American culture is obvious. Our nation has been challenged again and again—by soil and climate, by foreign foes, by internal dissension, and, increasingly, by sheer size and cultural complexity. More than once it has risen triumphantly to the challenge and emerged from the ordeal stronger and wiser. Today America faces its greatest challenge, a dual challenge from without and from within. Few of us question our ability as a nation to meet successfully the external threat of a mighty and militant communism if we face the threat realistically and do everything in our power to protect ourselves against it. The crucial challenge is here at home, in our very midst. It is the challenge to our inner integrity—the integrity of our nation as a whole, of our major institutions, and of each of us as

[1] See the one-volume abridgment of Toynbee's work, *A Study of History*, by D. C. Somervell (Oxford University Press, New York, 1947).

responsible moral agents and citizens in a free society. Above all, it is a challenge to that in us which has distinguished us in the past from other cultures and from most of the nations on the globe—our love of liberty. Can we preserve and strengthen this traditional love of liberty by doing what is necessary to keep it from degenerating into a craving for irresponsible license? Can we so discipline ourselves, individually and corporately, in all our major institutions and in our private lives, that our freedoms will in fact be responsible freedoms rooted in respect for men as men and for the cosmos of which we are a part? Will we be able to preserve and enhance our freedoms by working for them and making for them all necessary sacrifices? These are the crucial questions of our time.

In this book I have identified the spirit of liberalism with the spirit of responsible freedom and with the spirit of America at its most reflective and its most courageous. I have insisted that this spirit is not self-sufficient but is rooted in a distinctive conception of human nature—of man as evaluator, responsible moral agent, and finite creature able to respond to ultimate mystery with awe and reverence. It is this basic conception of man which constitutes the unwritten liberal creed, the creed we live by when we most respect ourselves and one another and the creed that so sharply differentiates us from those who adhere to communism. The crucial questions of our time can therefore be restated: How deeply do we believe in this creed? To what extent does it really motivate us? What are we willing to sacrifice in its defense?

The liberalism we have been exploring is not, indeed, the whole of life. It is no substitute for all the loyalties by which men live and work. The faith of a liberal in no way weakens his faith in government, family, school, or church, in nature, persons, or God. Every human being must have a substantive faith in whatever he deems to be real and valuable, and he must live by this substantive faith, however liberally or illiberally. But liberalism is, as we have here conceived of it, the crucial condition of *mature* faith and of *responsible* freedom; it is precisely what distinguishes reflective and responsible loyalty from blind and bigoted loyalty. It is not essential for religion but only for the responsible religious faith of a free man. It is not a prerequisite to social solidarity but only to the solidarity of a free community. In short, it is not the sufficient but the absolutely necessary condition of all the freedoms which men

211

most prize and to which we as a nation have been dedicated. Our future as a *free* nation will therefore depend entirely upon our complete allegiance to the cause of liberalism. We shall be as free as we are liberal and only to the extent to which our liberalism is an essential part of our inner being.

Will we as a people rise to this greatest of all the challenges that have confronted us in our brief history? Will we continue the Great American Experiment with confidence and courage? The answer will depend entirely upon us and our capacity to respond. Toynbee has noted the tendency of a small minority in every society to lead and of the majority to follow. He has also distinguished between two types of leadership and two ways in which leaders can be followed. Leaders can lead with primary reliance on force. In a state subjected to such leadership the masses must either obey with docile servility or, if they can, rebel with violence. But leaders can also lead by persuasion, and such leadership tends to evoke willing co-operation rather than blind obedience dictated by fear. The highest cultures, those which have achieved the most in the creation and enjoyment of man's most satisfying cultural values, have been those which have had persuasive leadership. If this analysis is correct, we can restate the crucial questions of our times in still another way: How successfully will we, as a nation, find and educate leaders in every walk of life who will lead us wisely and with persuasion, and how responsibly will we follow their lead? In the language of our own historical past, how vital is the spirit of Jeffersonian democracy in us today? How well do we understand the need for wise and responsible leadership and for wise and responsible citizenship?

Man's greatest vice is pride and arrogance. His greatest human asset is his capacity for humility and awe. The more he yields to his characteristic vice, the more he renders himself inhuman and incapable of concern for others. The more he cultivates his sense of finitude and his ability to respond with enlightened devotion to what is greater and finer than anything he himself can produce, the richer will be his own life and his associations with his fellow-men. The liberalism we have been studying is, above all, a liberalism rooted in humility and awe, a liberalism purified and deepened by an abiding faith in what can best complement man's incorrigible finitude and redeem him from his sinfulness. We have taken full cognizance of the fact that men search for this ulti-

212

mate holiness in many different ways and that they worship the ultimately worshipful as their hearts and consciences dictate. Liberalism honors all these divergencies. All it insists on as essential is authentic humility and honest search—the open mind and the receptive heart here above all, where men's souls are put to the supreme test. We can therefore ask the crucial question of our time in this final way: What is our corporate capacity for genuine spirituality and for the profound humility that is the fruit of such spiritual dedication?

This, then, is no dogmatic manifesto, no rigid creed, no dictated philosophy or enforced pattern of behavior. Ours is the infinitely more challenging task of understanding one another and of working together in every area of life as free men, not obedient slaves—of seeking, each in his own way, for an ultimate faith worthy of free men, and of living by that faith in mutual respect and concern. Ours is indeed a glorious heritage. Will we be worthy of it? Will we preserve it and enrich it for our children and our children's children? It is we who, at this very moment, are forging our own history and determining our own future. If our faith in our cause is strong enough, nothing can destroy what we most cherish. We have it in our power to endure and prosper as a free nation and a champion of freedom throughout the world.

Index

Index

217

Index

DATE DUE
